Creating
Walkable Places

Compact Mixed-Use Solutions

Adrienne Schmitz and Jason Scully

**Urban Land
Institute**

ULI–the Urban Land Institute
1025 Thomas Jefferson Street, N.W.
Suite 500 West
Washington, D.C. 20007-5201

Library of Congress Cataloging-in-Publication Data

Schmitz, Adrienne.

    Creating walkable places : compact mixed-use solutions / Adrienne Schmitz and Jason Scully.

        p. cm.

        ISBN-13: 978-0-87420-938-9 (alk. paper) 1. City planning—United States. 2. City planning—Health aspects—United States. 3. Pedestrian areas—United States. 4. Real estate development—United States. 5. Mixed-use developments—United States—Case studies. I. Scully, Jason. II. Urban Land Institute. III. Title.

      HT167.S264 2006

      307.1'2160973—dc22

                            2006029466

10 9 8 7 6 5 4 3 2 1

Printed in the United States of America.

About ULI

ULI–the Urban Land Institute is a nonprofit education and research institute that is supported by its members. Its mission is to provide responsible leadership in the use of land to enhance the total environment. ULI sponsors education programs and forums to encourage an open, international exchange of ideas and sharing of experiences; initiates research that anticipates emerging land use trends and issues and documents best practices; proposes creative solutions based on that research; provides advisory services; and publishes a wide variety of materials to disseminate information on land use and development. Established in 1936, ULI has more than 28,000 members in 80 countries representing the entire spectrum of the land use and development disciplines.

Project Staff

Rachelle L. Levitt
Executive Vice President, Policy and Practice

Gayle Berens
Vice President, Real Estate Development Practice

Adrienne Schmitz
Director, Residential Community Development
Project Director and Author

Jason Scully
Senior Associate, Policy and Practice
Author

Nancy H. Stewart
Director, Book Program
Managing Editor

Sandra F. Chizinsky
Manuscript Editor

Betsy VanBuskirk
Art Director

Byron Holly
Book Design and Layout
Senior Designer

Karrie Underwood
Digital Images Manager

Craig Chapman
Director, Publishing Operations

Principal Authors
Adrienne Schmitz and Jason Scully
Urban Land Institute
Washington, D.C.

Contributing Authors
Steven Bodzin
Writer
San Francisco, California

Robert Dunphy
Senior Fellow
Urban Land Institute
Washington, D.C.

Claire Enlow
Writer
Seattle, Washington

Steven Fader
Principal
Steven Fader Architects
Los Angeles, California

Laura Million
Writer
Franklin, Wisconsin

Sam Newberg
Market Research Analyst
Dahlgren, Shardlow, & Uban, Inc.
Minneapolis, Minnesota

Andrew Overbeck
Writer
Columbus, Ohio

Erinn Dowling Torres
Project Manager
George Washington University
Washington, D.C.

Reviewers
Robert Dunphy
Senior Fellow
Urban Land Institute
Washington, D.C.

Helen Hatch
Senior Principal
Thompson, Ventulett, Stainback, & Associates
Atlanta, Georgia

Christopher Leinberger
Founding Partner
Arcadia Land Company
Albuquerque, New Mexico

Arthur Lomenick
Managing Director
Trammell Crow Company
Dallas, Texas

Anne Vernez Moudon
Professor
Department of Urban Design and Planning,
 University of Washington
Seattle, Washington

Marilee Utter
President
Citiventure Associates LLC
Denver, Colorado

Preface

Real estate development has a major influence on everyone's life. Real estate developers create people's homes, neighborhoods, and places of commerce and recreation, all of which determine how they live day to day. One aspect of how people live has been drawing increasing attention in recent years: how development patterns affect people's health.

Public health experts have been making the case for more pedestrian-friendly development as a means of enabling people to integrate physical activity into their daily lives. It is a fact that people walk and bike for transportation much less than they used to. It is also a fact that Americans are increasingly overweight. Certainly, overeating is part of the problem, but lack of exercise is a contributing factor.

Many people would lead more active lives if they *could,* but their environments prevent them from doing so. Most development gives paramount importance to vehicle access, and little or no consideration to pedestrian accommodations. Land uses are separated, distances are large, and sidewalks are inaccessible or missing altogether.

What we hope to accomplish with this book is to show that there are alternatives to the status quo, and that many people want such alternatives. Developers can create more pedestrian-friendly places, and in so doing can improve their bottom line. Among the components of pedestrian-friendly places are mixed land uses; more and better sidewalks and trails; safer, slower traffic; and more accessible and convenient public transit.

In some places, things are already moving in the right direction. The nine case studies in this book show how forward-thinking developers and designers are finding ways to accommodate pedestrians, giving their projects wider appeal and generating great success. More and more examples can be cited, in both urban and suburban areas, that integrate transit, walking, and biking into the transportation networks. Some are new construction; others are redevelopments. Many of these creative solutions are discussed here, and new ones are breaking ground every day.

In the same way that activists worked together to curb smoking and drunk driving, concerned individuals and organizations are now tackling obesity. The Robert Wood Johnson Foundation, which made significant inroads in the war on tobacco, is spearheading the effort. The foundation is spending $70 million over a five-year period on studies and programs to encourage more active lifestyles as a means of stemming obesity and the diseases it causes. In its outside-the-box style, the foundation sees real estate development and land use patterns as a critical piece of the puzzle.

A final note: while this book was in the final stages of development, various studies came out disputing the link between sprawling development patterns and obesity. We acknowledge these studies and realize that there is ongoing controversy. That is the nature of research. But creating environments where people have choices, where walking and biking are viable pieces of the transportation network, is nevertheless an important goal. Any healthy environment must give people choices about the kinds of neighborhoods and homes they inhabit, and about how they get to school, to work, and to the neighborhood park.

Adrienne Schmitz

Jason Scully

Acknowledgments

Many professionals contributed their time and talents to this book. First, much appreciation goes to the contributing authors, Claire Enlow, Steven Fader, Laura Million, and Sam Newberg, who researched and wrote the case studies that illustrate the principles discussed in the book. We would also like to thank Steven Bodzin and Andrew Overbeck for their contributions to chapter 2; some of Robert Dunphy's writings on parking and transportation were also adapted for that chapter. Erinn Dowling Torres researched and wrote portions of chapter 3. Finally, we are grateful to the developers, architects, and designers of the projects featured in this book, who worked with us to accurately describe their efforts and provided the attractive visuals that bring this publication to life.

We would like to thank the reviewers—Robert Dunphy, Helen Hatch, Christopher Leinberger, Anne Vernez Moudon, and Marilee Utter—and especially Art Lomenick, who spent a great deal of time bringing us up to date on the issues. We would also like to thank the participants in the forum on pedestrian-oriented real estate development that was held to generate ideas for this book—particularly Nancy Graham, the forum chair, and speakers Juan Cameron, Richard Heapes, and Harrison Rue.

We would like to thank the ULI staff members who worked on this publication. Gayle Berens and Rachelle Levitt provided direction and insight. Nancy Stewart managed the book's production. Sandra F. Chizinsky edited the manuscript. Byron Holly designed the book and cover, and did the layout. Karrie Underwood helped manage the digital images that illustrate the book.

This book would not have been possible without the grant ULI received from the Robert Wood Johnson Foundation. Through its innovative approach to promoting better health, the foundation has brought land use issues to the forefront, as part of its active-living initiatives. Katherine Kraft, our main contact at the foundation, provided direction and encouragement.

Contents

Creating
Walkable Places

Chapter 1

Introduction

"The street is the river of life."—William Whyte

The typical American today leads a sedentary lifestyle—sitting all day at work, taking the elevator instead of the stairs, driving instead of walking, and watching television for recreation. People spend a large part of the day in cars—isolated from others, dealing with road rage, and looking for the best possible parking space at each destination. Although the amount of time people spend exercising as a leisure-time activity has remained constant for years,[1] what has dropped is the amount of exercise that people get from their daily activities—in particular, from walking or biking for transportation.

Today's sedentary habits represent a significant lifestyle change that has occurred since the mid-20th century. The built environment that has emerged over the past half-century is now designed to support inactive lifestyles. Communities and commercial districts are vehicle oriented: they offer an abundance of parking and are accessed via wide, high-speed roadways with little accommodation for pedestrians or bikers. Workplaces are isolated in office or industrial parks, so that workers must

More people would get exercise as part of their daily lives if the built environment supported pedestrians, bikers, and transit. Mixed-use, transit-oriented developments, like Pentagon Row, in Arlington, Virginia, are a step in the right direction. RTKL Associates

ity, including heart disease, diabetes, high blood pressure, colon cancer, and depression. A 2003 report, "The Relationship between Urban Sprawl and Physical Activity, Obesity, and Morbidity," is the first national study to find a clear association between the built environment and activity levels, weight, and health.[2] The report, which analyzed 448 counties across the United States, found that the residents of the most sprawling county in the country weighed an average of six pounds (2.7 kilograms) more than the residents of the most compact county. The study also cites national polls indicating that 55 percent of Americans would like to walk more and that 52 percent would like to bike more. The researchers concluded that many more people would get exercise as part of their daily activities if the environment in which they lived and worked supported a more active way of life. The study suggests a number of solutions:

drive to run errands or to go out to lunch. Stores are separated from neighborhoods and from each other, so that shoppers cannot complete errands on foot, but must instead drive from one store to the next. People are isolated in residential neighborhoods, in which their homes are increasingly likely to offer the amenities and entertainment options that used to be available only in public places.

A growing body of evidence points to connections between physical and mental health and the built environment. According to the Centers for Disease Control and Prevention (CDC), regular physical activity reduces the incidence of some of the leading causes of death and disabil-

■ Invest in infrastructure that will support bicycles and pedestrians;

■ Calm traffic;

■ Create safe routes to school;

■ Build transit-oriented development;

■ Retrofit sprawling communities to make them more pedestrian- and bike-friendly;

■ Revitalize walkable neighborhoods;

■ Educate and encourage the public.

All of these recommendations can be made part of the tool kit to create places that are more active, more pedestrian-friendly, and ultimately more profitable for developers.

The Landscape Today

America is a nation of drivers. On the surface, the nation's reliance on automobiles seems quite fitting for a modern society. But allowing the automobile to shape the environment, and everyone's lives, neglects the civic and social infrastructure that supports community. As architect and author Jan Gehl has said, "Life takes place on foot."

Since the 1950s, widespread automobile ownership has opened larger, less expensive tracts of land to millions of people and made possible the sprawling land development patterns that have emerged, including the suburban model of separated land uses. Today, most residential areas are located miles from the shopping districts, workplaces, schools, and recreational and cultural facilities that support them. Widely dispersed residential developments, many of which lack sidewalks altogether, and massive stretches of retail, with their attendant moonscape of parking lots, make walking or biking more than just difficult; it can be unsafe, unpleasant, and often impossible. As Robert Dunphy, Senior Resident Fellow for Transportation at the Urban Land Institute, has noted, "Currently, conventional greenfield development patterns make transit expensive and underused, render carpooling ineffective, and discourage walking and biking."

Although a growing number of national retail establishments are oriented toward pedestrians, the majority employ designs that favor the automobile. Standard suburban strips and big-box retail centers, in particular, give preeminence to automobile access. Retailers conduct market research by traffic counts and select locations on the basis of highway access and visibility. They require large swaths of visible, convenient parking right out in front. If a sidewalk exists at all, using it is unpleasant and often dangerous—as is traversing the football field of asphalt between the sidewalk and the store. It is equally difficult to walk from one shopping center to an adjacent one because connections are lacking. Shopping centers

Human-scale open space is being reintroduced to shopping centers. Santana Row, in San Jose, California, includes a variety of interesting public squares and an attractive sidewalk environment. Jay Graham, SB Architects

Ground-breaking developments like Mizner Park, in Boca Raton, and Seaside, Florida, have shown the value of distinctive, pedestrian-oriented environments. Left: Cooper Carry, Inc. Right: Adrienne Schmitz

are often separated by grass swales, untamed wooded areas, fences, loading areas, or other obstacles.

Long commutes rob working people of their free time, but the dispersal of uses hits the oldest and the youngest particularly hard. Children must rely on parents for transportation; few kids can walk down the street to the park for a game of baseball or to the corner store to buy candy. Seniors who can no longer drive are effectively trapped, unable to shop in their neighborhood or to get out and see friends and family without assistance.

Parks, squares, and other open spaces that contribute to the public realm are often either missing from today's commercial districts and residential communities or are inappropriately located or designed. By the mid-20th century, most cities had invested in major park systems, yet their residents were moving to the suburbs, where they believed there were better opportunities for recreation. In fact, the very suburbs to which city dwellers moved had little parkland—and in many of these areas, it was already

too late to create major public parks because the best sites were being transformed into residential subdivisions. Moreover, most residents were unwilling to dedicate the funds to pay for public parks. The result is that suburban residential subdivisions—unless they are very large—lack public open space. In many areas where small clusters of development dominate, there are no greenway systems or parks to speak of.

Numerous impediments remain to the development of compact, walkable, mixed-use development; architect and planner Andrés Duany summarizes them as follows:

■ Environmental regulations, such as mandatory greenways and buffers, prevent connectivity between projects. Requirements for on-site stormwater retention limit density and discourage infill redevelopment. Lot-coverage limits and high parking requirements also discourage density.

■ Most planning and zoning regulations are based on Euclidian single-use zoning, which prohibits mixed-use development. Mandatory setbacks preclude spatial definition and the intimate, pedestrian-scale streetscapes that are created when buildings are set close to streets.

■ The public approval process can undermine innovative development; specifically, the public often resists mixed uses, higher density, affordable housing, and connectivity between uses.

■ Financing entities tend to favor what has been done in the past. Secondary mortgage markets prefer standard, single-use properties. High parking requirements are typically a precondition of financing.

■ Marketing efforts for new communities promote images of idyllic and pastoral living featuring "anti-urban" amenities: gated, single-income enclaves; private civic buildings; and golf courses. Square footage is emphasized over community.

■ Traffic engineering often dictates the shape of development, with roadway capacity designed independent of context. The elimination of on-street parking encourages higher traffic speeds and adds to the need for parking lots. Excessively wide rights-of-way preclude the planting of street trees and make it impossible to situate buildings close to the sidewalk. Especially in suburban areas, public transit tends to be viewed as less important than accommodations for private vehicles.

Despite these and other obstacles, the landscape has begun to change. Had this book been written five or ten years ago, conditions would have been described in far more bleak terms. Throughout the country, communities are beginning to reflect the positive changes—in particular, the emphasis on a pedestrian presence—brought about

by smart growth and the new urbanism. Downtowns are being rebuilt with a mix of commercial and residential land uses side by side, or stacked one above the other. Some cities have even torn down outmoded and unnecessary highways that ripped through their cores.

Many new towns and villages—beginning with Seaside, Florida, in 1980—are designed primarily to support pedestrians rather than vehicles. In CityPlace, in West Palm Beach, Florida, local government and private developers worked together to create a strong, pedestrian-oriented downtown where none had existed. In 1990, Reston Town Center, in Northern Virginia, was developed as the walkable downtown core for a vehicle-oriented suburban community originally developed in the 1960s.

Steiner + Associates, based in Columbus, Ohio, has built its reputation on pedestrian-oriented retail development. According to Yaromir Steiner, president of the firm, today's town centers are becoming places that

■ Serve as hubs of social, civic, and commercial activity, with public spaces as focal points;

■ Have a more balanced, integrated mix (based on local market needs) of residential, hospitality, and office space;

■ Include a flexible, versatile design that will outlast initial building uses;

■ More successfully balance the need to be pedestrian-friendly with the need to accommodate cars.[3]

Walkable places are nothing new, nor are they obsolete. Major American cities like Chicago, New York, San Francisco, and Washington, D.C., have always been defined by their pedestrian focus and have remained viable and strongly competitive centers of business and culture. Smaller towns and cities—from Asheville, North Carolina, to Boulder, Colorado—have remained desirable places to live and work largely because of their pedestrian focus. Many college towns are prime examples of viable, pedestrian-oriented communities. In fact, part of what makes the college years so memorable for so many people is the way of life afforded by these intimate, pedestrian-scale communities and campuses. Some developers of master-planned communities are even beginning to look to college campuses as models for their projects.

Less Active Lifestyles

According to the surgeon general of the United States, 60 percent of Americans do not engage in physical activity on a regular basis, and 25 percent do not engage in any physical activity at all.[4] When asked why they don't exercise more, many people cite time constraints. For this reason, researchers believe that integrating exercise into people's daily routines—in the form of walking or biking to a destination—is the best way for more people to get the exercise they need. And because so many people live and work where walking and biking are not even possible, creating more pedestrian-friendly environments is critical to that goal.

More than one-quarter of all trips made by households are of one mile (1.6 kilometers) or less. Of those, 75 percent are made by car.[5] Of all trips of one to two miles (1.6 to 3.2 kilometers), 89 percent are made by car.[6] Because much of the built environment developed in the past 50 years has been designed for cars instead of people, it is no surprise that walking has taken a back seat to driving. Creating places that are easy and enjoyable to reach on foot or by bicycle could cut out many of the short trips that people now make by car, but until pedestrian-friendly development becomes more common, the only rational choice for most people is to drive everywhere—even for short distances.

As both homes and workplaces have sprawled away from cities and towns, walking has dramatically declined as a mode of transportation. In 1960, 9.9 percent of workers walked to work. By 1990, the percentage had fallen to 3.9 percent; and by 2000, only 2.9 percent of workers arrived on foot. It is worth noting, however, that in the more compact places, one-third more people walk to work than in the most sprawling places.[7]

Children are also walking less. In 1969, 48 percent of students (age five to 15) walked or biked to school. In 2001, fewer than 15 percent of students walked to school, and 1 percent biked.[8] Why the decline? Parents cite excessive distances, a poor walking environment, and concerns about safety. The consolidation of neighborhood schools—which requires larger sites—is largely responsible for the greater distances that students must travel.

The Current Health Crisis

Decades of vehicle-oriented development, coupled with poor health and nutrition habits, have resulted in a dramatic rise in the portion of the population that is overweight or obese.[9] Between 1991 and 2001, the prevalence of obesity in the American population grew from 12 to 21 percent—a 75 percent increase—and the rate is continuing to climb.[10] Obesity is linked to a number of serious health problems, most notably diabetes and heart disease. According to the American Diabetes Association, more than 18 million people—over 6.3 percent of the population—have been diagnosed with type 2 diabetes, now the sixth-leading cause of death in the United States.[11] Previously, this form of diabetes was known as "adult-onset diabetes" because it had historically been diagnosed only in middle-aged adults. However, the name was changed when doctors noted a rapid increase in the disease among younger people—even children.[12]

Figure 1-1: Diabetes Trends among Adults in the United States (Includes Gestational Diabetes)

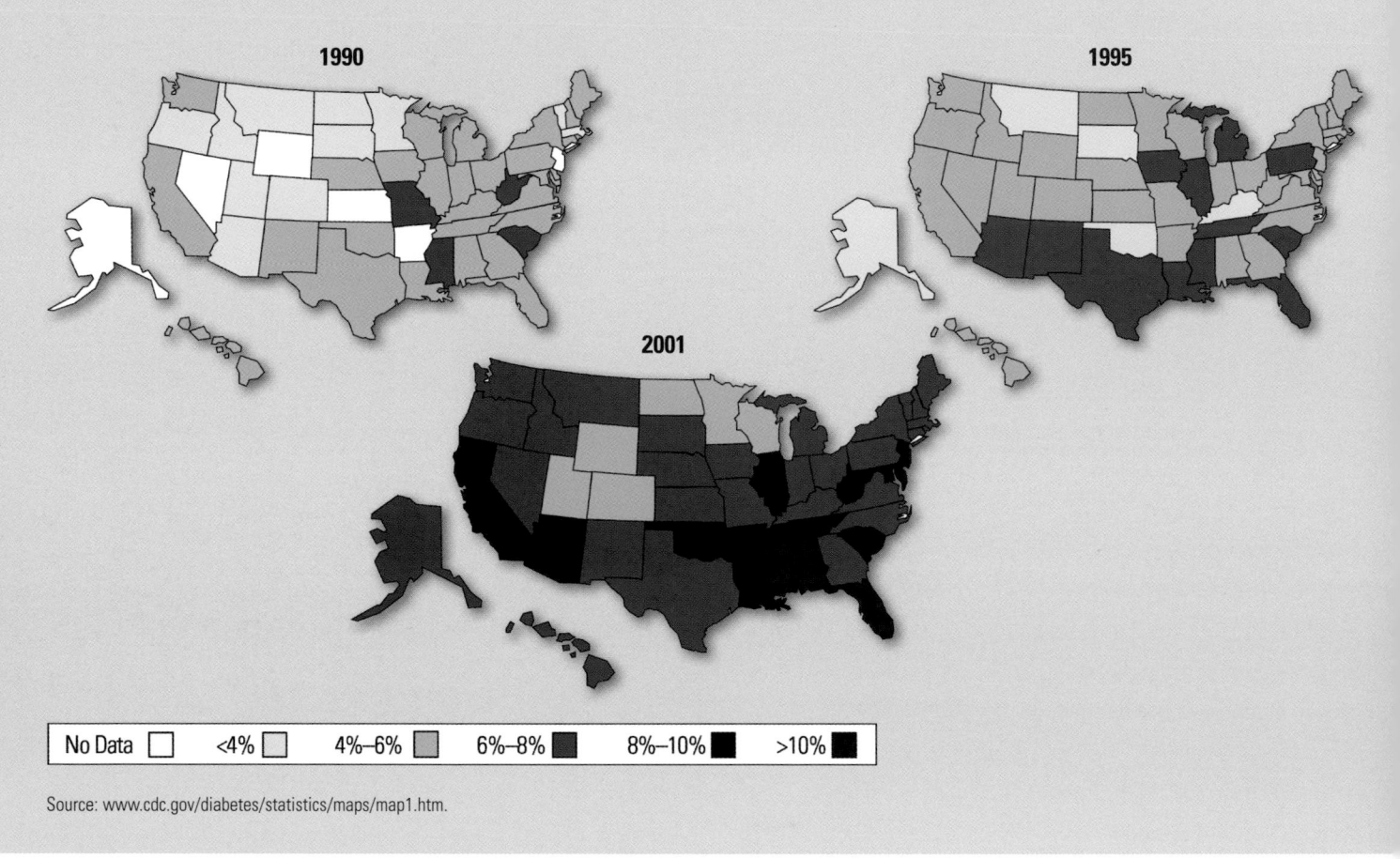

1990

1995

2001

No Data ☐   <4% ☐   4%–6% ☐   6%–8% ■   8%–10% ■   >10% ■

Source: www.cdc.gov/diabetes/statistics/maps/map1.htm.

According to the RAND Corporation, a nonprofit research organization, the increase in obesity has also people. A RAND study shows that from 1984 to 1996, among those age 30 to 39, the rate of disability increased from 118 per 10,000 to 182 per 10,000, a 54 percent increase. During the same period, among those from 40 to 49 years of age, the rate increased from 212 to 278 per 10,000, a 31 percent increase.[12] "Obesity is the only trend that is commensurate in size with what we found happening with disability," notes Darius Lakdawalla, lead author

of the RAND report. Further, RAND researchers believe that about 60 percent of the increase in obesity rates is attributable to sedentary behavior, and 40 percent to poor dietary choices.

Lack of exercise and the isolation created by vehicle-oriented environments also affect mental health. The prevalence of clinical depression has increased significantly in recent years. In *Bowling Alone,* author Robert Putnam notes that depression is ten times more common in the current generation than it was in the last. Putnam also notes that social interaction has health benefits. According to his research, the risk of dying during a one-year period doubles if a person is not a member of any group in which social connections can be made.[13] Similarly, one of the main points of Ray Oldenburg's *The Great Good Place* is that people who are isolated tend to be less happy and less healthy.[14]

Sedentary behavior and the resulting weight increases take a large toll on the American public in terms of monetary costs, quality of life, and premature death. Daily physical activity can help control weight; reduce the risk of heart disease; manage high blood pressure and high cholesterol; and help prevent osteoporosis, back pain, and even colds and infections. In addition, mental health conditions such as depression, stress, and insomnia can be reduced or prevented through regular exercise.

One study conducted by the National Institutes of Health found that patients who lost weight and walked more reduced their risk of becoming diabetic by 58 percent. The health benefits for older patients are even greater, with a 71 percent reduction in risk.[15] The combined annual cost of three chronic diseases linked to physical inactivity (type 2 diabetes, obesity, and coronary heart disease) is estimated at nearly $0.5 trillion a year,[16] and some studies have estimated that physical inactivity and obesity resulted in as many as 400,000 deaths in 2000. Using these data, only tobacco consumption is responsible for more lives lost in the United States, with an estimated 435,000 preventable deaths per year.[17]

Wide sidewalks with plantings at the curb offer protection for pedestrians. Eighth and Pearl, a mixed-use infill project in Boulder, Colorado, provides a transition between the main business street and a historic district. Wolff Lyon

Traffic Injuries and Fatalities

Limited opportunity for physical activity is not the only threat to health found in pedestrian-hostile environments. In 2001, 4,955 pedestrians were killed in automobile accidents in the United States, and an additional 78,000 were injured.[18] In a nationwide study on the relationship between land use patterns and traffic fatalities, researchers found that the more compact the county, the lower the traffic fatality rate; the more sprawling the county, the higher the traffic fatality rate.[19]

Researchers have identified some street design elements that offer protection against traffic injuries or fatalities: single-lane roundabouts; brighter lighting; "pedestrian refuges," such as median strips; and, perhaps most impor-

tant, sidewalks.[20] Lower traffic speeds are another means of decreasing the risk of pedestrian injuries. A pedestrian who is struck by a car traveling at 40 miles (25 kilometers) per hour has a 20 percent chance of surviving—but at 30 miles (19 kilometers) per hour, the chance is 60 percent. Lower speeds offer even more favorable survival rates: at 20 miles (12 kilometers) per hour, the survival rate is 95 percent.[21] Pedestrian-oriented environments control and channel the vehicular flow (generally through traffic-calming methods) in ways that reduce pedestrian accidents.

Pedestrian-Friendly Golf Courses

When Mark Twain described golf as "a good walk spoiled," perhaps he was envisioning the game as it is played in the United States today, where golf carts have replaced feet as the primary conveyance around the links. Once a walking game, golf is now dominated by players using golf carts.

The use of golf carts is so pervasive that revenue from rental fees is built into the pro formas of virtually every new golf course development. Cart fees, which range from $12 to $20 a round, have become an irresistible profit center. Many courses now build those fees into the overall greens fee, so that even at courses where walking is allowed, the decision to ride is an easy one, since golfers are paying for carts no matter what. Marketing efforts by golf cart manufacturers have also made carts more attractive to golfers. With add-ons such as global positioning systems (GPS), which can measure yardage, and features that make it possible to order lunch from the clubhouse, golf carts are more enticing than ever. Ten percent of courses in the country have installed GPS units on their golf carts.

The current design of many golf courses in residential communities makes walking nearly impossible. The functional needs of the golf course often take a back seat to the goals of real estate developers, who want to maximize profitable golf course frontage for homesites. As developers squeeze in more homes, distances of over 300 yards (274 meters) between a green and the next tee are not unusual. Needless to say, such long distances do not encourage walking.

But all is not lost. There is a movement afoot to return golf to its traditional roots. The United States Golf Association (USGA), golf's ruling body and a staunch defender of the game's traditions, started a movement in 1995 to encourage walking golf. The USGA has promoted walking through a manifesto that espouses the health benefits and superior design quality of courses that can be walked. While improving a course's aesthetics is an admirable cause, encouraging more Americans to get exercise by walking the five miles (eight kilometers) that, on average, are covered during an 18-hole round of golf provides quantifiable health benefits. So far, some 48,000 USGA members have signed a pledge never to use golf carts.

Although pedestrian-oriented courses are commonplace in the British Isles, they have been slow to regain ground in the United States. Nevertheless, in recent years, several American resorts have taken advantage of this emerging trend and have successfully built and marketed walking-only or walking-friendly golf courses.

In the late 1990s, when first-time developer Mike Keiser set out to build two walking-only, links-style golf courses on rural land on Oregon's coast, everyone thought he was nuts. The risk, which gave the new resort an instant marketing edge, has paid off big-time: Bandon Dunes is now one of the top golf destinations in the country, annually hosting 80,000 rounds. Keiser plans to build two more walking-only courses over the next few years at Bandon Dunes.

In 1998, the Kohler Company opened the first of two walking-only courses at Whistling Straits, in Haven, Wisconsin, and has been just as successful. Kohler's sister courses at Blackwolf Run allow golfers to use golf carts, but that hasn't kept golfers away from the walking-only Straits courses. According to general manager Steve Friedlander, each resort generates almost exactly the same number of rounds, and 25 percent of golfers at the Blackwolf Run courses choose to walk.

Golfers at Pinehurst Golf Resort, in Pinehurst, North Carolina, also have the choice between walking and riding. At the club's famed #2 course,

Vulnerable Populations

Any discussion of the link between health and urban form must give special consideration to the problems of vulnerable populations. People who cannot drive because of age or disability, or who cannot afford a car, are at a particular disadvantage in environments that lack pedestrian amenities or access to public transportation. Risks include social isolation, loss of independence, and health problems.

Members of minority groups tend to face greater health risks than the population at large, and this pattern is true in the case of obesity and its effects. Obesity rates are highest among African Americans, Latinos, and low-income households. The CDC estimates that nearly 25 percent of African American and Latino children are overweight. If current trends continue, the CDC estimates that one-third of all children and one-half of African American and Latino children will eventually develop diabetes.[22]

Children

The built environment plays a strong role in children's health. In pedestrian-oriented environments, children can walk to school, participate in extracurricular activities, and visit friends—all without having to rely on their parents to drive. In automobile-oriented environments, children rely on their parents for transportation, which decreases their opportunities for physical activity. As a result, many children are not meeting the U.S. Surgeon General's recommendation of one half-hour of moderate physical exercise a day. Only half of all youths between the ages of 12 and 21 regularly engage in vigorous physical activity, and 25 percent of those in this age group engage in no vigorous physical activity at all.[23]

nearly one-half of the 40,000 annual rounds are played by walking golfers.

Bandon Dunes, Whistling Straits, and Pinehurst all report significant savings on development and maintenance, especially on walking-only layouts. While the resorts offer caddies, which increase their personnel costs, the "core" golf courses are cheaper to build because they don't require as much land; nor do they require cart paths, which can cost upward of $750,000 per 18 holes to construct. Walking-only courses also avoid the cost of purchasing golf carts, as well as the associated costs for liability insurance, maintenance, labor, and upkeep. Because golf carts are not damaging the turf, walking-only layouts also need less grounds maintenance. Finally,

walking-only courses have also reported faster play; a round at Bandon Dunes, for example, averages four hours and fifteen minutes.

While walking-only golf is practical only in certain markets, industry experts have plenty of advice when it comes to designing a golf course that caters to those who want to leave the golf cart behind. Five basic design tenets are required to encourage pedestrian-friendly golf courses:

■ Tees and greens should be no more than 100 yards (91 meters) apart.
■ Slopes from tee to green should be as soft as possible.
■ Large topographic features should be broken into small increments.

■ The course should have multiple bridges and boardwalks to help golfers cross wetlands, streams, and environmentally sensitive areas.
■ Holes should have proper spatial separation and multiple access points; for example, if the tee for the next hole is to the right, there should be no right-hand bunkers on the previous green.

In addition to supplying plenty of benches and water coolers, course operators can take other steps to encourage more golfers to walk. Offering discounts for golfers who walk, creating a weekly walking-golf league, and requiring golfers who tee off before 8 a.m. to walk are popular strategies that have worked at golf facilities across the country. Operators concerned about the loss of revenue from golf cart fees need only look to Europe and Asia, where renting electric pull carts to golfers who walk is a profitable service.

As both residential and resort developers look ahead to the next wave of more active retirees, pedestrian-friendly golf courses could be a key amenity. Several resorts have already succeeded in creating a market niche for core golf courses that return the game to its traditional roots. Who knows? A walking-only golf course could be just the ticket in a fitness-themed community that caters to the active lifestyles of the baby boomer generation.—***Andrew Overbeck***

In 1969, 48 percent of students walked or biked to school, but by 2001, the percentage had fallen to less than 15 percent. Much of the decline was caused by the long distances created by school consolidations. RTKL Associates

Physical inactivity puts children at greater risk for a wide range of chronic diseases and a lifetime of ill health. The prevalence of childhood obesity has nearly tripled since the 1960s. In 2003, approximately 14 percent of children were considered obese.[24] By the time they are ten, 60 percent of overweight children will develop at least one risk factor for heart disease.[25] As a result of higher levels of obesity, the onset of type 2 diabetes in adolescents increased tenfold between 1982 and 1994.[26] Obese children are also at higher risk for high blood pressure, hypertension, sleep disorders, lower pulmonary capacity, osteoporosis, and emotional problems.[27]

Health professionals and community activists have targeted walking to school as a means of increasing physical activity among children and youths. In 1969, 48 percent of

Some states and localities are attempting to reverse such trends by reducing school size and reinstating the school as a community anchor. For example, in 2003, South Carolina eliminated minimum size requirements for school sites and buildings to encourage smaller, neighborhood-based schools. Nonprofit organizations are also involved. The Safe Routes to School program has developed educational programs and incentives to promote walking and biking to school. It also addresses safety concerns by encouraging greater enforcement of traffic laws and exploring ways to create safer streets. The National Trust for Historic Preservation, the U.S. Department of Education, and numerous community-level groups have begun to advocate small neighborhood schools—which, by facilitating more walking, can help lower the risk of obesity and reduce congestion and air pollution as well. Neighborhood schools can also become focal points for the social life of the community. Grass-roots programs such as Safe Routes to Schools and International Walk to School Day reflect citizens' interest in increasing opportunities for children to walk to school.

Senior Citizens

Like children, older people are more susceptible to the damaging effects, both mental and physical, of pedestrian-hostile environments. The dearth of opportunities for physical activity puts many older people at greater risk for chronic diseases. Not only can physical activity reduce the risk of chronic diseases, but for those who already have chronic conditions, regular exercise can often help relieve symptoms. Social isolation is also a problem for older people who, once they can no longer drive, may become virtual prisoners in their homes.

Although older people are, on average, more active and healthy than ever before, decreased physical abilities—diminished vision, a slower gait, and slower reaction times, for example—put them at risk for traffic accidents, both as pedestrians and drivers. Currently, 32 percent of all nonfatal pedestrian injuries and 22 percent of all pedestrian fatalities involve people age 65 and older.[30] Walkable neighborhoods, where residents can run errands and visit friends on foot instead of by car, have the potential to

Solavita, an active-adult community in central Florida, was built around a town center that provides a place to stroll. Canin Associates

students (ages five to 15) walked or biked to school. As of 2001, fewer than 15 percent of schoolchildren walked to school. Although traffic safety is a significant concern, the distance between home and school is by far the greatest impediment to walking to school. In a survey conducted in the spring of 2003, 66 percent of respondents said that their children do not walk to school because it is too far away.[28] In a trend that began after World War II, small neighborhood schools within walking distance of most of their students have gradually been phased out in favor of larger schools that are often built at the edges of communities, where land is more affordable. One of the reasons for this trend is bureaucratic guidelines that favor larger schools.[29]

A Map That Tells Time

Imagine that you have just completed a business trip in an unfamiliar city, and you have some free time before your trip home. After sitting in meetings all day, you'd like to take a relaxing walk and maybe do a little sightseeing, but your train leaves in three hours. Where can you go? What sights can you see in that short amount of time?

Amble Time, a software program developed at the Media Lab Europe (a research organization funded by the Irish government and affiliated with the Massachusetts Institute of Technology), was created with such scenarios in mind. Designed for a handheld personal assistant such as a Palm Pilot, Amble Time uses a global positioning system to generate a map of your location that shows what is within walking distance,

given your time constraints. So, for example, if you have a half-hour to walk, Amble Time shows a map with a bubble around your current location; anything within that bubble can be reached in half an hour.

Like all maps, an Amble Time map shows the distances between landmarks and destinations; but unlike most maps, Amble Time maps also show how places relate in terms of how long it takes to walk from one place to another. The scientists at the Media Lab refer to this as the temporal scale. Temporal scale is one of the concepts behind the "pedestrian shed"—the boundary that encompasses what lies within a short walk of a site. Urban planners and designers use pedestrian sheds when they are trying to make a

neighborhood more pedestrian-friendly. Unlike the pedestrian shed, however, which is based only on distance, Amble Time also takes into account a pedestrian's walking speed when calculating the temporal scale.

Programs like Amble Time reveal an increasing emphasis on walking and on the need to make walking easy and convenient. In walkable communities, programs like Amble Time may soon become indispensable, as people begin using them to schedule their day and plan their errands. With Amble Time, a pedestrian can easily determine which stores or restaurants can be reached in the time available. By making such information readily available, Amble Time may help more people choose to walk instead of drive.—*J.S.*

improve health and quality of life for older people while reducing their risk of traffic accidents.

Although the members of the baby boom generation can look forward to longer life spans and better health than members of previous generations, the sheer size of the aging baby boom cohort will intensify concerns about the health and transportation needs of older people.

How Much Activity Is Needed?

How much physical activity is needed to maintain good health? According to the American Diabetes Association, improved diet and moderate activity—such as walking two-and-a-half hours per week—can prevent type 2 diabetes. For overall health, the Surgeon General recommends at least 30 minutes a day of moderately intense physical activity, such as brisk walking. Moreover, it is not necessary to walk all 30 minutes at one time: three ten-minute walks, for example, will yield the same benefits.

Walking advocates recommend a minimum of 10,000 steps a day to maintain fitness and to reduce the risk of chronic disease, and 12,000 to 15,000 steps a day for successful and sustained weight loss. (A pedometer or step counter can be used to measure the distance or the number of steps walked per day.)

According to researcher James O. Hill, even a minimal increase in activity can stem the typical annual weight gain of most Americans. Hill's research shows that the average weight gain between ages 20 and 40 is 1.8 to 2.0 pounds (0.8 to 0.9 kilograms) per year; this gain could be eliminated by increasing activity enough to burn an additional 100 calories per day, which amounts to walking an extra mile (1.6 kilometers), or 15 to 20 minutes, each day.[31] Most people could easily achieve such a goal, simply by adding the kind of trip that is currently impossible in so many communities because of the lack of pedestrian connections and amenities.

Increasing Physical Activity

Research has established that people who live in pedestrian-oriented areas generally walk more and are healthier than people who live in areas where walking is difficult.[32] A 2003 study, for example, found that after controlling for demographic factors, increases in urban sprawl were linked to increases in weight.[33] (For this study, sprawl was defined in terms of low residential density, the absence of mixed land uses, the lack of a definable center, and inaccessible streets.) The study also found, as noted earlier, that residents of the county with the highest levels of sprawl were six pounds (2.7 kilograms) heavier than those who lived in the county with the lowest levels of sprawl.

In another study, conducted by researchers at San Diego State University and the University of Cincinnati College of Medicine, two neighborhoods in San Diego, California, were compared on the basis of walkability. The researchers measured each participant's daily physical activity and surveyed residents on a wide range of health-related topics. The study found that residents of highly walkable neighborhoods engaged, on average, in an additional 70 minutes per week of moderate to vigorous physical activity—a level of activity that could lead to an annual weight loss of almost four pounds (1.8 kilograms), or could prevent that much annual weight gain. The researchers also found actual weight differences between residents of the two neighborhoods: 60 percent of the residents of the low-walkability area were overweight—a figure that is close to the national average. But only 35 percent of the residents of the high-walkability neighborhood were overweight. Clearly, living in a place that facilitates walking (and biking) can make a significant difference in residents' weight and health.

Pedestrian-oriented communities offer numerous health benefits, including increased opportunities for physical activity and decreased likelihood of traffic casualties. In addition, by reducing the number of automobiles on the road, pedestrian-oriented development decreases the overall level of air pollution in a region.

Can people be persuaded to get out of their cars and walk more? Perhaps not everyone. But if more destinations were within walking range, many more people would choose to walk more often. A common misconception is that most car trips are made to commute to work. But the vast majority of trips are actually short-distance, nonwork trips. If more people could walk, for example, from the drugstore to the post office; if more children could walk to school or ride their bikes to the park; and if more senior citizens could get out on their own to shop or visit a friend, the difference in health statistics could be significant.

Harbor Town, in Memphis, is a pedestrian-friendly community. Completed in 2004, it includes a wide variety of housing types, commercial space, a school, and parkland. Jeffrey Jacobs/Mims Studios

Town centers like Birkdale Village (left) and Santana Row (right) are meeting the growing demand for places to walk. Left: Shook Kelly. Right: SB Architects

The Demand for Change

Today, 60 percent of America's downtowns are undergoing urban revitalization. Many of these cities had been in decline for decades. But from San Diego to Baltimore and from Seattle to Chattanooga, renewed demand for urban and walkable environments is generating a wide range of residential and commercial redevelopments.

Earlier trends, in which businesses were leaving downtowns for the suburbs, have reversed in most major cities. A comparison of vacancy rates for office space in cities versus suburbs now shows a national preference for downtown business locations. In the first quarter of 2005, for example, the national downtown office-vacancy rate was 13.8 percent; the corresponding rate for suburbs was 16.3 percent. During the same period, the pedestrian-friendly city of Washington, D.C., boasted the nation's lowest vacancy rate—7.8 percent—while its suburbs had a vacancy rate of 12.4 percent. Nearly every city that offers a clean, attractive, safe, pedestrian-focused downtown shows lower vacancy rates, and higher rents, than its suburbs.

Even in suburban areas, pedestrian-focused town centers are meeting the growing demand for walkability. Pioneering projects like Reston Town Center, in Virginia, and Miami Lakes Town Center, in Florida, are thriving. Newer town centers, like Birkdale Village, in North Carolina (see case study), and Santana Row, in California, are exceeding financial projections. Older, automobile-oriented shopping centers are deteriorating as consumer demands change, and some (like Belmar, in suburban Denver) are being reconfigured into pedestrian-oriented mixed-use districts.

Residential development in both urban and suburban locales is evolving to meet shifting consumer demand. New, high-style apartments and condominiums are attracting residents at both ends of the age spectrum. Neighborhoods based on the new urbanism are an increasing phenomenon, a shift that addresses the need for higher density as well as the demand for a more pedestrian-focused, community-oriented lifestyle.

What Makes a Place Walkable?

There are two primary kinds of pedestrian trips: those for recreation and those for function. And, of course, there are trips that combine the two. The purely recreational trip is relatively easy to accommodate on a trail through parkland or along the edges of a neighborhood. As long as the trail is safe and comfortable, it will serve its purpose and people will use it. The utilitarian pedestrian trip is more difficult to provide for. It requires an understanding of origins and destinations, and the routes that connect them.

"It's not about transportation, but about land use," says Dan Burden, executive director of Walkable Communities, Inc., a nonprofit consulting group that helps communities create better pedestrian environments. To create places that encourage and facilitate pedestrian activity, a number of elements must be in place:

■ There must be destinations that draw people.

■ The community must be built at a pedestrian scale, meaning that distances are short enough to walk and that buildings are close to the sidewalk.

■ Destinations must be reachable, and interconnected by means of a continuous network of safe, convenient, comfortable, and interesting sidewalks and paths.

■ Walkers must feel safe from crime, traffic, and weather conditions. Achieving this perception of safety requires careful design, including "eyes on the street," safe traffic speeds, and shelter at frequent intervals.

According to researchers Anne Vernez Moudon and Chanam Lee, of the University of Washington, the walkability of a place is determined by three characteristics: the quality of the route, the quality of the destination, and the quality of the area. When designing places that are walka-

The quality of a pedestrian route determines whether people will actually use it. At Bridgeport Village, in Tualatin, Oregon, developed by Center Oak Properties and Opus NW, pedestrians are encouraged to linger and explore on the way to their destination. Perkowitz + Ruth/ Paul Turang Photography

ble, developers should keep in mind that because of impediments, safety concerns, or other undesirable conditions, pedestrian routes may vary considerably from vehicle routes and that the route, the surrounding area, and the destination must all be attractive to pedestrians

Walking is discouraged at many shopping centers—which, by design, establish unappealing pedestrian routes because they cater to vehicles rather than to people. If a shopper wants to walk from one big-box retail store to another, the trip will most likely involve walking across one large parking lot, crossing a street or driveway, then crossing another parking lot to get to the destination. When walkways do exist between stores, they are often an afterthought—too narrow, unprotected from traffic or weather, and without good views of signage or storefronts. Because the environment is hostile, shoppers will opt, more often than not, to drive between stores instead of walking. And

From Mall to High-Density Downtown

For nearly four decades, North Hills Mall, one of the first fully enclosed shopping malls in the South, was considered as trendy as the upscale Raleigh, North Carolina, neighborhoods it bordered. But Raleigh's continued suburban expansion and the advent of larger, more contemporary retail complexes gradually took their toll on the cachet and economic viability of North Hills. Customers still came to the mall's anchor stores and ancillary commercial developments, but the mall hardly commanded the number of visitors or the market clout that would be expected of such a location.

With the best days of North Hills clearly over, local developer John Kane began to formulate a new vision for the two-level complex. He imagined something very different from the typical suburban mall surrounded by parking lots. The center's history, and its location alongside the state capital's major perimeter expressway, created an opportunity to augment the site's existing retail components with commercial, residential, and entertainment uses within a high-density environment—in short, to make North Hills a "downtown" for the very suburbs it had helped spawn.

The $200 million redevelopment program for North Hills Mall began in 2001 at a small, plaza-style shopping center across the street. Renamed the Lassiter, the 15-acre (six-hectare) site will ultimately integrate 300 rental apartments; an eight-story, 65-unit luxury condominium tower; and a retail component—all surrounding a newly renovated plaza. These and other community-oriented businesses and amenities will serve both future condominium and apartment dwellers and residents of the adjacent neighborhoods.

At the 30-acre (12-hectare) mall site itself, redevelopment includes a self-contained village with more than 725,000 square feet (67,360 square meters) of restaurants and retail shops oriented around a town square and a pair of shopping streets; a 14-screen cinema; a Renaissance Hotel with banquet facilities; and 300,000 square feet (27,870 square meters) of office space.

A classic downtown is an exercise in evolution, with design styles and uses that complement and influence each other over time. In addition to

North Hills Mall, in Raleigh, North Carolina, was converted from an enclosed mall to a pedestrian-oriented town center named Lassiter. At completion, the 15-acre (six-hectare) site will include rental apartments, condominiums, and 725,000 square feet (67,360 square meters) of shopping, dining, and entertainment facilities. Carter & Burgess, Inc.

providing the components of a trendy, energetic downtown, the real challenge was to capture the look and feel of an urban area. "From a planning perspective, that meant balancing a diversity of uses, maximizing density without sacrificing function or appearance, and ensuring that the distinctiveness of individual components fits within the site's overall context," explains John Larsen, associate principal at Baltimore-based Carter & Burgess, which provided master planning, architectural design, and full architecture and engineering services. "At the same time, we had to make North Hills serve as a reasonable transition area from the Beltline [Interstate 440] to the existing neighborhoods. It was one of those cases where the dictum of 'location, location, and location' fostered possibilities for a more vital confluence of uses and a higher level of energy than are found in many suburban environments."

The solution for these divergent requirements was the adoption, early in the planning process, of a "new midtown" design philosophy—one that goes beyond that found in conventional lifestyle center and urban retail projects. "We wanted to incorporate things that add to and expand the quality-of-life experience and speak to a more urban/local community," says Carter & Burgess project designer Dale Ciapetti. "The

design needed to capture the nuances of the 1920s midtown rather than contemporary suburban retail facades."

Instead of relying on the bright colors and brickwork common at developments across the Southeast, the structural facades at North Hills are as varied as those found in more established downtowns. The palette features a light-to-medium range of neutral colors; the building components include stuccolike materials, cast stone, concrete, and aggregates. "It's the same oversized weave of colors one would see walking down Fifth Avenue in Manhattan," explains Ciapetti. "Commercial tenants have the liberty to add the complementary signage and interior colors distinctive to their brand, completing the mosaic in the process."

To emphasize the walkability of the North Hills village, the project team integrated pedestrian-scale elements into the neo-urban environment, and added entry monuments that link the heart of the shopping district to the condominiums on the periphery. A commons area with a storefront pavilion is surrounded by outdoor seating and includes a freestanding, 24-hour ticket booth for the nearby cinema complex. The commons features a glass-canopied plaza with landscaped seating areas outside the pavilion's two food tenants; a separate, trellised public area faces the cinema court.

Source: Adapted from Jim Parsons, "From Mall to High-Density Downtown," *Urban Land*, February 2004.

In residential neighborhoods homes should be close to the sidewalks and to each other to minimize walking distances and create an inviting streetscape. At Stapleton, in Denver, houses are close to the sidewalk and feature front porches for greater interaction among residents. Adrienne Schmitz

Although route, destination, and area should be the focus for the design and development of large pedestrian-oriented shopping districts, smaller projects should be situated in areas that are already walkable. Alternatively, the developer can work with surrounding businesses, local government, and residents to create a pedestrian-friendly environment (Business improvement districts are an excellent tool for achieving this objective.) At the very least, smaller developments must be connected to the various pedestrian routes in the area, particularly the sidewalks, and must become part of a streetscape that is friendly and appealing to pedestrians. An appealing streetscape helps market the project, helps define a place as a destination, and helps the project become part of the larger pedestrian network.

Residential neighborhoods require similar considerations. Homes should be close enough to the sidewalks and to each other to facilitate walking from one to another. Sidewalks should be safe, comfortable, and convenient. Architecture and landscaping should establish an inviting, pedestrian-scale environment. The front doors, porches, and windows of homes—not garages or blank walls—should address the street. (These and other design criteria are covered in further detail in chapter 2).

once a potential customer is in the car, she might decide not to shop at that second destination at all, if parking is not readily apparent, if there is too much traffic congestion, or if her attraction to the destination is weak.

Designers and developers can do a great deal to improve the quality of a destination. Does the store address the pedestrian? Its entrance should be easily visible and approachable from the sidewalk. Signage should be visible, not just from the distant roadway and parking lot, but also from the sidewalk that runs alongside the building. By focusing on the quality of the destination, the route, and the area, developers can build places that people want to explore, spend time in, and return to.

Overview of This Book

This chapter highlights the relationship between physical and mental health and the built environment in the United States—including how that relationship has changed and continues to change. It discusses the need and demand for more walkable places, describes the benefits of walking (both for the public and the business community), and examines what makes a place walkable.

Chapter 2 examines the important design considerations and features of pedestrian-friendly places. Chapter 3 discusses the market for pedestrian-oriented development and shows how the real estate financing industry can help or hinder developers in their attempts to create walkable places. Chapter 4 covers the importance of the public sector in the creation of more pedestrian-friendly environments, with a particular focus on the key role of public/private partnerships and zoning and building codes that are more responsive to pedestrian-oriented development. Chapter 5 summarizes the key findings of the book and examines new trends in pedestrian-oriented development. It also introduces the nine case studies, explains why they were chosen, and describes the strengths and weaknesses of each project.

Notes

1. Centers for Disease Control and Prevention, "Physical Activity Trends—United States, 1990-1998," *Morbidity and Mortality Weekly Report* (March 9, 2001); available at www.cdc.gov/mmwr/preview/mmwrhtml/mm5009a3.htm.

2. Reid Ewing, Tom Schmid, Richard Killingsworth, Amy Zlot, and Stephen Raudenbush, "The Relationship between Urban Sprawl and Physical Activity, Obesity, and Morbidity," *American Journal of Health Promotion* (September–October 2003).

3. Yaromir Steiner, speaking at an Urban Land Institute Place Making Conference, Reston, Va., September 2003.

4. U.S. Department of Health and Human Services, Centers for Disease Control and Prevention, *Physical Activity and Health: A Report of the Surgeon General* (Atlanta: CDC, 1996).

5. Surface Transportation Policy Project, "Transportation and Health"; available at www.transact.org/library/factsheets/health.asp.

6. John Pucher and Lewis Dijkstra, "Promoting Safe Walking and Cycling to Improve Public Health," *American Journal of Public Health* 93 (September 2003).

7. Ewing et al., "Urban Sprawl and Physical Activity."

8. U.S. Environmental Protection Agency, *Travel and Environmental Implications of School Siting*, EPA 231-R-03-004 (Washington, D.C.: EPA, October 2003).

9. According to the CDC, being overweight is defined as having a body mass index of 25.0 to 29.9; obesity is defined as having a body mass index of 30.0 or higher.

10. A.H. Mokdad, M.K. Serdula, W.H. Dietz, B.A. Bowman, J.S. Marks, and J.P. Koplan, "The Spread of the Obesity Epidemic in the United States, 1991–1998," *Journal of the American Medical Association* 282, no. 16 (1999): 1519–1522; and A.H. Mokdad, E.S. Ford, B.A. Bowman, W.H. Dietz, F. Vinicor, V.S. Bales, and J.S. Marks, "Prevalence of Obesity, Diabetes, and Obesity-Related Health Risk Factors," *Journal of the American Medical Association* 289, no. 1 (2003): 76–79.

11. Centers for Disease Control and Prevention, "National Diabetes Fact Sheet"; available at www.cdc.gov/diabetes/pubs/estimates.htm#prev (accessed March 2004).

12. Darius N. Lakdawalla, Jayanta Bhattacharya, and Dana P. Goldman, "Are the Young Becoming More Disabled?" *Health Affairs* (January–February 2004): 168–176.

13. Robert Putnam, speaking at an Urban Land Institute Place Making Conference, Reston, Va., September 2003.

14. Ray Oldenburg, *The Great Good Place* (New York: Marlowe and Company, 1999).

15. Ewing et al., "Urban Sprawl and Physical Activity."

16. F.W. Booth, S.E. Gordon, C.J. Carlson, and M.T. Hamilton, "Waging War on Modern Chronic Diseases: Primary Prevention through Exercise Biology," *Journal of Applied Physiology* 8, no. 2 (February 2000): 774–787.

17. A.H. Mokdad, J.S. Mark, D.F. Stroup, and J.L. Gerberding, "Actual Causes of Death in the United States, 2000," *Journal of the American Medical Association* 23, no. 1 (2004): 1238–1245.

18. Surface Transportation Policy Project, *Mean Streets* (Washington, D.C.: STPP, 2002).

19. R. Ewing, R. Schieber, and C. Zegeer, "Urban Sprawl as a Risk Factor in Motor Vehicle Occupant and Pedestrian Fatalities," *American Journal of Public Health* 93, no. 9 (2003): 1541–1545.

20. R.A. Retting, S.A. Ferguson, and A.T. McCartt, "A Review of Evidence-Based Traffic Engineering Measures Designed to Reduce Pedestrian–Motor Vehicle Crashes," *American Journal of Public Health* 93, no. 9 (2003): 1456–1463.

21. W.A. Leaf and D.F. Preusser, *Literature Review on Vehicle Travel Speeds and Pedestrian Injuries* (Washington, D.C.: National Highway Traffic Safety Administration, 1999).

22. See www.cdc.gov/diabetes/pubs/pdf/ndfs_2003.pdf.

23. U.S. Department of Health and Human Services, Centers for Disease Control and Prevention, *Physical Activity and Health: A Report of the Surgeon General* (Atlanta: CDC, 1996).

24. R. Strauss, "Childhood Obesity," *Current Problems in Pediatrics* 29, no. 1 (1999): 5–29.

25. U.S. Department of Health and Human Services, Centers for Disease Control and Prevention, *KidsWalk-to-School: A Guide to Promote Walking to School* (Atlanta: CDC, 2005); and Mokdad et al., "Obesity Epidemic."

26. O. Pinhas-Hamiel, L.M. Dolan, S.R. Daniels, D. Standiford, P. Khoury, and P. Zeitler, "Increased Incidence of Non-Insulin-Dependent Diabetes Mellitus among Adolescents," *Journal of Pediatrics* 128, no. 5 (1996): 608–615.

27. Strauss, "Childhood Obesity"; J.F. Sallis and N. Owen, *Physical Activity and Behavioral Medicine* (Thousand Oaks, Calif.: Sage Publications, 1999).

28. Belden Russonello & Stewart: Research and Communications, "Americans' Attitudes toward Walking and Creating Better Walking Communities"; available at www.transact.org.

29. The Council of Educational Facility Planners International recommends ten acres (four hectares) for elementary schools; 20 acres (eight hectares) for middle schools; and 30 acres (12 hectares) for high schools. The council further recommends that an acre (0.4 hectares) be added for every 100 students. See National Trust for Historic Preservation, *Why Johnny Can't Walk to School* (Washington, D.C.: National Trust for Historic Preservation, October 2002).

30. Sandra Rosenbloom, *The Mobility Needs of Older Americans* (Washington, D.C.: Brookings Institution, July 2003), 10; available at www.brookings.org/es/urban/publications/20030807_Rosenbloom.htm.

31. James O. Hill, Holly R. Wyatt, George W. Reed, and John C. Peters, "Obesity and the Environment: Where Do We Go From Here?" *Science* (February 7, 2003): 853–855.

32. B.E. Saelens, J.F. Sallis, and L.D. Frank, "Environmental Correlates of Walking and Cycling: Findings from the Transportation, Urban Design, and Planning Literatures," *Annals of Behavioral Medicine* 25 (Spring 2003): 80–91.

33. Ewing et al., "Urban Sprawl and Physical Activity."

Form and Function: Creating the Pedestrian Experience

"It is difficult to design a space that will not attract people. What is remarkable is how often this has been achieved."
—*William Whyte*

What makes a place attractive to pedestrians? From a design standpoint, there is no set formula; such places are the product of the right location, a suitable mix of land uses and amenities, and design elements that enhance the walking experience. Not all locations can support pedestrian-oriented development. Walkable places benefit from high density, good access (both to and from the site, as well as good access to all components within a site), good transportation infrastructure, and proximity to compatible uses. These features all work together, creating multiple synergistic effects that, taken as a whole, determine how walkable an environment is.

High density, good access, and a mix of compatible uses are some of the basics for pedestrian-friendly places. Sasaki/Craig Kuhner

Additional factors that must be considered are convenience, safety, and visual appeal. Walking must be viewed as convenient when compared with driving. Pedestrians need to feel safe from crime, from traffic, and from weather conditions such as hot sun and sudden storms. And the environment must be aesthetically pleasing, stimulating, and changing. A boring walk feels much longer than an interesting one.

The National Center for Chronic Disease Prevention and Health Promotion, a division of the Centers for Disease Control and Prevention (CDC), has identified the characteristics of what the center calls "active community environments"—places where people of all ages and abilities can easily enjoy walking, bicycling, and other forms of activity. These places support and foster physical activity by providing the necessary infrastructure—including sidewalks, on-street bicycle facilities, multiuse paths and trails, parks and open space, and recreational facilities. Such places may also take the form of mixed-use developments with grid street plans, where everything is accessible by foot or bicycle. This description gives planners a rough outline from which to begin, but it takes much more to create an active place. Every decision should be made with consideration for the pedestrian and bicycler. If distances are kept short, and routes safe and interesting, walking or biking can be made the better option. A combination of carrots and sticks can make walking pleasurable and driving inconvenient.

West Palm Beach, Florida, initiated a downtown renaissance by developing a mixed-use core for the city. Elkus/Manfredi Architects brought together all the elements of the plan, which draws from European town squares. CityPlace Partners, L.P./C.J. Walker, photography

Creating pedestrian-oriented environments is complex, and designers need to consider a range of perspectives and disciplines, including urban design, transportation, environmental protection, education, crime prevention, pedestrian safety, and environmental psychology. Typically, an urban design or planning firm develops a master plan that arranges the mix of uses and elements on the site; various architects design the individual buildings; and landscape architects and other specialists see to important details (such as signage and color palettes) and provide other design services.

Creating Destinations

The average household makes about six vehicle trips each day. Of those, the majority are not commuting trips but local trips.[1] If destinations were conveniently located within walking or biking distance, many of these trips could be made on foot or by bicycle, reducing trip generation dramatically.

Because land uses are segregated in most communities, it is unusual to live or work in places where walking to school or to a store is part of the daily routine. Allowing land uses to be mixed, however, changes this pattern, triggering a chain of events that improves the pedestrian environment and increases pedestrian activity. While only a small percentage of people will be able to live within walking distance of their workplace, denser, mixed-use environments can enable many people to live or work where they can walk to other daily activities. For example, when office buildings are designed with ground-level restaurants, shops, health clubs, daycare centers, and other conveniences, workers do not have to drive to lunch or to pick up their dry cleaning. Similarly, in residential neighborhoods that include a logical mix of uses, residents can to walk to school, to the library, to the post office, or to dinner at a neighborhood restaurant.

How far will people walk? Some planners cite the five- or ten-minute walk—which translates to about one-quarter to one-half mile (0.4 to 0.8 kilometers)—as an optimal distance for pedestrian-oriented districts. In cities, people will walk farther than in the suburbs, simply because walking typically is more convenient than finding parking and dealing with traffic congestion. As traffic worsens, people may be willing to walk even farther. Also, city sidewalks usually feel safer because there are other people walking, and are more interesting because cities are designed to be experienced on foot. A good project design can increase the actual distance that people will walk by reducing the perception of distance.

Pedestrians need a reason to be in a place. One reason is social contact: people want to be around other people. Thus, if a place has a healthy street life—a critical mass of activity—people are more likely to incorporate it into their daily lives. Mixed-use destinations are key to generating pedestrian activity, and the mix must be carefully orchestrated on the basis of market research. Generating the kind of dense street life that can sustain itself requires the following:

■ A mix of commercial tenants and noncommercial activity that will keep people coming back;
■ A nearby population base of residents, workers, or both;
■ Daytime and evening uses, to keep life on the streets for as much of the day as possible.

The best pedestrian districts include national retail tenants for economic sustainability, plus regional and local businesses to create a unique character and sense of place.

Triangulation is a concept promoted by the Project for Public Spaces (PPS), a nonprofit group committed to improving the quality of urban outdoor spaces. Triangulation means organizing elements—both public and private—in ways that increase the activity around them. Triangulation can bring together seemingly unconventional combinations of uses; the PPS cites an example: "There is something that goes on if you take a playground, a children's reading room in a library, a coffee shop, and a Laundromat, and put them all together near a bus stop."

Third Places

Successful mixed-use developments provide at least some goods and services that meet people's daily needs. In addition, they facilitate casual social interaction. In *The Great Good Place,* sociologist Ray Oldenburg describes those environments that are neither the home nor the workplace but a "third place" where people can interact with others informally. Several features are characteristic of successful third places:
■ They are free or relatively inexpensive to enter.
■ They are easily accessible, preferably on foot.

■ A number of people can be expected to be there.

■ Everyone feels welcome. It is easy to start a conversation, easy to find old friends, and easy to make new ones.

Such places—corner stores, barbershops, neighborhood bars, and coffee shops—are crucial for creating a sense of place in a community. They enrich public life and allow casual contact with others in ways that do not occur at home or at work. People crave such places, as is evidenced by the number of Starbucks and other coffee shops that have appeared on almost every block of every commercial district of every city and town. Yet third places are largely missing from much of the modern landscape, where single-use office parks and residential communities dominate, and where commercial establishments are prohibited or economically infeasible.

"Third places" can include neighborhood cafés, town squares, or the local library. Increasingly, bookstores include a café where people can interact informally. Top: Clear Springs. Right: Adrienne Schmitz

A Sense of Place

Designing pedestrian-oriented places means embracing the human scale over vehicular convenience, while still accommodating vehicular traffic and parking. Ideally, blocks are kept short, and manageable for those on foot. Land uses are mixed, so that destinations are within short walking distances of one another. Developments connect to each other in meaningful ways: through streets, sidewalks, and paths that connect neighborhoods; and through shared open space, commercial districts, and public facilities. Barriers—such as wide, high-speed roadways; walled or gated neighborhoods; and culs de sac—are minimized. Parking is available but does not dominate the streetscape.

Place making occurs when multiple layers of design and utility are integrated into a plan that creates an attractive and functional environment for the people it serves. From a design perspective, successful place making requires elements that define and identify a particular location.

Lively streets are an important element in successful place making. Activities—both planned and unplanned—can be an excellent means of enhancing street life and attracting visitors to a place. Planned activities are the regular events that residents, visitors, and workers count on: farmers' markets, arts fairs, festivals, parades, and musical and cultural events. Unplanned activities are the spontaneous events sparked by the vibrancy of street life—people watching, chance meetings with friends, and conversations among strangers.

"Place" can be communicated by signage distributed throughout a site, with greater emphasis at gateways or entry points. Good signage tells the story of a place or conveys what makes the site special and interesting to visitors. Further, the signage at gateways defines nodes of activity. The inclusion of public art and historical and other landmarks helps give an area a distinctive identity. Public art and landmark features also provide points of interest and opportunities for social interaction. A foun-

At Santana Row, a lively, urban sense of place was created. SB Architects

tain with steps that double as seating, a sculpture that children can climb, and an antique railroad car are all examples of landmarks that help establish a sense of place, and encourage interaction with others.

Some planners favor a coordinated streetscape, with themes that carry from the residential to the commercial core, and common design elements for all storefronts and signage. Others believe that too much consistency in design can undermine the sense of authenticity.

Crime happens where there aren't people. At City Heights, crime subsided when new development created an atmosphere conducive to strolling and socializing on neighborhood streets. Adrienne Schmitz

Andrés Duany, of Duany Plater-Zyberk & Company, has long objected to "banners, berms, and bricks" as expensive and unnecessary design elements that do little to make a place desirable but distract planners from the real issues of function. Imagine walking down a brick-paved sidewalk lined with surface parking lots. Now imagine a sidewalk lined with a variety of shops, each with window displays. There might be a coffee shop with two or three outdoor tables, a bench for bus riders to wait. Whether the pavement is brick or the signage is beautiful matters much less in such a lively district.

The Perception of Safety

Lively public spaces and healthy street life cannot exist unless visitors, workers, and residents feel safe. And safety is not just a matter of actual crime or traffic levels but of perception.

One of the most effective ways to ensure a safe neighborhood is to create a self-policing environment. Jane Jacobs coined the phrase "eyes on the street" to describe the self-perpetuating phenomenon in which the more people are out on a street, the safer it will be—and the safer the street is, the more people will venture out.

In the words of British architect Richard Rogers, "Crime happens where there aren't people";[2] thus, many of the same design characteristics that bring people to a place will also discourage criminal activity. Residential communities should be designed with casual street surveillance in mind. Homes include front porches and windows facing the streets. Lots are platted to minimize blind areas between buildings. In commercial areas, retailers are prohibited from covering storefront windows. Instead, shops allow clear visibility both from the sidewalk into the shop, and from the inside of the shop to the sidewalk. The goal is to maximize the number of eyes on the street.

Well-designed site plans minimize the need to use tall fencing, hedges, or walls for screening. Streets that are lined with high fences or walls isolate pedestrians and make walking feel unsafe. Although screening may shield public areas from unattractive views, it can also conceal criminal activity. Similarly, parks, squares, and plazas should be carefully sited and designed to ensure that they are not isolated, dark, or uninhabited; such places can quickly become shelters for criminal activity.

The quality and intensity of lighting are important: a well-lit park, neighborhood street, or commercial district is a safer one. Lighting should be bright enough to ensure safety but not so bright as to create glare; overly bright lighting can give a place the character of a prison yard. Streets, sidewalks, and building entrances all require different types of lighting. Residential neighborhoods need their own lighting plan.

Transit-Oriented Cores

Multiple transportation options strengthen pedestrian-oriented development. Public-transit users naturally incorporate walking into their travels as they head from the parking lot to the train, from the train to the office, from the train to shops, and so on. In addition, public transit offers a "Plan B" for those who are willing to walk to work or to shopping when weather is good or when they are not carrying packages, but who need to have alternatives in place. Without an alternative available, potential walkers are likely to just drive all the time.

In earlier times, the railroad station was part of the commercial core of cities and towns. Transit stops were focal points in streetcar suburbs and commuter villages. But the more recent "park and ride" models tend to locate the transit stop on the least desirable land at the periphery of a community—in a location that is difficult to walk to, and where adjacent multiple uses are discouraged. The historic models—with the transit station at the center of the community and a mix of uses surrounding it—are the better ones for today's transit-oriented developments. The mixed-use component should extend outward from the center so that a variety of services are available within a five-minute walk (about a quarter-mile, or 0.4 kilometers).

Transit systems should be integrated into the design of the community, with stops in prominent and easily accessible locations. From the developers' perspective, embracing transit as a community's focal point makes better use of the land surrounding the transit station, increases property values, and generates foot traffic at all times of the day—a boon for commercial districts.

Ideally, parking lots for transit stations are not located immediately adjacent to the transit stop, because they waste the most valuable sites—land that could more effectively be used for income- and activity-generating development. Instead, parking is best located within a five- to

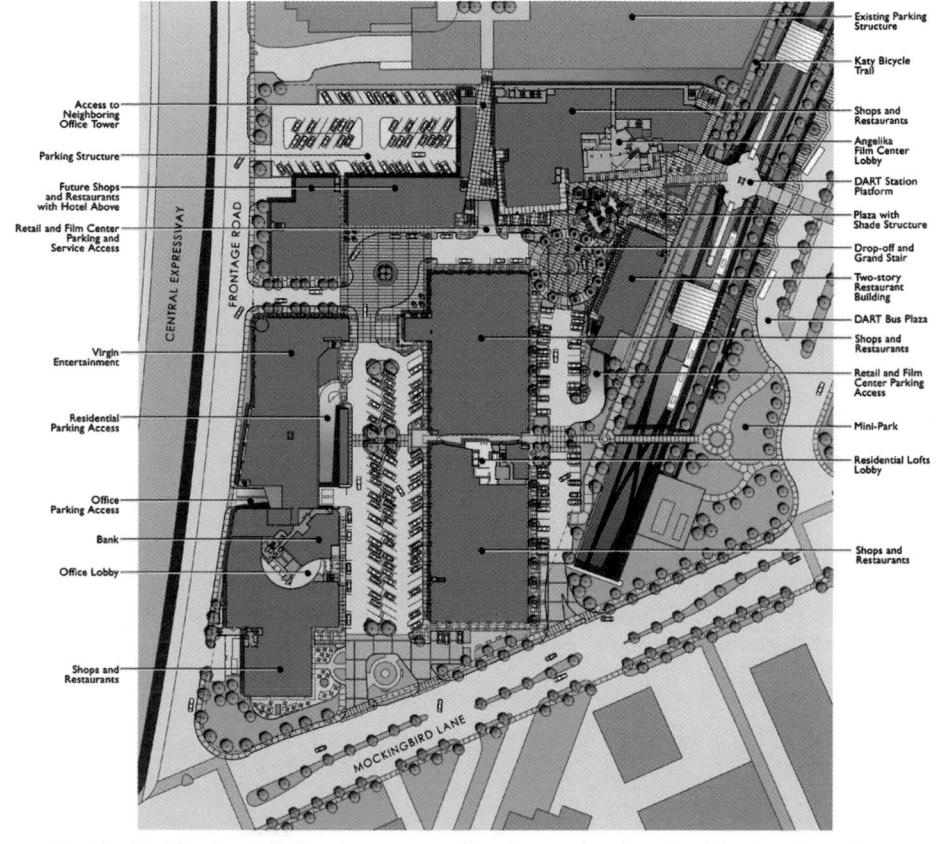

Mockingbird Station, in Dallas, is a ten-acre (four-hectare) pedestrian-friendly urban village designed to connect the transit station to its surroundings. The development includes apartments, a cinema, office and retail, and an enclosed public plaza. RTKL Associates

seven-minute walk from the station or transit stop. Shared parking arrangements can then be implemented for the commercial uses surrounding the transit stop.

According to Robert Cervero, a transportation expert at the University of California at Berkeley, the success of transit-oriented development depends on the "three Ds": density, design, and diversity of land uses. Of those, density is the most important because it brings the number

example, is constructing a $1.1 billion light-rail system that will feature pedestrian-friendly commercial hubs around stations. The economic impact of transit-oriented development is substantial. A proposed commuter-rail hub in New Jersey is projected to pump $1 billion into the state's economy.

Block by Block

Pedestrian-oriented development gives rise to complex planning and design issues. The site plan must not only provide for pedestrian connections, but must also accommodate parking and manage vehicular movement. The needs of all users must be considered: residents, retailers, shoppers, business owners, and workers. Often, these needs conflict, and designers and planners must work out the best compromises.

Synergies between uses must be accommodated and planned for. Synergies are enhanced by connections—both horizontal and vertical—between uses. For example, when residences or offices are located above shops, the residents and workers of those upper levels help to support the retailers. At the same time, the shops make the offices and residences more attractive by becoming on-site amenities. How people get from one place to another is also of utmost importance. If it is difficult or time-consuming for office workers to reach a shopping district, they will not be able to support it.

Amenities and attractions should be designed to enhance the pedestrian experience and to foster lingering, gathering, and purchasing. Large, uninterrupted streetscapes are not only uninteresting, unpleasant, and potentially unsafe: they also encourage, or even compel, driving between uses instead of walking.

To create a pedestrian-friendly balance between streets and walkways, a project should be designed as a district of short blocks divided by streets. According to planner and professor Jonathan Barnett, a block should have dimensions no greater than 600 by 300 feet (183 by 91 meters) or 700 by 200 feet (213 by 61 meters). Short blocks not only make a place more walkable, but can also increase connectivity by transforming a collection of geographically close but segregated real estate projects into

of riders that is necessary to ensure the viability of public transit. And at the same time as mixed-use developments provide the density to sustain transit, transit can help to support more mixed uses.

Connected nodes of mixed uses along a transit line will be more successful than a stand-alone mixed-use project. In fact, with the transit option available, a resident could work in one node and live in another without ever having to use an automobile to commute between the two. Nodes can also be developed to emphasize specific uses: some may be primarily residential, others primarily retail, and still others primarily office. A transit connection makes it possible to mix different types of development nodes.

From a financial standpoint, transit-oriented development has proven to be a boon to developers and cities alike. One of the best examples in the country is Arlington County, Virginia, where development along the Orange Line (part of the Metrorail system of Washington, D.C.) helped revitalize an entire portion of the county. By emphasizing redevelopment within a quarter-mile (0.4 kilometers) of Metro station entrances, Arlington County planners created a pedestrian-oriented, high-density environment containing a wide range of residential, commercial, and office uses. The concentrated development around the Orange Line now includes 21 million square feet (1,951,000 square meters) of office space and 25,000 residential units. And, although the development along the Orange Line yields nearly one-third of Arlington County's tax revenue, it occupies only 7.6 percent of its land area.

Cities from coast to coast are expanding existing transit systems and intensifying land uses near transit, creating significant opportunities for developers. Phoenix, for

Street widths, building heights, and the distances between buildings are all important to the character of a place. Mizner Park, designed by Cooper Carry, gets these right, and has influenced the design of other walkable districts. Cooper Carry, Inc.

integrated places, allowing people to patronize a variety of establishments more easily.

Establishing a network of short blocks can set off a chain of events, all of which serve to make places even more walkable. For example, when it is possible to walk from home to office, to shop, to restaurant with ease, more people *will* walk, and they are more likely to patronize businesses along the way, improving the viability of those businesses. Similarly, when people can park once and walk between several destinations, they are also more likely to make extra stops along the way. Reducing the number of vehicle trips within the area translates into lower levels of congestion and allows the width and capacity of internal roads to be reduced, saving on infrastructure costs and further improving the pedestrian environment.

Architect Richard Heapes, of Street-Works, advises planners and designers to imitate the best of the older developments. "Find a great street, measure it, and copy it." The widths of streets and sidewalks, the building heights, the distance between buildings, and the curb radii all contribute to a street's character. Early-20th-century suburbs offer some outstanding examples to imitate. Country Club Plaza, in Kansas City; Forest Hills, in New York; Shaker Square, in Shaker Heights, Ohio; and Worth Avenue, in Palm Beach, all offer lessons for designers of pedestrian-oriented retail districts. The Market Common, Clarendon (see case study), in Arlington, Virginia, was inspired by Cooper Carry's now classic Mizner Park, in Florida, which was itself inspired by Rome's Piazza Navona. The residential neighborhoods in Kansas City, Forest Hills, Shaker Heights, and Palm Beach—along with those in other districts and towns, such as Chevy Chase, Maryland, and Winter Park, in Orlando—offer similar examples for those designing pedestrian-focused residential communities.

Retail and Entertainment Districts

To generate more pedestrian activity in commercial cores, planners and designers should eliminate blank street-fronts and instead use most of the ground-level space for shops, restaurants, entertainment, and other pedestrian-focused uses. In cities such as Dallas and Atlanta, office and retail uses have historically been segregated, creating block after block of empty downtown sidewalks. Recently, however, in these and other cities, the shopping street has begun to emerge as a viable form. And in suburbs, town centers have become de rigueur among savvy developers. Many of the newer mixed-use commercial developments are walkable, with a pedestrian scale and a definite main-street character, and have offices and housing components located nearby.

Design. Yaromir Steiner, developer of Easton Town Center, in Columbus, Ohio, describes the characteristics of well-planned retail and entertainment districts:[3]

■ Parking is abundant, clean, safe, and convenient. Parking lots are not located in front of buildings.

■ Stores do not turn their backs to the street, but have front doors that open onto the sidewalks.

■ Well-merchandised and well-designed public spaces are an important part of the design. Streets and squares are the urban hubs that integrate the mix of uses.

Michael Beyard, a senior fellow at the Urban Land Institute, warns against "every storefront looking alike, every sign so controlled they all look identical, the same color, style, and shape. Both consumers and retailers are looking for elaborate environments, diversity in their

Grid streets, wide sidewalks, and well-articulated buildings are among the characteristics that help Bethesda Row fit into the urban fabric of an old suburban downtown. Cooper Carry, Inc.

presentation to the public."[4] Richard Heapes also believes that the best pedestrian districts are those that do not look programmed but give the sense that they have evolved over time, with various designers, retailers, and others making separate design decisions. Increasingly, instead of dictating uniform standards for signage and facades, Heapes leaves the design decisions to the individual commercial tenants; the result is a kind of "messiness" that makes a place feel authentic.

Bethesda Row, in Bethesda, Maryland, is a development that revitalized a portion of an existing suburban downtown. With its grid streets, wide sidewalks, and low-scale, well-articulated buildings, the project fits into the urban fabric of the older downtown. The design of the buildings is secondary to the urban pattern and to the carefully assembled mix of local and national restaurants and retailers that has leased space in the development. When necessary, the developer, Federal Realty Investment Trust, even subsidized the rents of small local retailers for the sake of the total experience.

At Santana Row, in San Jose, California, Heapes used some of the lessons learned at Bethesda Row to create

a main-street experience amid unwalkable sprawl. The 42-acre (17-hectare) project, previously a strip shopping center, now offers 18 blocks of fashionable shops and restaurants, with luxury rental apartments on upper levels. While the project is currently an island of urbanity, the ultimate goal is to connect Santana Row to its surroundings and to continue the pedestrian network. Over time, Santana Row is expected to be a catalyst for more main-street-style development, which will expand the walkable district.

Density and Diversity. To succeed, a retail district must address the needs of both retailers and shoppers. The key is to ensure enough density for businesses to thrive while relying largely on pedestrian traffic. To create the critical mass required for economic success, the retail core must draw a diverse mix of people, and must therefore incorporate a diverse mix of uses. According to one rule of thumb, at least 200,000 square feet (18,600 square meters) of retail and other commercial space and at least 2,000 dwelling units should be located within a ten-minute walk of each other. According to Richard Heapes, a ten-minute walk translates to about six blocks. If both sides of the street are used, six blocks offer enough space for about 120,000 square feet (11,150 square meters) of retail. Heapes also notes that retail must line both sides of the street; there are no successful one-sided retail streets.

Street-oriented storefronts enhance walkability. First-floor retail gives an "edge" to the street and helps provide definition to an area. Buildings that enclose and frame streets are more attractive to pedestrians: it is more stimulating to walk along a street of storefronts than to walk along the blank walls of an office complex or through the open, undefined space of a parking lot.

To achieve both density and appropriate scale, it is desirable for buildings to include two levels, often more. The ratio between the width of the street and the height of the buildings lining the street is also an important design consideration. Most zoning ordinances set maximum building heights and lot coverage, enforcing a sense of inhospitable openness that is directly contrary to the sense of enclosure that most pedestrians prefer. Moreover, limits on building heights and lot coverage undermine the chance for economic success. When zoning requirements demand overly wide streets, a row of street trees can help to create a sense of enclosure by narrowing the visual space and providing a canopy overhead.

Vertical mixed use is one way to achieve density, but it is not the only one—nor is it easy. Horizontal mixing can be equally effective, and it does not create the design, construction, and permitting problems associated with vertical mixing. But despite the problems, vertical mixed use is becoming more common, and the financing, approval process, and design for vertical mixed use have come a long way.

Multilevel retail space is also increasingly common. Although it was once considered impossible to lease upper floors for retail use, that is no longer the case. Now that pedestrian-oriented street frontage is considered desirable, retailers are reconfiguring their designs to suit more vertical spaces, enabling them to compete for attention at the sidewalk but to have a large space on upper levels. Starbucks, for example, has multilevel outlets in some locations. Bookstores such as Borders and Barnes & Noble have many multilevel outlets in both urban and suburban locales. And several big-box chains, including Target and Home Depot, have created more urban-style models to fit multistory spaces. At Reston Town Center, in Reston, Virginia, the entrance to the multiplex cinema is at the street level, but most of the theater space is on the second level, which is accessed by escalators. As long as a highly visible street-level presence can be attained, secondary levels—either above or below the ground floor—have proven acceptable. Office and residential space can occupy upper levels as well.

Downtowns, town centers, main streets, and other commercial districts are made up of a diverse mix of market-driven uses. Yet the mix of businesses needs to be carefully orchestrated. A block lined with banks, real estate agents, and tax preparers does not generate pedestrian buzz. Such uses are needed, but are best interspersed with attractive and unique shops, eateries, and entertainment facilities.

Unlike residential or office development, retail development must attract customers on a daily basis. To do so, it must continually provide the newest, best, most interesting experiences. In addition to density, pedestrian-

Multilevel retail is no longer taboo. Even big-box retailers are redesigning their buildings to fit urban streetscapes. Ellerbe Beckett

oriented retail districts should achieve a unique sense of place and an immersive quality. The best shopping districts integrate leisure uses into retail environments, to encourage people to come and linger.

Edges and Timing. The edges of a retail district can be difficult to lease if they are not well planned and properly marketed. To get the best visibility, the larger, destination retailers will want to locate on the main streets, which leaves the edges of the retail district available for secondary uses. Such sites can be ideal for neighborhood-serving establishments such as dry cleaners, copy centers, pharmacies, and grocers. Expanding the tenant base to include such secondary uses creates a better mix and a more "real" place than if only destination retailers are included.

Loading ramps are an unattractive but necessary feature of commercial buildings. To minimize their impact, they must be carefully located and designed early in the planning process. With their associated noise, odors, trash, and truck traffic, loading areas can be particularly difficult to site when a commercial district includes residential units above the commercial level. At the Market Common, Clarendon, loading ramps are hidden in an alley, along with the garages for the residential townhouses.

When a retail district is first envisioned, there may not be enough of a market to sustain the level of retail ultimately desired. Yaromir Steiner recommends that developers "start smaller, with a kernel of 'place.'"[5] Projects can be broken into districts for phasing. At Seaside, Florida, the area that eventually became the town center began with temporary kiosks, which housed a limited amount of retail activity until a large enough market had developed to support more permanent investment. Once a market base has been established, live/work spaces can be converted from housing to retail or office uses. Vacant sites can be used as temporary parks, for farmers' markets, or to host outdoor performances. Vacant buildings can be used in various ways as well, to prevent the space from appearing dead. Retailers can use storefronts for additional display space. Local schools or arts groups can be invited to display their work. At Santana Row, a group of artists—Red Ink Studios, which calls itself a "guerrilla art movement of nomadic artists"—briefly took up residence in unleased second-level commercial space. In addition to using the space for their studios, the Red Ink artists held weekly gallery events, and thereby brought in more foot traffic to the district and added to the evening activity.

The Details: Storefronts and Signage. The best commercial districts feel as if they've evolved over time. Too much coordination of visual elements creates the sense of being in a theme park. Retail buildings should look like what they are. To create the rich and varied appearance of a street in an older city, tenants should be allowed to pick their own storefront designs, awnings, signage, and so on. That said, a certain amount of coordination is useful. For example, building heights, massings, and setbacks need to be carefully controlled to create the right scale for pedestrians. Parking should be coordinated and shared among all tenants. Unified landscaping, including significant street trees, can help to create a sense of place. And a program of events (such as festivals and holiday celebrations) should be developed in which all tenants are encouraged to participate.

At Bridgeport Village, in Tualatin, Oregon, designers allowed each each storefront to maintain its own identity, while becoming part of a harmonious environment. Perkowitz + Ruth/Paul Turang Photography

Retail tenants should be encouraged to use store windows for interesting displays of merchandise. They should be prohibited from papering over or bricking up street-facing windows.

Well-designed and well-coordinated signage can contribute to an effective circulation and landscape plan. It can also be important in establishing a strong identity for a place. By making the development easy to negotiate, consistent directional and orientation signs enhance the pedestrian experience. Prominent, clear, and attractive signage is also critical for retailers' success.

The design concept for the development should influence the signage. For example, if the intent is to integrate the project into its surroundings, the signage should be in keeping with that on the surrounding streets. To maintain their individual identities, however, retail and restaurant tenants require a certain amount of flexibility and control of their own signs and facades. Overregulating signage often leads to a bland, boring "project" feel rather than to the vibrant authenticity that is desired. At the same time, the corporate identity of a chain store should not be allowed to alter the overall character of the district.

Well-designed signage provides separate messages for both drivers and pedestrians. Large, high-mounted storefront signs that can be seen from the road are rarely visible to pedestrians, whereas pedestrians walking from one shop to another can easily read "blade" signs that hang overhead, perpendicular to building facades. Saffron, in Sammamish, Washington (see case study), has several different levels of signage: large storefront logos let drivers

From Birkdale Village, in North Carolina, to Santana Row, in California, living over the store has become a popular lifestyle option and a way to mix uses. Left: Patrick Schneider, courtesy of Crosland and Pappas Properties. Right: SB Architects

on the adjacent arterials know what services are available, while lighted blade signs create an appealing and inviting atmosphere for pedestrians passing by.

Residential Districts

A residential component is crucial for creating viable mixed-use developments. Commercial districts that do not include housing or have housing nearby become dead zones after business hours and on weekends, and have limited economic success.

The principal factors in designing the residential components of pedestrian-oriented developments are security, privacy, amenities, style, and views. Residential districts are usually located at the edges of a mixed-use area to emphasize quiet and privacy over activity. Or

they may be stacked above commercial uses. In that case, privacy is maintained by elevating the residential uses above the activity of the street, rather than by horizontally separating them.

In a mixed-use district, the simplest way to incorporate residential uses is to place them in separate buildings; this approach is cost-effective, minimizes potential conflicts, reduces building and fire code requirements, and is easier to finance. But the idea of combining residential and commercial uses in the same building has gained favor in recent years. For one thing, it offers a way to use upper floors, which may be difficult to lease for retailing or office use. In addition, "living over the store" has come to represent an urban lifestyle that has growing market appeal. Once regarded as unmarketable, "residential over retail" has become a highly successful development form, both in urban downtowns and in suburban town centers from Celebration, Florida; to Birkdale Village, in North Carolina; to Santana Row, in San Jose, California. In Celebration, the highest apartment rents per square foot are for those above the main-street shops.

Getting More Feet on the Street. The residential component is key to the success of pedestrian-oriented developments: it provides the synergy and the critical mass that ensure round-the-clock activity and enable neighborhood businesses to succeed.

As with the commercial component of mixed-use development, diversity expands market potential. A mix of housing types targeted toward a range of income groups and lifestyles broadens the demand for homes. From a design standpoint, a mix of housing types allows land to be used more effectively because a suitable product type can be developed for each land parcel. Live/work units, apartments above stores, and a good mix of multifamily units, townhouses, and single-family houses all have a place in a mixed-use housing plan. Generally, the highest-density housing types are located closest to the commercial core, while townhouses and single-family homes are situated farther from the commercial core but are still within walking or biking distance.

Designing Residential Districts for Pedestrians. Residential neighborhoods should be planned with as many homes as possible situated within walking distance of the commercial core. Parks and schools should be sited to allow children to walk to them. Residential neighborhoods should be designed with the least mobile residents in mind—children, senior citizens, and disabled people. Good neighborhood design emphasizes a sense of community without compromising privacy. To facilitate walking or biking between homes and other destinations, street patterns should emphasize connectivity and minimize distances between residences and other uses. Ideally, residential blocks are no more than 220 feet by 600 feet (67 by 183 meters) in size. Narrow lots increase the number of homes on a street and improve its character. Most homes should include usable front porches; instead of

Residential neighborhoods that appeal to pedestrians are built with generous sidewalks and planting strips, shaded by a row of street trees. Houses with front porches add "eyes on the street," enhancing the perception of safety. Urban Design Associates

turning their backs to the street, houses should have windows that face the street. All streets should have sidewalks, and they should be at least five feet (1.5 meters) wide, so that two people can walk comfortably side by side. Sidewalks should be bordered by a tree lawn (also called a planting strip), which should also be at least five feet (1.5 meters) wide and should be planted with shade trees at regular intervals. Richard Heapes notes that the best "pavement material" for sidewalks is the dappled shade that comes from mature street trees.

The goal is not to eliminate vehicular traffic but to tame it. Pedestrians and bicyclists can navigate easily when traffic moves at slow speeds. Two ways to calm traffic are to narrow roadways and to shorten the distances between intersections. Neighborhoods made up of short blocks of intersecting streets create better connections for pedestrians and keep traffic from picking up speed the way that it would on longer stretches. A grid street pattern also has the advantage of dispersing traffic more evenly than a hierarchical street system. Roadway systems dominated by curving streets are disorienting to walkers and drivers alike. Because one-way streets only encourage higher speeds and decrease convenience for drivers, two-way traffic is preferable. When traffic lights are needed, they should be on short cycles to keep both vehicles and pedestrians moving efficiently.

Culs de sac are appealing to homebuyers but can create inefficient circulation patterns that make walking difficult and channel auto traffic to a few main streets, leaving the others underused. Compromise plans, which maintain privacy and discourage cut-through traffic without sacrificing efficiency and pedestrian access, can be as marketable. One option is a grid street pattern in which homes are located on short courtyards: this design affords homes the privacy of a cul de sac, but the grid permits easy access. When only culs de sac will do, pedestrian rights-of-way with paths can add a circulation network for those on foot.

It Takes a School to Make a Village. The idea of living where children can walk to school has long been part of the American dream. For families, schools are often the focal point of community life. Neighborhood schools are often a primary consideration for homebuyers, and therefore a significant selling tool for residential development.

Many parents and educators believe that smaller, neighborhood-based schools are better for students, and that students' independence suffers when they must rely on a school bus or a parent chauffeur. But, like transit stops, schools are often relegated to the least valuable land on the periphery of a community, far from homes and community amenities. Consolidation has pushed schools onto larger and larger sites, ever farther from students' homes. However, a number of communities are bucking this trend. At the Kentlands, in Maryland, the Rachel Carson Elementary School is indeed the focus of community life. Located on a prime corner near the entrance to the development, the two-story, red-brick building is accessible by foot for most of the community's schoolchildren. At Stapleton, in Denver, the developers viewed community-based schools as a critical element of their marketing plan. Stapleton's first elementary school, which opened in 2003, is a 350-student, two-level school located on a residential street and surrounded by houses on three sides. Playing fields are at the rear of the school, backing up to a linear park. A larger school, not yet built, is planned on a similar model: the building will be close to sidewalks and have playing fields behind, and will also back up to parkland.

Children and the Built Environment

While much has been learned over the past 50 years about the influence of toxic environmental and chemical agents, little attention has been paid to the significant influence of the built environment on everyday life—especially the everyday life of children. Yet urban scholars believe that the physical environment has the power to demoralize or to depress, and can also contribute to emotional anesthesia, violence, or even suicide.

Though hundreds of new neighborhoods and towns where children will reside are being constructed around the country, architects, planners, and developers seldom consider the effect of their designs on the lives of children and young adults.

Issues that are of concern to urban scholars include the following:

■ Accessibility and autonomy (areas of town that children can reach on their own by foot, bike, or public transportation);
■ Opportunities for social interaction and learning in urban public spaces;
■ Legibility and "imageability" (characteristics of the built environment that make it possible for children to orient themselves and to visualize their town or suburb);
■ Stimulation value of architecture, building uses, public art, and monuments;
■ City and neighborhood identity;
■ Sense of community reinforced by the built environment.

Accessibility, Mobility, Autonomy

At every age, children acquire an increased level of autonomy—the ability to take steps on their own, safely and unaided by parents. Toddlers, as soon as they can stand, are encouraged to walk by themselves; it is the parents' responsibility to ensure that if a toddler falls, he will not hurt himself. A five-year-old should be able to explore his immediate neighborhood and make short trips on his own to a friend's house down the street. The block on which a child lives should be safe for him to negotiate alone. A ten-year-old is curious about the larger world of town or city and should be able to explore it. Clearly, the degree to which children can develop autonomy is influenced strongly by the degree to which their neighborhoods and their cities are safely accessible by foot, bicycle, and public transportation.

Traffic policies; speed limits; the width of streets and traffic lanes; and the presence or absence of traffic-calming mechanisms, pedestrian networks (with continuous sidewalks), and bicycle networks all play a role in helping children and youth to develop independence. For journeys to be short enough to be made on foot or by bicycle, and for public transportation to be feasible, there must be a moderately dense mix of land uses that creates a "city of short distances." Schools should be close enough to homes so that children can walk or bicycle to them. The ice cream parlor, the movie house, and the library should also be within easy reach by foot or bike. Creating "cities and towns of short distances" would also increase children's opportunities for physical activity during the normal course of a day, thus reducing childhood obesity.

Opportunities for Social Learning: Shared Public Spaces

Many people are required to provide suitable models for the socialization of children. The skills involved in speaking with others, making contact, resolving differences, and taking pleasure in social relationships cannot be acquired only from one's own family. Much can be learned if children can share in the social life of their city and observe how adults act in their encounters and relationships.

To become fully developed socially means engaging in the whole spectrum of human interaction—learning to be attentive, to respond appropriately, and to live with the different kinds of people in one's neighborhood, town, or city. Children and young people often lack these social skills and competencies—which is not surprising, considering the impoverished state of urban public spaces, few of which provide a setting where good models of relationships may be observed and where dialogue and general discourse skills may be practiced. The urban fabric should be reconstructed so that streets and squares become vibrant places for social discourse and community life. As Jane Jacobs says, "The people of cities who have other jobs and duties . . . can, and on lively sidewalks they do, supervise the incidental play of children and assimilate the children into city society. They do it in the course of carrying on their other pursuits."

Orientation, Legibility, and Imageability

For a child to find his way around in a neighborhood or city, the urban structure must be easily recognizable and understandable. According to child psychologist Jean Piaget, children first recognize their environment by a series of landmarks, and then learn the relationships between these points of reference. According to city planner Kevin Lynch, we create an image of the city by its overall shape and form, and by identifying landmarks such as distinctive buildings and squares, and familiar paths and routes. Towns and districts are more easily visualized if they have identifiable boundaries. "A highly image-

City Heights Urban Village, in San Diego (see case study), integrated the elementary school into the urban fabric through shared recreation facilities, including a swimming pool, tennis courts, and playing fields. At Belle Creek, near Denver, the "family center" is the core of the community, both physically and philosophically. The idea behind the facility—which includes a public charter school, a community center, a shared gym, a daycare center, and public meeting rooms—was that residents would form relationships through the school and through the community center activities.

Healthy environments encourage increasing levels of independence for children as they mature. Left: Cooper Carry, Inc. Right: RTKL Associates

able city would seem well formed, distinct, remarkable," Lynch observes.

New neighborhoods and towns should create an environment so "legible and visualizable" that children can get to know it as well as the backs of their hands; as the Italian educator Walter Baruzzi has put it, children should "have the city in their pocket."

Meaning of the Built Environment

Researchers studying dysfunctional families have noted that the dialogue in such families is often disconnected and lacks meaning. Dysfunctional urban environments may be thought of as analogous to dysfunctional families: buildings are constructed with total disregard for the character of adjacent buildings or local traditions, creating a fragmented and meaningless city. For children who lack strong and meaningful family experiences that would tend to neutralize the effects of "toxic" surroundings, an adverse, fragmented, urban environment could lead to the belief that their world makes no sense.

For the city to make sense to a child, the majority of buildings should be connected and related in character and scale. A continuous urban fabric gives the feeling of a community in which cooperation and negotiation take place, and can continue to take place. Within this urban fabric, special civic buildings—schools, libraries, theaters, museums—should be identifiable by their design and appearance and easily distinguishable from factory and office buildings.

Sense of Community Reinforced by the Built Environment

In the Italian city of Siena, every neighborhood has its own flag and neighborhood song; its own community kitchen, museum, and meeting rooms; and its own fountain—in which, each year, a formal *battesimo* ceremony is performed to induct children into the community. At the heart of each neighborhood is a main street or square where community dinners are held, with several thousand people eating together many times a year. Children grow up with a strong sense of their priv-

ileges and responsibilities as community members, and the intense rivalry among neighborhoods is played out in the annual Palio horse race. This strong system of neighborhood identity, in which teenagers and youths play some of the most valued roles in historic celebrations, has enabled the city to be virtually free of crime, social problems, vandalism, and teenage delinquency.

Shared public spaces and community facilities within a compact, mixed-use neighborhood can reinforce a sense of community. To reconnect children and youth with their fellow city dwellers requires a balanced urban fabric supporting a vibrant public realm that is hospitable and accessible to adults and children. As Colin Ward notes, "If the claim of children to share the city is admitted, the whole environment has to be designed and shaped with their needs in mind, just as the needs of the disabled" today are being accepted as crucial elements in design.

Source: Adapted from Suzanne H. Crowhurst Lennard, "Children and the Built Environment," *Urban Land,* January 2004, 69–70.

When planning school sites, developers need to consider the school's relationship to the overall community and to amenities such as libraries, playing fields, daycare centers, and commercial districts. Safe walking routes should be laid out so that students from most neighborhoods can walk to the elementary school. The siting of the

school building on the property is also important. Locating the building at the back of the site, with access by way of long driveways, is less effective than placing it nearer the street, with playing fields at the rear.

At City Heights Urban Village, in San Diego, a core of public facilities includes a continuing education facility, an elementary school, and a Head Start center (shown here). Martinez + Cutri

Making Connections

Successful pedestrian-oriented streets provide a safe and pleasant environment where pedestrians feel comfortable and neighbors can interact. A good street plan is essential for creating connectivity within and between developments. Streets should be woven into the public domain. They must be pedestrian-friendly and still move traffic effectively. Pedestrian-friendly streets are narrow enough to minimize traffic speed and to allow safe crossing.

Developments must be planned so that they mesh with adjacent communities and are linked by streets, sidewalks, parks, and trails. Without such connections, pedestrians are effectively trapped in their immediate neighborhoods, unable to reach nearby destinations. When new developments are closed off from old, and connectivity between uses is reduced, driving becomes imperative, even for short trips. Creating public spaces and commercial districts that bridge communities and developments, and integrating sidewalks and bike paths to allow access to different uses, helps support a number of different transportation choices, makes public transit more possible, and ultimately makes communities more livable.

Traffic Calming

Pedestrians benefit from controlled traffic patterns that provide for greater safety and connectivity between uses. A number of traffic-taming practices can be used to better manage automobiles. In the words of pedestrian planning expert Dan Burden, America could use a "road diet." Too often, roads are designed to meet future demand, which becomes a self-fulfilling prophecy. Burden points out that many standard five-lane roadways (two lanes in each direction, plus one center turn lane) could be redesigned to have two travel lanes, a landscaped median, and bike paths and on-street parking on both sides—and still handle the traffic load. Generally, the center turn lane adds little to traffic capacity, so eliminating it still allows traffic to move efficiently.

The type of road Burden recommends will still handle the traffic load, but it will do so at slower speeds; the road will be safer for motorists as well as for pedestrians and bicyclists, and it will be more attractive. And on-street parking reduces the need for large off-street surface lots. Furthermore, slower speeds can actually *decrease* travel times. At higher speeds, the distances between cars increase, which decreases the volume of cars on a stretch of roadway while creating pockets of stop-and-go traffic.

Several built-in safety measures in Burden's design protect the pedestrian, maximizing walkability. The bike lane and on-street parking serve as added buffers, and the median allows pedestrians a point of refuge if the street cannot be crossed all at once. The on-street parking allows curb extensions to be used at intersections, which further reduces crosswalk distances. Curb extensions at the end of a block also slow down the cars turning the corner.[6]

Other traffic-calming devices include traffic circles, the use of islands or median strips (to narrow roads), and the use of various pavement surfaces (for example, where pedestrian use is high, brick or cobblestone pavers can be used to slow traffic).

Of all the traffic-calming tools available, speed bumps should be considered only as a last resort. They increase

The street and sidewalk right-of-way requires ample space for buffers such as bike lanes, on-street parking, and tree lawns. The best streets include all of these elements as a series of buffers that serve other purposes as well: bike lanes offer bikers their own space; on-street parking provides convenience for shoppers making a quick stop; and tree lawns provide a sense of enclosure and help define the street edge.

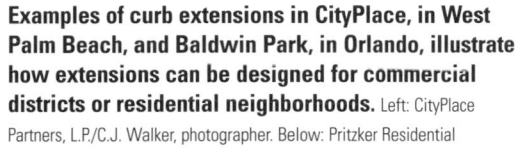

Examples of curb extensions in CityPlace, in West Palm Beach, and Baldwin Park, in Orlando, illustrate how extensions can be designed for commercial districts or residential neighborhoods. Left: CityPlace Partners, L.P./C.J. Walker, photographer. Below: Pritzker Residential

noise, are difficult to maneuver, and are not especially effective; they often fail to slow traffic except at the point of installation. Speed tables, which are flat surfaces with a gradual ascent and descent, are somewhat better, and can effectively delineate a midblock pedestrian or bikeway crossing. Better still, however, are streets with built-in traffic-calming measures—narrow streets with short blocks, for example.

Some arterials need to carry higher loads of traffic at greater speeds than can be accommodated with traffic-calming measures in place. In such cases, landscaped buffers along the median and along the sidewalk edge should be increased to protect pedestrians; in some

Curb extensions and pavement treatments like these, at North Hills, in Raleigh, North Carolina, send a signal to drivers that this is a pedestrian zone and that they must slow down. Such traffic-calming devices are more effective than speed bumps.
Carter & Burgess, Inc.

cases, separate paths may be appropriate to accommodate bicycles. Framing wide-open streetscapes with landscaping is also a good way to bring the street down to the human scale. Broad streets with limited tree cover do not feel as secure and comfortable as narrower streets that are lined with buildings and that offer enough trees to provide a canopy overhead. In areas of high traffic but low speed, minimizing building setback requirements—and allowing buildings to enclose and frame the corners—can help identify an area, give greater definition to the street edge, and make the streets more pedestrian-friendly. This is especially important at major intersections.

Planners can take a number of steps to ensure proper crosswalk design, which is essential for pedestrian safety: reduce curb radii; square off curbs at intersections or use curb extensions to shorten the crosswalk; provide refuge areas on medians; narrow roadways; and make crosswalks more visible to motorists. With respect to visibility, the standard zebra stripes provide the bare minimum. An effective alternative is to raise intersections slightly and to use different pavers, such as brick, stone, or colored concrete, to distinguish the crosswalks visually and contextually for drivers. Positioning crosswalks at an angle can help to differentiate them from the street and can also give pedestrians an angled view into the street, so that they can lock eyes with the drivers of oncoming cars. Midblock

Good wheelchair access requires careful planning. Too often, ramps exist but are not usable because of obstacles, steep grades, or missing connections. Michael Ronkin

crosswalks can sometimes increase safety by reducing the temptation to jaywalk. Finally, crosswalks should have adequate and easily distinguished signage, and intersections should be well lit so that pedestrians are highly visible at night.

Universal Access

It is important to develop a comprehensive plan for universal access so that all public spaces are completely wheelchair accessible. In addition to being able to fully navigate and enjoy sidewalks, parks, and squares, people who use wheelchairs or walkers, or push strollers, should be able to take the shortest routes from parking to all public spaces and commercial facilities. Signage should be visible from a seated position, and accommodations should be made for users whose sight is impaired. (Braille signs mounted at eight-foot heights do not work!)

The Americans with Disabilities Act specifies detailed requirements for parking, curb ramps, signage, and other elements of project design.

Sidewalks

The sidewalk is the most important public open space and the focal point of community life. In retail districts, the sidewalk is the generator of commerce. In residential neighborhoods, it is the social connector. Places must be designed to be experienced on foot—that is, on a human scale. Pedestrians feel most comfortable in places with well-defined edges, and sidewalks are an essential means of achieving that definition. Street trees, grass strips, bollards, and specialty curbing can further reinforce the street edge.

Designing Accessible Parks, Gardens, and Playgrounds

Public parks, gardens, and play areas can be designed to accommodate people with a range of abilities. Here are just a few things to think about:

■ *Access.* All entryways must be as level as possible. On a walking surface, the maximum grade for wheelchair passage is 5 percent; it should be no more than 2 percent in areas where wheelchairs will be loaded and unloaded from cars. To

Hadley's Park, in Potomac, Maryland, is designed to accommodate people with a range of abilities.

accommodate wheelchair width, paths should be three feet (0.9 meters) wide. If two chairs might need to pass each other, the path should be widened accordingly. Turnaround space requires a diameter of five feet (1.5 meters).

■ *Changes in grade.* Steps leading down from a deck or terrace should be replaced with, or supplemented by, a ramp. If the drop is not too far, create a switchback or a curved path with an attractive, stable surface and accent it with planting areas. Screen a plain ramp with plantings, placing taller plants at the back and shorter ones in front; this arrangement is more graceful than a single line of shrubs, which tends to emphasize the starkness of the lines. Curving

lines in planting beds also soften sharp angles. Use plants that have year-round interest or plants that bloom at different times.

■ *Curbs and borders.* Curbs can be useful guideposts for people who are visually impaired. Concrete edges or railroad ties along the edges of paths make it easier to follow the path with a cane. Texture changes along a path or across grounds will also help people with vision impairments find their way, as will sharp contrast changes, such as black to white, or white to dark green. Edges or kickboards should be no more than 27 inches (69 centimeters) high. Railings of 30 to 34 inches (76 to 86 centimeters) in height should be added for people whose mobility is impaired.

■ *Wheelchair safety.* Curbs and kickboards can be impediments to people who use wheelchairs. Curb cuts create easier access. It's important to make the edges safe for people in wheelchairs. At Hadley's Park, a playground in Potomac, Maryland, a one-inch- (2.5-centimeter-) high lip edges the playground—enough to signal that the edge is there and to stop a wheelchair from rolling out of the playground.

■ *Surfaces.* People with limited mobility need a smooth, stable surface to walk on; children on a playground need something relatively soft to fall on. Several types of paving are wheelchair-friendly. Walkway surfaces need to drain completely and not become slippery when wet. Some surfaces that look smooth can be uncomfortable or even treacherous for a person in a wheelchair or for someone who uses a walker. According to one young wheelchair user, "Bricks are not fun." The pathways at Hadley's Park are made of rub-

berized material (shredded tires) that can be poured to whatever depth is needed to meet standards for surface safety.

■ *Themes and cognitive aids.* Hadley's Park uses themed designs—a castle, a pirate ship, Main Street—to encourage creative play. Signs can be used to teach and to provide cognitive benefits. Some signs at Hadley's Park are in three forms: letters, sign language, and Braille. Globes and maps are contoured to indicate features. Simple signs could be used in a community garden to teach plant names or spelling.

■ *Plantings and comforts.* People with no or low vision can enjoy fragrance, texture, and taste. Herbs that can be pinched and identified by smell, and shrubs with fragrant flowers or foliage offer sweet or savory rewards for anyone venturing into the garden. Gardens should include plants that can be touched and examined at wheelchair level, such as butterfly bushes or rosemary shrubs. Raised beds can be designed so that visitors using wheelchairs can touch the vegetables and herbs, smell the flowers, and pull the weeds. Appropriate tools can make working in the garden more comfortable for people with disabilities: lighter, recoiling hoses; ergonomically designed hand tools; containers for hauling plants and debris; faucet extensions; watering wands; and knee pads.

Americans with Disabilities standards are available at www.ada.gov, or at 800-514-0301 (voice) or 800-514-0383 (TTY). Playground guidelines can be found at www.access-board.gov. The American Horticultural Therapy Association in Denver (800-634-1603, www.ahta.org/contact) can recommend books and other resources. Learn about Hadley's Park, Inc., at www.hadleyspark.org.

Source: Adapted with permission from Joel M. Lerner. © 2004, Joel M. Lerner, APLD. All rights reserved. Originally published in the *Washington Post*, January 24, 2004, F-1.

In commercial districts, sidewalks should be able to accommodate outdoor cafés and still allow room for pedestrians to pass. At the Market Common, Clarendon, in Arlington, Virginia, sidewalk life is enhanced by cafés. Adrienne Schmitz

Sidewalks should be ample for the setting and anticipated use. In a commercial area, sidewalks should be wide enough to accommodate café-style seating and still allow two pedestrians to walk side by side comfortably. In most residential neighborhoods, sidewalks should be at least five feet (1.5 meters) wide. They should also be well lit at night, for safety and visibility, and should be installed on both sides of the street.

Bike Lanes and Bike Paths

Safe bicycling requires a certain amount of separation from automobiles. Commercial streets should include bike lanes, recreational areas should provide bike paths, and residential areas should provide a mix of the two. Bike racks should be located at convenient places in commercial and recreational areas. Ideally, collector and residential streets should offer bike lanes, and separated bike paths should be limited to larger arterial roads or other roads where bike lanes are not safe or feasible. In many communities, bike paths along natural features and greenways are a value-added amenity and provide attractive, safe, and auto-free connections within and between communities. In the case of both bike lanes and bike paths, planners must take care to remove impediments to bicycles (such as large grates or rough railroad crossings). Bike

The Importance of Planting Strips

Sidewalks can either be built right at the edge of the street or can be separated from the curb by a planting strip. Just a few feet of grass between the sidewalk and the street can make a big difference. There are many benefits to planting strips, among them the following:

■ *Increase pedestrian safety.* Every now and then, a reckless driver will run up on the sidewalk. The separation makes collisions with pedestrians less likely. It also protects pedestrians from overhanging cargo on large vehicles.

■ *Increase pedestrian comfort.* It is very uncomfortable for pedestrians to walk close to traffic. A green buffer makes a sidewalk much more comfortable for walking.

■ *Provide space for groups of pedestrians.* When pedestrians travel in groups, they will not fit on a narrow sidewalk. If the sidewalk is set back behind a grassy strip, people walking in groups will spill over onto the grass rather than into the street.

■ *Direct pedestrians to desired crossing locations.* Pedestrians are less likely to cross the street where they have to cross grass to get to the street. A grass strip gently encourages pedestrians to cross at paved access points.

■ *Reduce problems with dips and cross slopes at driveway aprons.* This is particularly important for pedestrians using wheelchairs.

■ *Reduce the amount of road spray striking pedestrians in wet weather.* In addition to the dramatic splashes from large puddles, cars generate a tremendous amount of fine spray close to the roadway.

■ *Discourage parking on the sidewalk.* Physical separation from the street can do more to discourage this practice than law enforcement.

■ *Keep the apparent street width narrow.* Sidewalks at the curb make a street appear wider, which encourages drivers to speed. Sidewalks set back behind a planting strip—particularly when trees are planted in the strip—will make the street appear narrower.

■ *Help drivers identify pedestrians who are about to cross.* When the sidewalk is at the curb, all pedestrians are just a step away from crossing the street. When the sidewalk is set back, pedestrians planning to cross the street will have moved away from the pedestrians who are just walking along the sidewalk.

■ *Help drivers spot driveways.* When the sidewalk is at the curb, the entire length of the curb is paved. A grass strip at the curb will make driveways stand out.

■ *Provide a place to plant trees.* In the summer, pedestrians welcome the shade provided by a row of street trees. Trees also provide substantial environmental benefits.

■ *Absorb runoff when it rains.* Separating sidewalks from gutters and storm drains with a wide grassy area minimizes the environmental impact of sidewalks.

■ *Improve air quality at the sidewalk.* Exhaust fumes are most concentrated closest to the center of the traffic stream. Moving the sidewalk away from traffic, even a few feet, will keep pedestrians out of the highest levels of pollution.

■ *Provide a place to dump snow.* Plows pile snow high along the curb. If the sidewalk is built at the curb, it will be buried under the deepest part of the mound.

■ *Provide a place to pile leaves for recycling.* Without a planting strip, the only alternatives are either to block the sidewalk or to clog the gutter and storm drains.

■ *Provide space for fire plugs, utility poles, and road signs.* Without a planting strip, such necessary elements can form permanent obstructions to pedestrians, wheelchairs, and strollers along the sidewalk.

■ *Provide a place to put trash cans and recycling bins.* Trash cans and recycling bins can block the sidewalk on trash day if there is no planting strip.

■ *Provide a place to put street furniture.* In business districts, the grass is typically replaced by a paved surface to create a "furniture zone." Benches, bike racks, newspaper boxes, and other street furniture occupy the area between the curb and the "travel zone" of the sidewalk.

■ *Provide a place to put storm drains out of the street.* Storm drains can be recessed into the green space, keeping steep inlets and metal grates out of the curb lane. In-street storm drains can be hazardous to bicyclists and are difficult to keep free of debris. Also, the pavement around drains is subject to premature failure.

How wide should a planting strip be? A planting strip of six to ten feet (1.8 to three meters) will provide all the benefits enumerated in this list. If the planting strip is much wider, it can start to disconnect the sidewalk from the road, which can be a problem if pedestrians are out of the line of sight of drivers who are about to turn a corner. A narrow planting strip of just three feet (0.9 meters) is far better than nothing, but it will not be able to provide all the benefits of a wider strip.

Images of the same street, before and after an epidemic of Dutch Elm disease, show the value of street trees. The uniform row of arching elms provides a canopy over the street and gives the neighborhood a quality that is not recreated by the haphazard assortment of replacement trees. Jack H. Barger, Ph.D., U.S. Forest Service

Source: Adapted from John Z. Wetmore, "Sidewalk Placement," www.pedestrians.org/tips.htm, with permission from John Z. Wetmore.

paths should be designed to minimize surface crossing at busy intersections.

Public Spaces

Well-designed public spaces are the cornerstone of livable communities. And the essence of community is human connection: a sense of belonging to an identifiable place and to an active public realm. Pedestrian-friendly development is thus more than connectivity between physical land uses: it requires a paradigm shift—a new way of viewing design and architecture that is based on improving connections among people.

Parks, plazas, and other public spaces need not be large and expensive, but they do need to be properly designed and located. In *The Social Life of Small Urban Spaces,* William Whyte, one of the foremost thinkers on public spaces, describes in detail the design elements that are crucial for generating life in urban spaces.[7] Whyte conducted field research on how people use (or don't use) urban public space, and made two particularly important findings: first, good public spaces generate users; second, contrary to the conventional notion that people dislike crowds, people are most attracted to places that are well populated. It is essential, for designers of small parks and public plazas alike, to pay attention to Whyte's design tenets. Simply providing open space is not enough; the space must be welcoming, safe, and attractive. The most successful public spaces are those that are active; provide ample and comfortable seating; offer protection from extremes of sun, wind, and temperature; and connect seamlessly to the street but still maintain edges and definition.

The "pocket parks" championed by architect Peter Calthorpe are relatively small, ranging from one to four acres (0.4 to 1.6 hectares). At the residential neighborhood level, pedestrian planning expert Dan Burden takes this concept one step further, calling for even smaller parks that can be accessed easily on foot by all residents. In Burden's concept for neighborhood parks, the parks are approximately the size of one house lot and would be located within one-quarter mile (0.4 kilometers) of most

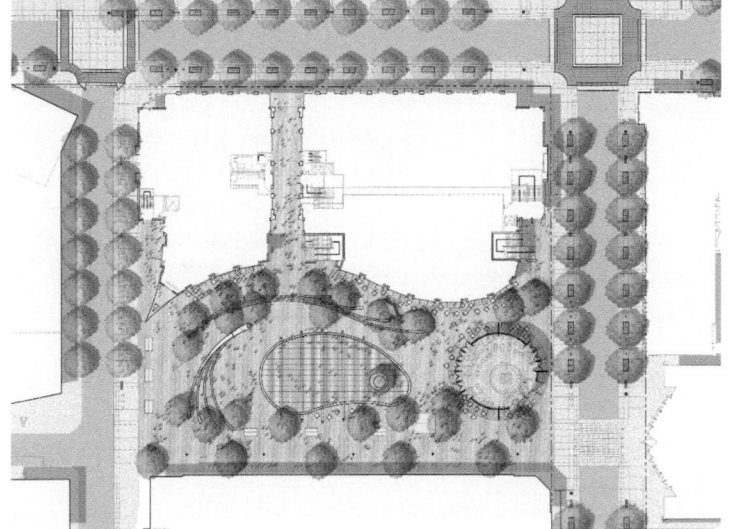

Belmar, in Colorado, was designed around a public plaza that brings together key design elements: trees, water, seating, shade, and kiosks. Civitas

homes. No matter how small, such parks can accommodate diverse facilities, including playgrounds, skating areas, playing fields, and community gardens. These kinds of public spaces provide people with opportunities for physical activity and a reason to venture out on foot. Integrating such spaces into residential neighborhoods, and allowing them to serve as bridges to commercial and other residential areas, gives residents a place to gather and encourages them to be more active.

Social Capital, Third Places, and Walking

"There's no there, there." Gertrude Stein is reported to have uttered this famous comment after a visit to her childhood home in Oakland, California. The house had burnt down, and nothing was left but Stein's memories. But the quote is now often used to refer to the absence of a sense of "place" that characterizes many post–World War II suburbs. In much of suburban America, all that is left are memories of "there."

What is "there"? What is it that makes a place special? While urban designers, planners, architects, and developers have been approaching this question from a perspective rooted in the study of the physical environment, social theorists are trying to understand what "there" is by examining social connections and interactions within communities. These scientists are trying to determine which environments are conducive to social interactions, and how people use their physical surroundings to create meaningful social relations.

In his ground-breaking book *Bowling Alone*, Harvard professor Robert Putnam popularized the concept of social capital—the strength of our social networks—and documented its steady decline in American society. All of us are embedded in social networks made up of family, coworkers, friends, and acquaintances—and their families, coworkers, friends, and acquaintances. For Putnam, social capital is the degree to which these networks can inspire trust, create or reinforce norms of behavior, and solve social problems.

Where social capital is high, it has the power to mobilize social networks to engage in a wide range of actions that benefit communities. The informal neighborhood watch, in which neighbors keep an eye on each others' houses, is an example, as are barn raisings, quilting bees, bridge clubs, and fraternal organizations.

The title of Putnam's book refers to one of the prime examples of social capital: the bowling league. Until the 1960s, bowling leagues were quite common. Members practiced bowling with their friends and then competed against each other in tournaments. Today, bowling is as popular as ever, but membership in bowling leagues is lower than ever. Most people who bowl now bowl alone.

Putnam sees the decline of bowling leagues as indicative of the decline in social capital everywhere in society. This decline, he believes, has resulted in historically low levels of civic participation and voter turnout. The decline has also impaired the ability to engage in social discourse

"Third places" are important for a community's social well-being. Such places have been excluded from many suburban communities, but they are being brought back by planners and developers who understand their importance. Shown here is Addison Circle, a mixed-use community in Addison, Texas. RTKL Associates

on controversial topics in a civil and meaningful way. Today, community organizations are more likely to be collections of individuals acting in their own self-interest than groups of people proactively trying to improve community life.

Following are some key elements for active outdoor spaces:

■ Seating may include benches, ledges, and movable chairs. It's best to give people choices about where to sit: in sun or shade; alone or in groups; out in front or away from the street. Low retaining walls can serve a double purpose if they are of the right height for sitting and are not pointed, sloped, or spiked to prohibit sitting.

■ Climate is a major consideration. In temperate climates, both sun and shade should be provided. In hotter regions, protection from the sun is important.

■ Trees provide shade, shelter, and a connection with nature. Ideally, native, long-lived, low-maintenance species that grow to the appropriate height for the space should be selected.

■ Natural or manmade water features can be an attraction. Pools, fountains, waterfalls, streams, lakes, and ponds provide a variety of sensory experiences. Water features should be sited to allow interaction. A fountain that children can run through is much more inviting than one surrounded by shrubbery or a wall.

■ In commercial areas, a certain amount of commerce should be allowed to spill over into parks or plazas. Food vendors, skate rental facilities, and street performers, for example, generate pedestrian activity.

■ An active space is a safe space: activity in itself discourages criminal elements from staking their claim to a space. "Eyes on the green" are as useful as eyes on the street.

■ The location of parks and plazas should encourage impulse use. They should be located in busy areas, and should be easy to see and to reach; they should not be sunk below grade or hidden behind walls or shrubs.

Social capital is not only important for civic life: it also offers health benefits. Putnam notes that over a dozen medical studies have shown that people who are socially disconnected are two to five times more likely to die from all causes than those who are more socially connected; people who are less connected are also more likely to suffer from heart attacks, strokes, cancer, and depression.

Although social scientists are not certain why levels of social capital have dropped in recent years, there are a few possible suspects. One possible culprit is the built environment. A study published in the *American Journal of Public Health* found a relationship between social capital and walkable neighborhoods: people living in walkable neighborhoods (as defined by the number of places that a resident could walk to without too much trouble) were more likely to know their neighbors, more likely to participate in political activities, more likely to trust others, and more likely to be involved socially.

A related concept is that of the "third place." In sociologist Ray Oldenburg's *The Great Good Place*, third places are where people go when they do not want to be at home (the first place) or at work (the second place). Third places are where people hang out—meet friends, make new friends, and engage in public life in an informal and relaxed setting.

According to Oldenburg, successful third places have low barriers to admission: entry is free or relatively inexpensive. The cost of admission to a coffee shop, for example, is the price of a cup of coffee. Successful third places are relatively easy to get to. They are also popular places, with a high volume of daily visitors. Finally, the successful third place is welcoming to both regulars and newcomers.

Television and film often depict third places. One prominent example is the bar on *Cheers*. The *Cheers* theme song is also the source of one of the most concise and accurate definitions of the third place: it's "where everybody knows your name." Other examples of third places in popular culture include the Central Perk coffee house in *Friends* and the barbershop in the movie *Barbershop*.

For most Americans, real-life examples of third places are unfortunately much harder to come by. The drugstore soda fountains of the early 20th century are now only memories. Post–World War II suburban development patterns, combined with strict zoning regulations, left little room for the creation of third places. Even in many cities, there are few true third places.

The decline in third places is likely linked to the decline in social capital. Third places generate, renew, and strengthen social capital. The informal and sociable atmosphere of the third place helps people make new friends and reinforces relationships with old ones. The combination of a third place and a social network can have some powerful results. The Wagon Wheel Bar, in Mountain View, California, for example, has become legendary as the birthplace of Silicon Valley. When the semiconductor industry was in its infancy, the Wagon Wheel was a third place where engineers from many different companies throughout the region would go to unwind, gossip, boast about their accomplishments, and just hang out. During these informal get-togethers, ideas and information were shared, technical problems solved, and alliances forged. Many technical innovations and successful businesses were born in the Wagon Wheel or in other third places in the Valley.

For the land use professional, the concepts of social capital and third places are essential to creating places that feel authentic. Understanding how people will use the spaces that are built for them, and the social implications of building and design, is the first step in creating authentic places that will meet the test of time. Without social capital and third places, there can be no "there" there.—*J.S.*

People on their way to an appointment, parents running errands with children, pedestrian commuters, or others might stop to play, rest, read, or chat with someone they happen to meet along the way. An active park or square is also an amenity for those who don't stop but who walk by and see the activity. It becomes part of the scenery that makes walking fun.

Whyte discovered that children play in the street not because they have no options but because they like to. Jane Jacobs made a similar observation. What children are really seeking is an active, visible place where friends can gather for impromptu play. Playgrounds should be located in public areas, including busy commercial districts. They need not be large or elaborate but should provide equipment for active play—swings, jungle gyms, and so on.

Parking: Carrot or Stick?

Ironically, parking is one of the critical elements of pedestrian-friendly design. Getting the parking right is more complicated and expensive in a dense, walkable area than in highway-oriented exurbs, where it may be as cheap and easy to pave the grass as to mow it.

There are two schools of thought on parking: the carrot and the stick. In other words, should a bare minimum of parking be provided at a high price, or should parking be ample, convenient, and free? Providing a delightful walking experience is generally more profitable than punishing drivers with overly expensive or hard-to-find parking. If people must drive to a destination, it is preferable to create an environment in which people park once and then are happy to walk between multiple uses.

but such businesses are probably not appropriate in the pedestrian-oriented core and should instead be concentrated elsewhere.

Surface parking lots in front of buildings are off-putting to pedestrians and create an environment that is welcoming only to cars. Instead, it's best to site parking behind, above, or below buildings. When land values warrant it, structured parking makes sense. Ideally, most parking should be located in structures that are shared by all businesses, and should be supplemented by on-street parking. Even if on-street parking does not account for much of the overall parking inventory, it allows people to cruise past shops on their way to a parking facility and adds to the pedestrian activity on

At Market Common, Clarendon, parking garages were carefully integrated into the plan. In this part of the project, parking is above the stores and is designed to look like the upper floors of commercial buildings. Adrienne Schmitz

Parking for Commercial Districts

Deciding how much parking to provide is a challenge. When calculating the number of spaces needed, planners need to take all factors into account, including transit users, walkers, and shared parking arrangements. Although zoning regulations and parking codes usually mandate a certain number of spaces per 1,000 square feet (93 square meters) of building floor area, pedestrian-friendly designs can often reduce the amount of parking that is required. Successful pedestrian-oriented developments match the amount of parking to the project's needs and design the parking to be as unobtrusive as possible. Some businesses may need large parking lots,

the street. High-turnover on-street parking (for example, metered parking with short time limits) is especially useful because it conveniently accommodates patrons making quick trips.

To make garages fit into the pedestrian-oriented streetscape, active retail or service uses can be incorporated at the street level. One alternative is to "wrap" the entire parking structure with another building. Miami architect Bernard Zyscovich believes in animating the pedestrian level by integrating the parking garage with other uses: his projects feature retail uses or narrow townhouses along the garage face, with gardens in front.

Creating shared parking districts served by central garages minimizes the total number of spaces that are needed. Shared parking can be used wherever the peak hours of demand differ for adjacent land uses. For example, a movie theater and a supermarket, or a church and an office, can easily share parking. The goal of a shared parking policy is to provide enough parking for commercial and other uses while taking up the smallest footprint possible. Shared parking reinvigorates neighborhoods by reducing unnecessary parking areas and allowing more land to be used for productive, activity-generating development.

Parking for Residents

Parking for multifamily residential development can require as much or more land as the housing itself. Excessive parking is wasteful, but insufficient parking is a guarantee of failure. Providing the right amount of parking requires a cooperative local government, a good understanding of the tenant mix, and a balance between parking development costs and land costs.

Typically, local codes require 1.75 parking spaces per residential unit, but actual demand can vary widely, depending on the location. To reduce the impact that parking has on the streetscape, developers can use on-street parking for some of the required spaces, create shared parking arrangements for residences and other uses, and integrate garages into other developments. (Because residents often expect to have a parking spot available for their exclusive use, shared parking arrangements with residential users can be difficult, but have worked in some cases.)

Reconfiguring Existing Development

People who dream of building walkable communities usually imagine building from scratch. They sketch neighborhoods with a Portland street grid, New York subways, and Boulder wilderness, all within walking distance of San Francisco bakeries. But in the real world, the public demands walkability in places that are already built. And these places often have characteristics that would seem

The apartments at Market Common, Clarendon, participate in a shared parking arrangement. A garage is located behind the stores, with the residences above. Adrienne Schmitz

Crystal City, in Arlington, Virginia, is being transformed from a 1960s office superblock into a lively, street-oriented, 18-hour office and retail environment. Courtesy of Cooper Carry, Inc.

to ensure that walking will forever remain a dangerous and inconvenient transportation option: they have oversized blocks, little or no transit, and long distances between where people live and their everyday destinations. For a development team or a municipality, converting sprawl into walkable neighborhoods is one of the most difficult but rewarding tasks. When such projects succeed, the payoff can be tremendous—financially; in terms of community spirit; and, eventually, in terms of improved public health.

Compared with greenfield development, retrofitting an existing area requires extra care in identifying the site, extra patience in the public process, greater cooperation between the developer and the municipal government, higher design standards, and a carefully developed long-term strategy. Still, from the malls of Florida to the suburbs of Seattle, development teams and public agencies are overcoming these challenges and creating unique, valuable properties that satisfy the public's hunger for walkable places.

Pedestrian-oriented retrofits can be initiated by either the public or the private sector. Publicly initiated projects tend to focus on an entire corridor or district, whereas private efforts usually target a single large lot, such as an old shopping mall. Or, as was the case at City Heights Urban Village, a for-profit developer may team with a nonprofit organization to initiate the revitalization of a whole neighborhood. Sometimes zoning changes enacted by the public sector can offer private developers the opportunity to make incremental changes on small properties, such as obsolete strip shopping-center sites, and even single-family home lots.

Regardless of the scale of the project or who initiates the retrofit, the development fundamentals are fixed: the lead entity must identify potential sites, learn about legal obstacles, find development incentives, work with competent designers, and develop a marketing program that will attract a healthy mix of commercial and residential occupants. In these respects, redevelopment is like greenfield development, but it requires even more expertise.

Each location requires addressing a different set of issues. At City Heights, for example, the community revitalization program had to include crime prevention measures, whereas at Market Common, Clarendon, a major issue was getting the neighbors to buy into the redevelopment concept. In all cases, however, redevelopment requires a multidisciplinary approach and partnerships between public and private entities.

Destinations Are the Goal

The main goal of pedestrian-friendly development is the creation of dense, mixed-use *destinations,* from shopping districts to schools, cultural facilities, and major workplaces. These are the places where people have always congregated: trading post, village center, or downtown. In most suburban areas today, destinations are typically surrounded by vast parking lots or by acres of landscaping, and are accessible only by way of wide, high-speed streets. Making these districts walkable means reconfiguring large stretches of asphalt or open fields to create fine-grained, pedestrian-scale districts. Because pedestrian improvements mean additional costs, they often require public/private partnerships for funding. When a public agency wants to foster the development or redevelopment of walkable destinations, it can make a collection of policy changes that add up to a new personality for the district:

■ Allowing housing above retail;

■ Permitting the construction of multifamily dwellings;

■ Allowing narrow streets;

■ On wider streets, allowing higher building heights;

■ Splitting up large blocks with new streets;

■ Reducing building setbacks;

■ Forbidding parking lots in front of new buildings;

■ Improving the quality of sidewalks;

■ Adding more streetlights, with shorter, more pedestrian-scale poles;

■ Providing safe bicycle routes;

■ Consolidating parking lots;

■ Providing or improving transit access;

■ Imposing architectural guidelines that address scale and character.

In San Mateo County, California, the local government changed the zoning and planning regulations for a strip arterial, El Camino Real. Setbacks were eliminated, and new and remodeled buildings had to be built directly adjacent to expanded sidewalks. The new regulations encouraged taller buildings at corners, fewer curb cuts, and parking lots that faced side streets rather than main streets wherever possible. Over time, the change in reg-ulations has had an effect: El Camino Real has become more walkable.

Private developers lack the authority to narrow an arterial, but many tools are available to improve walkability, especially on large sites like former office parks or shopping malls. Establishing short, walkable blocks, lining streets with wide, shaded sidewalks, and creating mixed-use districts are all within the realm of the private developer. And when zoning changes facilitate retrofitting for walkability, private developers can contribute to a larger revitalization effort by making changes on smaller, individual lots. In the suburbs of Minneapolis, for example, it is permissible to transform a single-family home into a multifamily dwelling in the course of renovating it, and this has become a popular form of infill development. San Francisco recently legalized "in-law," or accessory apartments, in less dense neighborhoods along transit lines.

Successfully redeveloped properties can become new regional destinations in their own right. In Boca Raton, Florida, an old shopping mall was converted into a walkable neighborhood that features street-level stores, a long urban green surrounded by a small street, multifamily and attached dwellings, structured parking, and an office tower. The result, Mizner Park, is now the city's prime attraction. It is a desirable workplace, office address, and shopping destination. Children, teens, working adults, and senior citizens all go there to shop, walk, eat lunch, or just people watch. All of these interactions and synergies spur high sales volumes—and, in turn, higher commercial rents. The everyday activity that Mizner Park generates means better health: physical health for residents, and financial health for pedestrian-oriented businesses.

American suburbs tend to have far more land zoned for retail than they need, which encourages sprawl. Municipalities must face the tough question of whether they have too much commercially zoned land. Sometimes, by focusing development on a few key intersections, local governments can transform them into attractive mixed-use nodes. Although the businesses at these nodes will benefit from an overall reduction in the allowable retail square footage for the region, such a plan can be a tough sell politically, and may encounter resistance from merchants and landowners outside the newly defined, smaller retail core.

Identifying an appropriate site for reconfiguring can be a difficult challenge. Not every failing mall, defunct airport, or undervalued large-lot subdivision is ripe for redevelopment. Most of the same factors that are important for new development also apply to redeveloped sites, including access to transportation, room for expansion, and a good regulatory climate.

Major Roadblocks

Developers need to be prepared for the obstacles to redevelopment; the more prepared developers are, the more likely that problems can be overcome. Nevertheless, it may take some time—even years—to surmount some of the obstacles. The most common roadblocks in redevelopment are complications involving ownership, resistance on the part of the local government, and the scarcity of successful examples.

■ *Ownership complications.* Some sites have long-term ground leases or other ownership structures that can give someone else veto power over a development. This is not necessarily a deal killer—several major redevelopment projects have involved multiple original land owners or leaseholders—but these complications must be considered ahead of time. Sometimes the municipality can help with lot assembly.

■ *Resistant government.* Because municipal governments often believe that residential development absorbs services but contributes little to the tax base, they are often resistant to increased housing density. The private "governments" or community associations that oversee an increasing amount of the suburban landscape can be even more resistant to change, as they often require a supermajority to rezone land.

■ *Lack of examples.* The lack of comparables can make everything more difficult, from financing to dealing with neighborhood concerns. One approach that can be helpful is to tour the best examples throughout the country, photographing places that match the local vision and interviewing residents of those locales about what they like and don't like.

Catalyst Projects

Too often, when local governments notice neighborhoods that are beginning to revive, they impose massive improvement schemes that do more harm than good. Convention centers, arenas, and other megaprojects have a place in

Mizner Park is the result of the redevelopment of an old shopping mall in Boca Raton, Florida. Today the project features retail, residential, and office development, all surrounding an urban green. Courtesy of Cooper Carry, Inc.

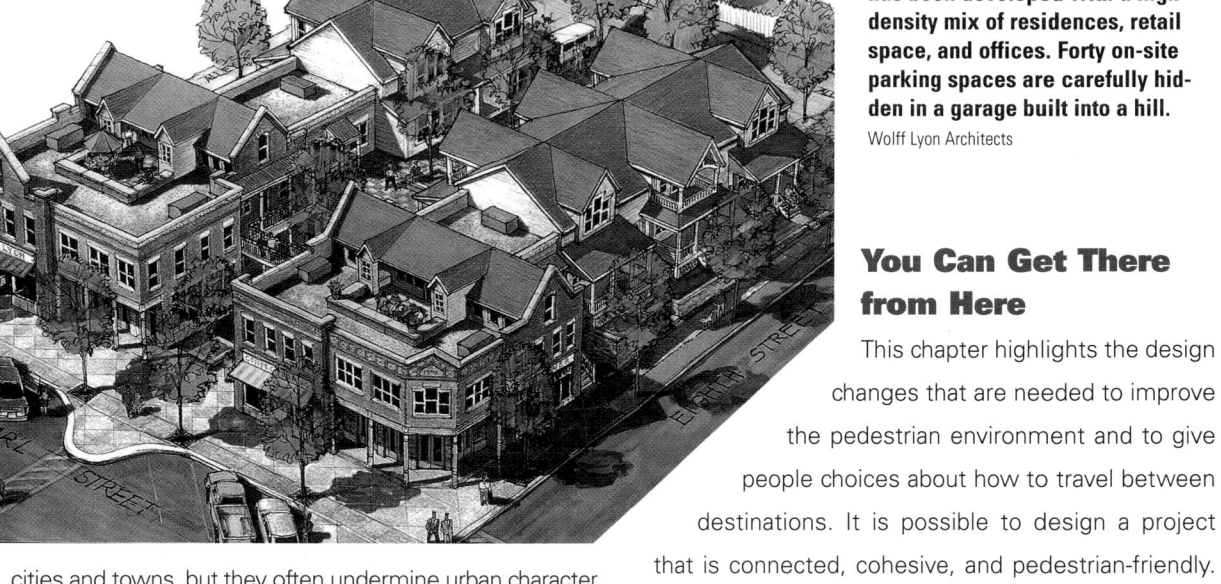

An infill site in Boulder, Colorado, has been developed with a high-density mix of residences, retail space, and offices. Forty on-site parking spaces are carefully hidden in a garage built into a hill.
Wolff Lyon Architects

You Can Get There from Here

This chapter highlights the design changes that are needed to improve the pedestrian environment and to give people choices about how to travel between destinations. It is possible to design a project that is connected, cohesive, and pedestrian-friendly. Designing for the human scale, creating destinations, and improving physical access will all help improve the definition, connectivity, and walkability of communities. It will also provide a greater variety of sensory experiences, which will invite people to stay, explore, and enjoy. Pedestrian-friendly and transit-oriented development improves livability by reducing air pollution and dependence on automobiles, by providing public gathering places and access to basic services, and by encouraging residents to walk and to use public-transit options. The strategies outlined in this chapter will help create healthy, sustainable, and more livable communities.

cities and towns, but they often undermine urban character and diminish walkability. Instead of thinking about how many dollars in tax revenue or how many jobs a project will yield, local governments need to ask whether the project will catalyze further private investment by creating a more desirable place for development.

For example, the city of San Francisco improved infrastructure and made zoning exceptions to allow the San Francisco Giants to build a new ballpark on the city's waterfront. In addition to requiring the project to be pedestrian- and transit-friendly, the city zoned the surrounding areas to take advantage of the attractive new ballpark. Today, the neighborhood has thousands of new residential units and dozens of successful businesses, many of which do business independent of the ballpark.

Reinvesting in the Streetscape

Though historic buildings have a charm of their own, it is in the streets where a city comes to life. Milwaukee and San Antonio are examples of cities that have invested in small streetscape improvements that unify their revived downtowns. Such improvements can include modest changes, like decorative tree planters, benches, and trash cans, as well as bigger investments, like new paving and new traffic signals. Streetscape projects succeed through attention to detail: there are no one-size-fits-all formulas.

Notes

1. U.S. Department of Transportation, Federal Highway Administration, "2001 National Household Travel Survey," available at nhts.ornl.gov/2001/html_files/introduction.shtml.

2. Richard Rogers, addressing the Urban Land Institute, District Council Meeting, Washington, D.C., January 14, 2004.

3. Yaromir Steiner, speaking at an Urban Land Institute Place Making Conference, Reston, Va., September 2003.

4. Michael Beyard, speaking at the Urban Land Institute/Joseph C. Canizaro Mayors' Forum, San Antonio, Tex., February 26–27, 2002.

5. Steiner, Place Making Conference.

6. Numerous traffic-calming measures are suggested in *Residential Streets* (Washington, D.C.: National Association of Home Builders, American Society of Civil Engineers, Institute of Transportation Engineers, and Urban Land Institute, 2001).

7. William Whyte, *The Social Life of Small Urban Spaces* (New York: Project for Public Spaces, 2001).

The Business of Pedestrian-Oriented Development

The popularity of pedestrian-oriented development is growing nation-wide, as people discover the benefits of living, working, and shopping in walkable places. And developers who are responding to this growing demand are finding that pedestrian-oriented development can be not only feasible but profitable. As the number of successful pedestrian-oriented developments grows, walkable places are taking on widely diverse forms: villages and town centers, new urbanist master-planned communities, suburban infill projects, urban redevelopment districts, main-street rejuvenation projects, rehabilitations of conventional retail centers, and transit-oriented developments.

Even though developers are finding success building pedestrian-friendly projects, the financing challenges are sometimes more complicated than those associated with more conventional developments. Lending institutions and equity sources are only now beginning to warm up to pedestrian-oriented development, and the financing methods that work well for conventional, single-use projects do not always take into account the unique circumstances of pedestrian-friendly projects.

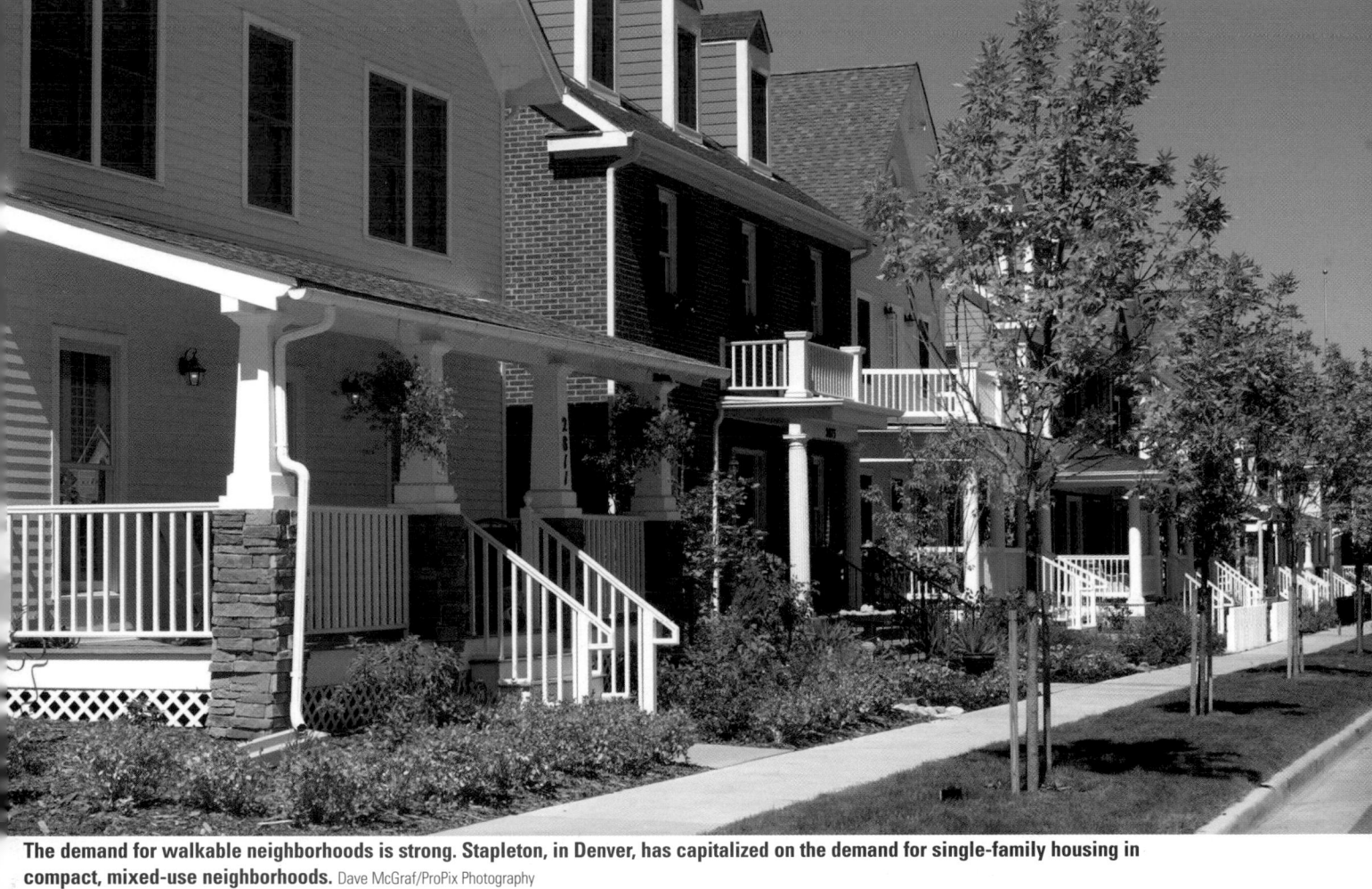

The demand for walkable neighborhoods is strong. Stapleton, in Denver, has capitalized on the demand for single-family housing in compact, mixed-use neighborhoods. Dave McGraf/ProPix Photography

This chapter documents the increasing demand for pedestrian-oriented developments, lists the challenges involved in financing such projects, and describes various strategies that can be used to overcome those challenges.

The Market

For many years, surveys of potential homebuyers have shown a strong, clear preference for single-family homes in low-density neighborhoods. However, new surveys and closer scrutiny of previous surveys reveal that the demand for housing is much more complex. Although there continues to be a market for conventional, vehicle-oriented development, a strong market is also evident for places that are walkable.

Analyzing Consumer Preferences

People want to walk more, and they want to live in neighborhoods that provide them with more opportunities to do so. A 2003 survey on attitudes toward walking, sponsored by the Surface Transportation Policy Project (STPP), showed that 55 percent of Americans would like to walk more than they do. Sixty-three percent said that they would like to be able to run errands on foot and walk to stores. When asked why they do not walk as much as they would like, 61 percent of respondents said that walking is too inconvenient and that things are too far away. Finally, 79 percent stated that the presence of sidewalks and other places to walk and to exercise are important in deciding where to live.[1]

found that many people (33 percent) would rather live in a neighborhood with sidewalks, narrow streets, and parks, than in large-lot suburbs with wide streets. Another consistent finding is that many people (37 percent in one study, and 57 percent in another) actually prefer higher-density developments.[4]

Thus, even though most people want low-density, single-family housing, a substantial segment wants something different. Moreover, the STPP findings suggest that even those who prefer conventional developments would like more opportunities to walk. The overall picture that emerges from available research is that many consumers want low-density neighborhoods composed predominantly of single-family homes, but with all the amenities and benefits of a walkable neighborhood. For example, a 2001 NAHB housing survey found that 58 percent of respondents wanted walking or jogging trails in their neighborhoods. Similarly, 48

Figure 3-1: Americans' Attitudes toward Walking

Viewpoint	Percentage of Respondents Who Agreed
Would like to walk more than they do	55
Would like to run errands on foot and walk to stores	63
Walking is too inconvenient and things are too far away	61
Presence of sidewalks and other places to walk and to exercise are important in deciding where to live	79

Source: Compiled from "Americans' Attitudes toward Walking and Creating Better Walking Communities," an April 2003 survey sponsored by the Surface Transportation Policy Project and conducted by Belden Russonello & Stewart.

Researchers such as Dowell Myers, at the University of Southern California, are echoing the findings of the STPP study. After closely reexamining market research on housing, Myers argues that there is a substantial unmet demand for homes in pedestrian-oriented developments. He notes that a consistent percentage of customers surveyed (1) prefer urban locations, (2) prefer attached or multifamily housing, and (3) want to live in high-density environments where they can walk to destinations.

In a 1999 study by the National Association of Home Builders (NAHB), 17 percent of respondents preferred living in a town-house in the city to living in a detached, single-family home in the suburbs.[2] Other surveys found that a significant percentage of respondents (9 percent in one survey, and 14 percent in another) would prefer condominiums to single-family homes.[3] Further, the 1995 American LIVES survey

Baxter Village, in Fort Mill, South Carolina, offers the sidewalks, narrow streets, and parks preferred by a large segment of homebuyers. Urban Design Associates

percent of those who responded to the 1998 Vermonters' Attitudes on Sprawl Survey preferred neighborhoods with stores and services within walking distance of their homes.[5]

Research conducted by Robert Charles Lesser & Co. (RCL), a national real estate advisory firm, offers further evidence that consumer tastes are shifting. RCL under-

Figure 3-2: Demand for Alternatives to Conventional Residential Development

Viewpoint	Percentage of Respondents Who Agreed	Source
Prefer a city townhouse to a suburban single-family home	17	1999 National Association of Home Builders (NAHB) survey
Prefer condominiums to single-family homes	9 14	1997 Mature Markets survey 1996 NAHB survey
Prefer neighborhoods with sidewalks, narrow streets, and parks to large-lot suburbs with wide streets	33	1995 American LIVES survey
Prefer higher-density developments	37 57	1998 *Professional Builder* survey 1996 NAHB survey
Want to be within walking distance of stores and services	48	1998 Vermonters' Attitudes on Sprawl

Source: Compiled from Dowell Myers and Elizabeth Gearin, "Current Preferences and Future Demand for Denser Residential Environments," *Housing Policy Debate* 12, no. 4 (2001).

took surveys of numerous metropolitan areas throughout the country to determine the level of demand for walkable, mixed-use communities. In all the regions surveyed, between 31 and 37 percent of respondents wanted walkable, urban-style living, but there were few such options in their metropolitan areas. It is logical to presume that once there are more walkable options available, and people can see and understand these examples, the percentage who prefer this lifestyle will increase. Regardless of whether the number is roughly one-third of all households or higher, there is significant pent-up demand for this kind of development.

Changes in preferences for amenities are in line with other findings on consumer tastes. For example, DMB, an Arizona-based developer of master-planned communities, found a marked difference between surveys of what consumers wanted in the early 1990s and what they were looking for in 2003. In the earlier surveys, consumers wanted golf courses and other recreational amenities. Today, consumers want walkability: communities with pedestrian access and a sense of connection to both their neighbors and adjacent uses.

Finally, data on purchases of new versus existing housing indicates the strength of the market for walkable neighborhoods. The 1999 American LIVES Community Preferences survey attempted to determine whether some people buy existing housing because new developments do not offer the types of housing or neighborhoods that they prefer. The survey confirmed that when compared with buyers of new housing, resale buyers are more likely to (1) prefer narrow streets; (2) prefer alternatives to driving; (3) believe that cities can be safe environments for children; and (4) be less concerned about the potential noise or privacy issues that can be associated with high-density development.[6]

Before-and-after photo simulations showing the benefits of increased density for the Streeterville neighborhood in Chicago.
Steve Price, Urban Advantage

But if there is a large demand for homes in walkable communities, why are most buyers of new homes purchasing in low-density environments where walking to destinations is difficult? Laurie Volk and Todd Zimmerman believe it is because most homebuyers do not have any viable alternatives, which inflates the perceived demand for lower-density housing.[7] According to a 2001 NAHB survey, only 38 percent of respondents said their first choice would be to buy an existing house;[8] however, in 2002, of the 6.5 million home sales nationwide, about 85 percent (or 5.56 million) were for existing homes.[9] These data suggest that there is a large group of potential new homebuyers whose needs are not being met by the new-construction product types.

Expanding Consumer Awareness

Findings such as those discussed in the previous section indicate a large unmet demand for pedestrian-friendly environments. But they also indicate that consumers may want something that is not described in most surveys: a neighborhood that combines single-family living with mixed uses in a walkable environment.

According to Zimmerman, Volk, and other market researchers, many Americans want walkable alternatives to conventional developments but are unable to imagine what these developments would be like.[10] Emil Malizia and Jack Goodman, like Zimmerman and Volk, believe that people have a difficult time imagining pleasant, high-density, walkable environments. Most surveys rely on written statements or questions that participants respond to, but using a visual preference survey in which partici-pants responded to pictures of various neighborhoods, Malizia and Goodman discovered that a majority of respondents actually prefer well-designed high-density environments to low-density ones.[11]

In other words, when it comes to pedestrian-oriented neighborhoods, seeing is believing. Many people are trapped by the notion that housing options are limited only to what they are familiar with: suburban low density or urban decay. But when they are shown images of well-designed neighborhoods, those who might other-wise oppose higher densities, clustered developments, and multifamily housing will often prefer such com-pact development. Visual images of successful, well-designed, pedestrian-oriented communities are thus essential in helping to unleash demand for pedestrian-oriented development.

The state of Florida offers many new walkable com-munities—possibly more than any other state—and, as a result, public acceptance of higher-density, mixed-use development is probably higher than elsewhere. Nancy Graham Lawler, former mayor of West Palm Beach, says, "Every time I get a chance, I talk about density. It's critical, but we don't do a very good job of educating people about what it is and how it can look. Visual preference surveys can help people understand."[12] To this end, computer-edited "before and after" photographs are being used more fre-quently in the marketing of pedestrian-oriented develop-ments. Organizations such as Urban Advantage specialize in the creation of images that depict what neighborhoods might look like after density has been increased by more intensive development. Software programs can be similarly helpful; Community Viz, for example, offers software prod-ucts that allow users to create three dimensional models based on real or hypothetical geographic information systems data.

Financial Benefits of Walkability

Studies have shown that people are willing to pay more to live in walkable communities. *Valuing the New Urbanism,* a 1999 Urban Land Institute publication, compared four new urbanist communities with their surrounding competitors and found that people spent an average of $20,189 more to live in pedestrian-friendly, new urbanist communities.[13] More recent studies are finding similar results.

In an attempt to determine which elements of walk-ability people are willing to pay for, researchers Yan Song and Gerrit-Jan Knaap examined sales information and characteristics of the urban form for 48,000 home sales in Washington County, Oregon.[14] They found that home-buyers are willing to pay more—an average of $24,255 more—for design elements that make walking easier, such as smaller block sizes, more street connectivity, pedestrian access to commercial uses, and proximity to parks and transit.

Demand for walkable retail districts is also strong. In Reston, Virginia, Reston Town Center, a pedestrian-oriented town center, filled a void in its suburban locale and now draws shoppers from all over Northern Virginia. The developers of Birkdale Village (see case study) report that while the project was still under construction, people were so eager to have places to walk that they climbed over barricades to explore the newly built streetscape.

Not only are people willing to pay more to live in walk-able areas, but real estate analysts also believe that these places offer the best investment potential. According to the yearly Urban Land Institute and PricewaterhouseCoopers *Emerging Trends in Real Estate* surveys, it is less risky to invest in the mixed-use central business districts of healthy, 24-hour cities than to invest in single-use assets in the sub-urbs. Since 1995, the *Emerging Trends* reports have been steering investors in suburban commercial and residential developments toward districts that have a more urban character, including foot traffic.

The *Emerging Trends* reports also indicate that there are strong potential markets in emerging subcity nodes, which *Emerging Trends* defines as pockets of high-density urban development in locations that were once considered suburban; examples include Buckhead, in the Atlanta region; Old Town Alexandria, in the Washington, D.C., area; and downtown Bellevue, on the shore of Lake Washington across from Seattle. All of these areas already have mixed-use, pedestrian-focused development. There are also major opportunities to create walkable districts in employment centers that now have no mix at all. Hundreds of edge-city business and office complexes could be expanded into mixed-use districts, especially if transit can be added.

The recommendations in the *Emerging Trends* reports are based on two factors: first, analysts believe that as traffic congestion intensifies and distances between destinations increase, the American public will become less enamored with suburban development. Second, analysts believe that people are beginning to recognize the value of the mixed-use approach, which brings together in one location the various services and amenities that people want. According to the 1999 *Emerging Trends* report, "People want to live closer to where they work and play. Hectic lifestyles demand convenience. Golfers may gravitate to more suburban locations, and art collectors and restaurant lovers to the city. Whatever the orientation, commercial real estate markets will thrive if they have attractive adjacent residential districts."[15]

Mixed-use projects can cater to those who enjoy walking to stores, restaurants, entertainment, and work. Moreover, employers are discovering that more urban and walkable locations can be used as marketing tools for worker recruit-

Mockingbird Station, in Dallas, is a transit-oriented suburban downtown. RTKL Associates

ment and retention. The higher occupancy rates, sales revenue, and return trips made by customers of pedestrian-oriented retail districts speak to the positive response of consumers, who are willing to pay a premium for the pedestrian experience.

The fact that there is a limit to the distance that people are willing to walk—generally about 1,500 feet (457 meters)—benefits developers of walkable projects. An area with a radius of 1,500 feet (457 meters) covers about 80 to 100 acres (32 to 40 hectares), which limits the potential competition. AvalonBay, an apartment real estate investment trust, concentrates its ownership of projects in walkable districts. For example, it owns the majority of the apartment units surrounding the Ballston Metro station, in Arlington, Virginia, and in downtown Stamford, Connecticut, within walking distance of the AMTRAK station. Because any company developing within the walkable range has a limited available inventory of sites from which to select, this

Southside Works brings new life to an urban neighborhood near downtown Pittsburgh. Development Design Group, Inc./Walter Larrimore, photographer

Demographics and the Pedestrian Experience

Shifting demographic trends are further strengthening the demand for walkable environments. In particular, the aging of the baby boomers and a decrease in the number of households with children are fueling a shift in demand away from conventional suburban developments. As Dolores Hayden shows in *Redesigning the American Dream,* the residential, commercial, and office settings of post–World War II suburbs were designed largely to meet the needs of families that consisted of a working husband, a stay-at-home mother, and children.[16] But today, families with a breadwinner father and stay-at-home mother account for barely 10 percent of all households. By 2000, married cou-

ples with children represented only 23.5 percent of all households; the other three-quarters of American households were made up of singles, families with no children, and single parents with children. According to the 2000 census, one-quarter of all households currently consist of people living alone, and nonfamily households will soon account for one-third of all households.

Demand for conventional, low-density suburbs is highest among those between the ages of 25 and 34, the group most likely to have young children in the house. Further, for households with children, proximity to good schools is an important factor in choosing where to live. While families with children are more likely to prefer low-density neighborhoods, many families—especially single-parent and dual-income households—appreciate the convenience of walkable neighborhoods with nearby services and amenities.

Because women are responsible for the majority of household spending decisions, including home purchases, researchers are starting to focus specifically on women's preferences. At a panel discussion at the Urban Land Institute's 2003 Fall Meeting, Jacinta McCann, a managing principal at EDAW, reported that the top four characteristics that women want in a neighborhood are choices in transportation, access to good grocery stores, great parks, and high-quality landscape design. Transportation alternatives, especially walking, can go a long way toward reducing the amount of time parents spending chauffeuring their children to school and to various after-school activities. Moreover, many women realize that walkable environments create more opportunities for face-to-face contact with neighbors—and that it is through these contacts that community relationships are built.

Childless households, on the other hand, use much broader and more diverse criteria to choose residential locations. Households without children do not have to worry about locating near good schools; and, because they have fewer safety concerns, childless households may also be more adventurous in their housing choices. A survey conducted by the Yankelovich market research firm found that 64 percent of respondents prefer to live in areas that foster greater social interaction, while 33 percent prefer to live in areas that are quiet refuges isolated from neighbors and community activities.[17] This preference for "hiving" over "cocooning," along with the desire to live in less auto-dominated environments and to have lower maintenance requirements, are among the reasons that many aging baby boomers, empty nesters, and childless echo boomers are moving into more urban environments.

Safe, walkable neighborhoods like Baxter Village can reduce carpooling time for parents, and create more opportunities to socialize. Adrienne Schmitz

The demographic shifts enumerated here, along with the growing recognition of women's preferences and the general lack of diverse, mixed-use environments in America's suburbs, are fueling the demand for compact, walkable, less auto-dependent environments and bolstering the development of new town centers and urban villages.

Financial Returns

Pedestrian-oriented, mixed-use centers are more successful by virtually every measure: rental rates for apartments and for office and retail space, sales prices for residential units, sales and tax revenues, hotel-room occupancy rates, and property values. Overall, per-square-foot rates for retail and residential rents in mixed-use town center developments are 20 to 50 percent higher, absorption is two to four times faster, and appreciation is two to three times faster.[18]

Town Centers Outperform Traditional Suburban Real Estate

Town centers are one of the hottest trends in real estate today, as they consistently surpass standard suburban real estate products in office and retail lease rates, residential prices and rents, retail sales, and hotel occupancy rates.

■ *Winter Springs Town Center, Winter Springs, Florida.* This 240-acre (97-hectare) project broke ground in 2002 and will ultimately include 17 buildings. In the first phase, retail rents averaged $18 to $23 per square foot ($194 to $248 per square meter), compared with $16.50 per square foot ($178 per square meter) at the nearest competing shopping center. Despite higher rents, 90,000 out of 135,000 square feet (8,360 out of 12,540 square meters) of retail space was leased before the first building had been completed. The first completed residential units sold for $325,000—10 to 15 percent more than the price of comparable housing units in the larger market area.

■ *Keller Town Center, Keller, Texas.* This 360-acre (146-hectare) town center broke ground in 1999. Phase I office space was leased for annual rents averaging $12 to $13 per square foot ($130 to $140 per square meter), which was 25 to 35 percent higher than the rates charged for comparable space in the market area. Retail space in the center rented for $17 to $22 per square foot ($183 to $237 per square meter), compared with only $13 to $16 per square foot ($140 to $172 per square meter) in the rest of the market area. The town center's apartments opened with monthly rents ranging from $0.98 to $1.12 per square foot ($10.50 to $12 per square meter), while comparable properties rented for $0.89 to $0.92 per square foot ($9.60 to $9.90 per square meter).

■ *Easton Town Center, Columbus, Ohio.* Opened in 1999, this 1,200-acre (486-hectare) town center is slated for buildout in 2010. Office rents averaged $23 per square foot ($248 per square meter) at a time when similar properties rented for $15 to $19 per square foot ($161 to $205 per square meter). Retail rents averaged $35 per square foot ($377 per square meter), which were the highest rents in the metropolitan area. Occupancy was at 95 percent, and annual sales were over $400 per square foot ($4,306 per square meter). Daily room rates at the town center's hotel ranged from $134 to $219, while other

local rates ranged from $58 to $103. Hotel occupancy rates at Easton Town Center were at 85 percent, compared with an average occupancy rate in greater Columbus of only 59 percent.

■ *Southlake Town Square, Southlake, Texas.* The first phase of this 130-acre (53-hectare) town center was completed in 1999, and buildout is expected by 2020. Office rents are about 10 percent above those in the overall Southlake market. At the same time, the occupancy rate at the town center is 95 percent, compared with an occupancy rate of only 74 percent elsewhere in the market area. Retail rents also enjoy a 10 to 15 percent premium over the broader Southlake market, with retail occupancy at 98 to 100 percent, somewhat higher than the market average. Further, adjacent property values experienced a halo effect, gaining 5 to 10 percent over comparable properties elsewhere in Southlake.

■ *CityCenter Englewood, Englewood, Colorado.* A 55-acre (22-hectare) redevelopment that transformed a mall into a transit-oriented town center, CityCenter includes office, retail, residential, and civic uses. In 2003, office space averaged $21 to $25 per square foot ($226 to $269 per square meter) with a 100 percent occupancy rate, compared with $17 per square foot ($183 per square meter) with a 90 percent occupancy rate elsewhere in the market area. Retail rents at CityCenter averaged $18 to $20 per square foot ($194 to $215 per square meter) with a 90 percent occupancy rate, while retail rents in the market area ranged from $8 to $14 per square foot ($86 to $151 per square meter) with an 80 percent occupancy rate. Apartments at CityCenter commanded rents of $1,005 to $1,735, while market rents averaged only $550 to $750.

■ *Reston Town Center, Reston, Virginia.* One of the pioneer town-center projects, this 50-acre (20-hectare) development has become the central business district for Reston. Office and retail space continue to lease faster, and for higher rates, than comparable space in the surrounding market. Whether the local market is up or down,

Reston Town Center commands a premium of 10 to 15 percent. The Hyatt Regency Reston is one of the top two hotels in the region in terms of revenue and room rates.

Reston Town Center, in Virginia, continues to outperform surrounding suburban-style development. Sasaki Associates

Why are town centers outperforming standard suburban real estate products? "First, a pedestrian-oriented, mixed-use town center brings together everything people want in one attractive, interesting place, often generating two to three times the draw of a traditional shopping center," says Gary M. Cusumano, of Newhall Land. "Second, many people are hungry for homes in a town center that allows them to walk to stores, restaurants, entertainment, even work. Third, many employers want the wide mix of uses—all within walking distance—that a town center provides, because that turns their office location into an amenity workers particularly value, which aids in their recruitment and retention efforts."

While many town centers achieve higher-than-average values, that does not necessarily translate to outperforming the competition in terms of return on investment. The complexity of town centers may lead to substantially higher development costs and substantially longer time-to-market periods than are associated with conventional products. Developers and investors must be realistic in their pro forma analysis.

Source: Adapted from Charles Lockwood, "Raising the Bar," *Urban Land*, February 2003.

North Hills, in Raleigh, North Carolina, converted an enclosed mall into a pedestrian-oriented, mixed-use town center oriented around a town square. Carter & Burgess, Inc.

ment's ability to secure financing. Some developers, however, have found the cost differential to be much higher and believe that public investment is the only way to make such projects work.

In pursuing funding for pedestrian-oriented developments, it is important to keep in mind that these projects offer a number of significant advantages. Developers should use these advantages both to guide the development process and to market the project to potential investors, government officials, and the general public. Todd Zimmerman and Laurie Volk have identified some of the advantages to developing residential new urbanist projects. (New urbanism's focus on walkability makes these advantages equally applicable to pedestrian-oriented developments.) They have noted, for example, that such projects offer greater development flexibility, premiums for both the value of housing and the location, and higher projected long-term returns—all positive economic features that can make a project more feasible and more appealing to lenders.[20] Although Zimmerman and Volk focused on projects with housing, similar advantages can be found in compact, high-density, mixed-use retail, office, and town center projects.[21]

Particularly in the case of first-phase infrastructure, such as new streets and sidewalks, higher density may reduce the cost of land and infrastructure per unit (or per developed square foot), although this is not always the case. The provision of public services may also be less costly for pedestrian-oriented development. A study undertaken by the Canada Mortgage and Housing Corporation found that most public sector costs were 48 percent lower in a nonresidential pedestrian-oriented development than in a

infrastructure investment can be too high for all but the largest development companies. Compared with the low-cost infrastructure investments of strip retail, mixed-use retail in greenfield areas is considered both more expensive and more risky. By comparison, lenders believe that mixed-use projects developed at infill sites are risky, but can be quite profitable if done well.

Another interesting finding from the Gyourko and Rybczynski study is that while lenders believe that mixed-use projects generally cost around 10 percent more to develop, this cost differential is not a factor in a develop-

nonresidential conventional development plan, and that public sector costs were 5 percent lower in residential pedestrian-oriented development.[22]

The flexibility and broader market of mixed-use projects also offer advantages to developers. Mixed-use developments can be more responsive to market changes: when the market for one use weakens, another use can fill the space—a strategy that is largely impossible with single-use projects. Also, a certain amount of flexibility can be built into mixed-use projects: for example, live/work buildings can be converted to and from residential and commercial uses. This kind of flexibility is especially helpful early in the life of a project, when there may not be much demand for commercial space; as the project reaches maturity, space can quickly be converted to retail and commercial uses to meet the increased demand.

The Entitlement Process

One commonly held belief regarding the development of walkable places is that the entitlement process is a major obstacle for developers; this belief has been supported by many stories and examples over the years. However, new evidence suggests that the entitlement process is not always an obstacle to the development of walkable places. For example, Gyourko and Rybczynski found not only that investors did not consider new urbanist projects to be more difficult to entitle, but that many jurisdictions actually favor denser, more walkable alternatives to conventional suburban development.[23]

One explanation for the differing opinions on entitlement risk is that local jurisdictions vary so much. In jurisdictions that are favorably disposed to alternative forms of development, investors are less concerned about entitlement issues, whereas in a jurisdiction that wishes to maintain conventional zoning standards and land use regulations, investors are much less likely to fund an innovative development. Thus, for every story of a pedestrian-friendly development that failed because of stringent zoning regulations, there are an equal number of examples of public agencies that are working hard to foster walkable development. Today, many cities and towns have overlay zones that are designed to encourage the development of pedestrian-friendly districts or town centers. Some cities are even purchasing land, hiring architects to create master plans for the site that encourage walking, and then selling the land to developers under the stipulation that they follow the master plan.

Even the federal government has programs intended to encourage pedestrian-oriented development. For exam-

Today, many jurisdictions encourage the development of pedestrian-friendly districts. Kierland Commons, in Phoenix, offers a main-street ambience. D.A. Horchner/Design Workshop

ple, the Location Efficient Mortgage program (sponsored by Fannie Mae and the Institute for Location Efficiency) increases allowable loan amounts to people who buy homes within one-half mile (0.8 kilometers) of transit

Location-Efficient Mortgages

The location-efficient mortgage (LEM), a financing mechanism for homebuyers, emerged in 2000. The goal of LEMs is to increase the amount of money available for home purchases in urban areas. The underlying theory is that since urban residents can walk, bike, or use public transportation to shop, to get to work, and to meet their daily needs, they spend less on transportation and have more disposable income available with which to purchase housing—and that mortgage lenders should take this factor into account.

Unlike a traditional mortgage, which is granted on the basis of factors such as income earned, current assets, and the value of the property, LEMs also consider factors such as neighborhood density, amenities, and access to public transportation.

In Seattle, where the first LEM program was piloted, the city was divided into 518 zones, each of which was assigned a monetary value based on its location efficiency. LEMs start out with generous qualifying ratios (a maximum of 35 percent housing-to-income ratio, and a total debt-to-income ratio of 45 percent), then adjust those ratios upward, depending on the savings that can be generated by living in a location-efficient area. The maximum housing-to-income ratio is 39 percent, and the maximum debt-to-income ratio is 50 percent. All LEMs offer fixed-interest 15- to 30-year loans.

So, for example, a household of two with good credit standing, a total income of $50,000, and a 3 percent downpayment can qualify for an additional $43,840 on a mortgage at 6.778 percent interest, provided that the home being purchased is in a location-efficient neighborhood. (The neighborhood used in this example is zone number 290, on Seattle's Capitol Hill.)

The higher housing-to-income ratios of LEMs (39 versus the standard 28 percent) can significantly increase buying power. For example, under typical guidelines, a household earning $50,000 a year would qualify for a $163,000 mortgage at 7.65 percent interest over 30 years. With an LEM, the savings in commuting costs associated with location-efficient housing are estimated to be about $200 per month, so the same purchaser could qualify for a $213,000 mortgage.

LEMs can be a valuable source of support for pedestrian-oriented neighborhoods. Because LEMs include more than the traditional factors in mortgage calculations, they encourage prospective homeowners to examine the cost of choosing certain locations. LEMs thus have the potential to promote urban living and to make it a more economically attractive investment decision. As a result of the LEM program, builders might find a growing consumer preference for areas that provide better pedestrian access, as well as an expanded pool of households that are able to afford home purchases. A further result would be a decrease in the level of risk associated with developing pedestrian-oriented projects.

LEMs are currently available in the Chicago, Los Angeles, San Francisco, and Seattle metropolitan areas. As the program continues to be refined and expands to additional cities, it may become a significant mechanism for increasing the consumer market for walkable development. Nevertheless, the future viability of the LEM program remains unknown. Since it was rolled out as a demonstration project, it has been slow to gain acceptance. The reasons seem to relate to the limited number of participating banks, and to confusing marketing messages (which led to the mistaken belief that mortgage recipients must forgo the use of automobile transportation). The marketing materials and promotion mechanisms are being retooled, and efforts have begun to target specific population segments, such as recent college graduates and moderate-income households.

However, further hindrances to the wider use of LEMs also need to be addressed. For example, Fannie Mae's recent shift to automated underwriting systems, which allow a wider range of factors to be considered when determining loans, has enabled more borrowers to qualify for traditional mortgages, thus lessening the demand for LEMs. In addition, the extra step needed to calculate the value of location efficiency serves as a deterrent.

It is unclear how quickly the limitations of the LEM program will be dealt with. And, since the program is currently restricted to so few locations, efforts to make comprehensive and long-term adjustments to underwriting practices are necessarily limited. It is important to note, how-

Location-efficient mortgages allow greater buying power in walkable neighborhoods with transit. The Epicenter, in Seattle, is located in a pedestrian-friendly neighborhood with public transit. Bumgardner Architects

ever, that when Fannie Mae added location efficiency to its automated model, applications for LEMs spiked, demonstrating that there is consumer interest in this type of program; this increased demand may serve as a stimulus for the creation of a more viable LEM program in the near future.

More information on the location-efficient mortgage program is available at www.location efficiency.com.—*J.S.*

Creating a sense of place takes more time than just building projects. Pedestrian-friendly development must be evaluated on the basis of long-term returns. Dougherty Schroeder & Associates, Inc.

centers or pedestrian-oriented neighborhood centers (see feature box). This program can be useful for developers interested in creating and marketing pedestrian-oriented places that include a residential component.

Project Evaluation

Because conventional methods of evaluating project feasibility do not always take into account the development advantages, special circumstances, or requirements of pedestrian-oriented projects, feasibility analysis is sometimes an obstacle in securing financing for pedestrian-oriented development. Most feasibility analyses rely on discounted cash flow (DCF) methods, which evaluate projected cash flow by comparing investment to projected financial returns. DCF methods include the calculation of net present value (NPV), internal rate of return (IRR), and return on investment (ROI). Because DCF analyses are

based on the assumption that the value of a current dollar decreases over time, lenders generally demand a maximum return on investment within five to seven years.

With their focus on short-term returns, DCF methods of evaluating real estate do not adequately take into account the possibility of long-term financial gains. Much of the financial value of pedestrian-oriented developments is created by design elements that entice people to come to a project and then linger. Walkable places with these elements—including character, complexity, sense of community, and synergistic relationships with adjacent uses—need time to mature in order to reap financial dividends. And the amount of time needed is often longer than the five to seven years at which DCF analyses generally call for a maximum return on investment. In addition, pedestrian-oriented developments are more likely to hold or increase their value than many conventional projects.[24] And as new structures are added over time, they further enhance the sense of place, increase the number of destinations to walk to, and bolster the value of the surrounding properties.

While DCF will continue to be appropriate for assessing short-term projects, mid- and long-term projects may be better evaluated through analyses that take into account a wider range of factors, such as the amount of additional private investment leveraged, the resultant economic impact, and the amount of infill, rehabilitation, and open-space networks that results from the project. These and similar benchmarks are important to pedestrian-oriented projects because they reflect improvements to the quality and fabric of the neighborhood.

In sum, mixed-use, pedestrian-friendly projects—and their markets—must be evaluated differently than single-use projects. Specifically, each project component must be evaluated separately, to determine its ability to stand alone; at the same time, the components must be evaluated collectively to determine how they will create market synergy within the development. Thus, it is important to ensure that each component has viable market support, even if little or no synergy between uses occurs. Developers must also keep in mind that because separate analyses must be performed for each use, these evaluations are subject to greater miscalculation than those that are undertaken for single-use projects.

One of the goals of developing a walkable place is synergy. When synergy occurs, the whole of the project becomes greater than the sum of its parts. Each component of the project builds on the strengths of the other components to create a place that is interesting and dynamic. This dynamism, in turn, attracts even more people to the project. In some cases, the project itself can create demand for a product where none had existed previously. For example, the area surrounding Winter Park Village, in Winter Park, Florida, had no established market for office space. Inspired by the popularity of earlier phases of the project, however, the developer added an office component that immediately became quite successful. Synergy created market potential that had not existed previously.

Nevertheless, synergy is a tricky phenomenon. Overly optimistic assumptions about synergy have been the weak points in many mixed-use projects, particularly where uses were oversized or inappropriate for the location. Experts emphasize the need to ensure that each major component has viable market support on its own—a strategy that implies, essentially, that the project should be financially feasible even if little or no synergy occurs; if the synergy turns out to be significant, then that should be viewed as an attractive bonus. This conservative approach becomes even more important when retail, office, entertainment, hotel, and other uses are phased in over time, or when phasing is uncertain, as in the case of performing arts centers, museums, and similar facilities over which the master developer has little, if any, control. In general, developers attempting to assess synergy in a project must temper analysis with seasoned judgment and experience.

Another important consideration is that some of the initial costs for a pedestrian-oriented project will be higher than those for conventional developments; other costs will be lower. For example, because mixed-use projects need to appeal to multiple markets, the site must be well located, and land costs for such a well-located site can be considerably higher than for more isolated sites. In addition, because walkable developments are not standardized, they may require more time and planning than conventional developments. This translates into higher initial planning and architecture costs. Land-carrying costs and absorption rates may also differ for pedestrian-oriented and conventional projects. Parking costs could be lower over time,

In Miami Beach, Ballet Valet is a parking garage developed through a public/private partnership. The garage includes ground-level retail space. Arquitectonica

because of the potential for shared parking and because mixed-use projects may be subject to different regulations regarding the amount of parking required. On the other hand, if structured parking is part of the plan, parking costs for pedestrian-oriented development may be higher.

Developers of mixed-use projects must prepare themselves for unforeseen costs. An article in *Shopping Centers Today* warns that there are no firmly established methods for creating a budget for developing mixed-use projects.[25] Costs can arise in unlikely places. For example, a long entitlement process or NIMBY objections from neighbors are potential sources of additional costs. Or problems may arise in the construction phase, when plumbing, wiring, and ventilation from a retail component connect to the residential uses directly above. One major developer of

mixed-use projects, Federal Realty Investment Trust, discovered firsthand just how extensive these cost overruns can be. Phase I of Santana Row, in San Jose, California, was estimated to cost $500 million, yet at the end of the process the developer faced a debt of $660 million.

Dealing with Obstacles to Financing

Out of necessity, developers of walkable places have had to find innovative approaches to financing. It is in the best interest of developers to investigate all financing options, both conventional and alternative, and to keep in mind that there are no standard methods for obtaining the necessary funds. Alternative methods of securing financing include (1) seeking out lenders that are interested in long-term investments, (2) strategically phasing development, (3) seeking out public sector participation, and (4) using the strengths of pedestrian-oriented development to sell the project to potential lenders.

A number of the strategies that can be used to gain the interest of banks, equity partners, and future investors will be familiar to developers, but some of them bear repeating. Of course, all developers should look to industry leaders for examples and as possible business partners. This is especially important for developers of pedestrian-oriented developments because, as noted earlier, investors tend to prefer larger and more experienced firms—and the more complex the project, the more experience is desirable.

Breaking the project into smaller pieces for investors can address the higher perceived risks of developing a mixed-use project. This option has two advantages: it creates multiple possible exit strategies for investors, and it makes it possible for different investors to finance different uses within the mixed-use project. However, when many parties are involved in a development, it is important for the developer to minimize possible conflicts through clear communication, careful management, and meticulous attention to legal issues (such as the delineation of property lines).

Securing preleased anchor tenants in a retail development is an important prerequisite for obtaining financing from most investors. Anchor tenants can help to meet the requirement for a bondable entity, or for an entity with a strong credit rating. But as long as it can be demonstrated

Securing anchor tenants is an important prerequisite for obtaining financing for a retail development. Field Paoli/David Wakely, photographer

that a property has enough market potential that it will generate sufficient traffic, an anchor may not be necessary.

Finding Multiple Sources of Financing

While some investors remain skeptical of pedestrian-oriented developments in general, and mixed-use projects in particular, other investors are creating a name for themselves by funding such projects. These companies are forging new relationships between lenders and developers and paving the way for greater understanding of the financial potential of pedestrian-oriented development.

As more lenders are financing more mixed-use projects—and enjoying more successes with them—new lending sources are emerging, and pedestrian-oriented developments are gaining the interest and attention of established lenders. Both Freddie Mac and Fannie Mae, the two largest purchasers and securitizers of mortgages in the world, are making inroads in the funding of mixed-use projects. Both have funded pedestrian-oriented projects; Fannie Mae's American Communities Fund, in particular, has specifically targeted mixed-use projects, neighborhood retail, and single-family and multifamily housing for investment.

Another important lender that is exploring the potential of walkable environments is Wells Fargo Bank, which has a special division that finances mixed-use urban projects. The bank is participating as a construction lender in a complex downtown revitalization project in Albuquerque, New Mexico; the development also incorporates equity from the New Mexico Urban Initiatives Fund, a new equity fund that focuses on mixed-use real estate projects.

Bank of America has long been one of the strongest supporters of urban projects and other community-building efforts, including pedestrian-oriented development. This financial institution invested in inner-city projects back in the

financed mixed-use properties that integrate multifamily housing with retail space.

Getting to Smart Growth II: 100 More Policies for Implementation, published in 2003 by the International City/County Management Association and the Smart Growth Network, includes a directory of lending institutions that have funded and are interested in funding smart growth projects. Funders range from J.P. Morgan Chase & Company to the Ford Foundation.

Patient Equity

"Patient" equity is a prerequisite for investments with a mid- to long-term time frame for returns. Finding investors who are willing to offer patient equity may be essential for developers interested in innovative development. Pension funds and charitable organizations are among the entities that are discovering opportunities in long-term real estate investment. The California Public Employees' Retirement System (CalPERS), for example, has a history of investing in real estate and has recently branched out to focus on urban infill and walkable projects. Its California Urban Real Estate Program (CURE) specifically targets smart growth projects, low-income housing, mixed-use housing, and economic development and redevelopment in urban neighborhoods. Out of the $11 billion CalPERS has invested in real estate, over $211 million was allocated to CURE projects.[26]

Living over the store is a tradition that has become popular again. At Santana Row, in San Jose, California, apartments located above shops command high rents. Adrienne Schmitz

1970s, when few other funding sources were available for such development. More recently, Bank of America has committed billions of dollars to small-business loans and affordable housing, often to the benefit of urban neighborhoods.

GE Capital Real Estate is another lender that has supported walkable developments. In cities that include Washington, D.C.; New York; and Chicago, GE Capital has

Bethesda Row: Creating a Sense of Place

In 1993, Federal Realty Investment Trust saw an opportunity that it considered rife with potential: five contiguous blocks of underperforming properties controlled by a single owner, on the outskirts of a central business district that served one of the most affluent counties in the United States.

When Federal Realty began contemplating the project, 125,000 people lived within a three-mile (4.8-kilometer) radius of Bethesda, an inner-ring suburb of Washington, D.C. The average household income was $110,000, and 68 percent of the adult population was college educated. Also, the site is located within walking distance of the Metrorail stop in the heart of Bethesda.

Once a district of 1950s-era buildings housing storefront offices, small-scale distributors, service trades, and convenience retailers, the area had been targeted for redevelopment when, in 1992, the county built a metered, 950-space, five-level parking garage in the middle of one block. According to Federal Realty Investment Trust, the garage made the development economically feasible.

Montgomery County, where Bethesda is located, is known for its proactive land use controls and for its efforts to stem sprawl and concentrate growth in urban corridors. To facilitate the city's metamorphosis from a bedroom suburb to a lively, mixed-use urban center, the county built some half-dozen public garages in downtown Bethesda. The parking garages were essential to developing a strong, pedestrian-oriented business core where drivers could deposit their cars, then take to the sidewalks for shopping and dining.

Federal Realty Investment Trust created enough critical mass to attract retail tenants, while phasing the entire development, block by block, in order to generate enough cash flow to sustain forward momentum. Phase I took immediate advantage of the newly finished county parking garage by renovating 14,000 square feet (1,300 square meters) of adjacent specialty shops and adding a 37,000-square-foot (3,440-square-meter) Barnes & Noble bookstore. Phase II renovated 33,000 square feet (3,070 square meters) of retail space across the street and added 5,000 square feet (470 square meters) of new space.

Phase III added 30,000 square feet (2,790 square meters) of office space on two floors above 15,000 square feet (1,390 square meters) of main-street shops. Phase IV, completed in 2001, added 60,000 square feet (5,570 square meters) of street-level retail; a below-ground, eight-screen multiplex; and 80,000 square feet (7,430 square meters) of Class A office space on four floors above the retail space.

To make Bethesda Row feel like an authentic neighborhood, Federal Realty created a network of public gathering places—"third places"—where people of all ages come to meet and greet, stroll

Bethesda Row brought specialty retailers, restaurants, and a multiplex cinema to downtown Bethesda. Cooper Carry, Inc.

While the CURE program seeks long-term investment opportunities in pedestrian-friendly developments, the fund is also expecting higher rates of return for these projects than for more conventional real estate products. Further, although the CURE program has many altruistic aims, CalPERS explicitly states that the goal of this program is to achieve the highest total rates of return for its investments.[27]

Charitable foundations are also discovering the benefits of long-term investment in pedestrian-oriented development. A progressive development plan can tie together social, environmental, and economic interests in a way that allows developers to tap a diverse array of financiers who want to focus on particular aspects of such projects. For example, many of the nation's most prominent foundations (including Ford, Irvine, MacArthur, McCune, Packard, Surdna, and Turner) are among the 90 members of the Funders' Network for Smart Growth and Livable Communities, a clearinghouse of information and resources for philanthropic organizations interested in smart growth. Since its inception, in 1999, the Funders' Network has been creating opportunities for charitable organizations and foun-

and shop, dally and dine. In contrast to many urban entertainment districts, which feature large multiplex cinemas and themed restaurants like Planet Hollywood and the Hard Rock Café, "the main focal points," says Federal Realty's former president and chief executive officer Steven Guttman, "are the streets themselves, where the primary entertainment is people watching."

The developer knew that having people milling about is the best magnet for retailers. A main gathering spot is the corner fountain and plaza outside the Barnes & Noble bookstore. Located across the street from the popular, 11-mile (17.7-kilometer) Capital Crescent Trail, which runs from Georgetown, in Washington, D.C., to Silver Spring, Maryland, the plaza is a welcome rest spot for hikers and bikers and has become a favorite destination for Bethesda residents.

The sidewalks between the streets and shops were also designed as gathering spaces. Architect Richard Heapes, now of Street-Works—whose design for Boca Raton's Mizner Park made him something of a main-street guru—worked with Federal Realty to create an outdoor café zone along Bethesda and Woodmont avenues. Instead of following the usual practice, which is to place outdoor dining areas immediately adjacent to their restaurants, thus forcing pedestrians to walk close to the curb, Heapes pushed the outdoor cafés out to the curb. This arrangement puts pedestrians right where tenants want them—directly in front of their shops and restaurants. It also makes the sidewalk more interesting for pedestrians, who can peer into the store windows or look at the people dining in the outdoor cafés.

How do you create a main-street environment that feels neighborly? "Although we bring in strong nationals," says Guttman, "we don't want to overpower the existing urban fabric and destroy the special neighborhood flavor that local retailers and restaurants bring to a place. Too many streets have gone national, and you end up with a regional mall without walls."

Federal Realty's key strategy, with respect to both tenant selection and main-street design, is diversity. It's essential to offer a variety of reasons for people to spend time at main-street developments. At Bethesda Row, where local and regional specialty tenants outnumber nationals, shoppers can accomplish most of their errands in one shopping trip. The main-street district offers an assortment of neighborhood services—a chain grocery store, food specialty shops, a dry cleaner, hair salons, bagel and coffee shops, bookstores—plus a selection of fashion boutiques and specialty arts shops. To extend the life of the street, Federal Realty brought in a 24-hour Kinko's and strategically located the large-format store on the upper level, thus saving room on the street for shops that offer more visual interest.

Instead of looking like a planned redevelopment project designed by one hand, the developers wanted Bethesda Row to look eclectic, as if it had grown randomly over time. To achieve this effect, they arranged for a collaboration between three local architectural teams and the developer's main architectural firm, Cooper Carry, Inc. "We used a variety of architectural styles and building materials to create this idiosyncratic sense that the street grew organically," says Heapes. "We tried to make these main-street districts look spontaneous, as if they had been here forever and were not designed," he observes. "When we finish, we want to be able to sneak out of town without leaving a trace."

Federal Realty's efforts have transformed the retail economics of Bethesda. In addition to raising property values throughout the neighborhood, Bethesda Row is quite profitable itself. In the four years between the completion of Phases I and IV, retail rents nearly doubled, occupancy rates were 96 percent, and average annual sales were more than $425 per square foot ($4,575 per square meter). All this was accomplished through a self-funded real estate investment trust; the only exception was the county-owned municipal garage, which was in a sense a public subsidy.

Bethesda Row transformed a quiet and unappealing district into an authentic neighborhood with a network of public gathering spots, giving it a sense of place. The streets bring shoppers in from the neighborhood and beyond, and they also form the backbone of a pedestrian-oriented network of public spaces where people watching is the primary entertainment.

Source: Adapted from Terry Lassar, "Hitting the Streets," *Urban Land*, July 1999; and David Takesuye, "Bethesda Row: Creating a Sense of Place," *Urban Land*, February 2003.

dations to become active and influential players in the creation of walkable, smart growth communities.

In addition to serving as viable funding sources for development, charitable organizations and foundations are strategic partners in efforts to influence local or state policies affecting pedestrian development. In Vermont, for example, an alliance of ten organizations, ranging from the Vermont Forum on Sprawl to the Preservation Trust of Vermont, successfully lobbied the legislature to approve expanded incentives for development focused on downtowns and village centers.

Strategic Phasing

Phasing can help minimize the risk associated with pedestrian-oriented projects because it breaks the project down into smaller pieces with shorter development timeframes. It also allows for greater flexibility and responsiveness to unforeseen changes in the market. For example, in a mixed-use project, the housing component can be built first, to help establish a base market of consumers as well as to give the site a sense of vitality that will attract nonresidents to the project. The retail component can be put off until a sufficient market develops. (It is important

open spaces. It is not realistic to expect private owners to maintain public areas over the long term. (Partnering with public entities is discussed further in chapter 4.)

Mechanisms such as public/private partnerships, land writedowns, tax increment financing, the sale of municipal bonds, and public improvements made at no cost to the developer have played key roles in the realization of many projects to date. Partnerships have proven quite useful to developers facing political, legal, and financial hurdles, and have also helped to provide some assurance in what is often a new and untried market. For instance, help in overcoming community opposition, facilitation of land assembly, and financial support have been key. In addition, the flexibility of public/private partnerships makes it possible to tailor the project to meet both the public sector's needs and the private sector's financial requirements. And, because the partnership serves the interests

A public/private effort has yielded a pedestrian-oriented downtown with a park for Duluth, Georgia.

When a project's costs are higher than the market will bear, the municipality will often have to bridge the gap through tax abatements, loans, or other incentives. When market forces favor sprawling, auto-oriented development, public participation can tip the balance in favor of higher-density, pedestrian-friendly development. Because higher-density developments enhance the public realm and the tax base, such partnerships ultimately benefit the public. Public entities must also be involved in maintaining newly created

of both parties, the public and private sector participants will be strongly motivated to work hard for the project's timely completion.

Although the importance of public involvement should not be underestimated, it is crucial to understand that the vast majority of the funding for any project will come from private sources. Because most walkable places take many years to create (far longer than the typical politician is in power), in the most effective partnerships the private sector needs to take the lead.

Yerba Buena Center added major facilities, both public and private, and extended the pedestrian realm of downtown San Francisco.

In recent years, a number of communities have solicited developers to help them build pedestrian-friendly projects. With such help, many cities and towns are creating town centers or revitalizing downtowns and other walkable districts. The city of Denver, for example, solicited proposals for the development of the Stapleton airport site, which is now being developed as a new in-town community by Forest City Enterprises, Inc. Also, the Denver Urban Renewal Authority partnered with Trammell Crow Company to redevelop a former hospital site into a vibrant new neighborhood that includes 1,000 housing units and 35,000 square feet (3,250 square meters) of ground-floor retail space.

In response to the rapid, sprawling development occurring in the suburbs of Georgia, the town of Duluth hired developer Doug Spohn to help create a town center. The completion of Phase I of the project has yielded a five-acre (two-hectare) town green, which has become a central gathering point for the community. With shops, restaurants, and residences facing the park, Duluth now has a walkable downtown with a park as its central focus.[28]

Site Assessment

Several kinds of sites are especially suitable for pedestrian-oriented development. Because many suburban environments lack any kind of center or gathering point, suburban infill sites can offer a great opportunity to provide such an amenity and tap into an unmet demand for walkable places. Addison Circle, in Addison, Texas, and Birkdale Village, near Charlotte, North Carolina (see case study), are successful examples of efforts to anchor a sprawling suburb with pedestrian-oriented development.

Walkable projects can also serve as catalysts, revitalizing old neighborhoods or bringing new life to underused downtowns. Finally, pedestrian-oriented projects can stretch the boundaries of an existing pedestrian district by adding adjacent development to existing sites. Yerba Buena Center, in San Francisco, effectively expanded the downtown business district by redeveloping the area south of Market Street with convention and cultural facilities, hotels, and commercial and residential development.

Site selection for pedestrian-oriented projects can have many implications for financing, land costs, and the final project plans. As noted earlier, Joseph Gyourko and Witold Rybczynski found that investors are usually more open to mixed-use projects in urbanized settings than in outlying greenfields. Further, the fact that many walkable projects are mixed use means that diverse markets are required. The right location can maximize proximity to multiple (and often overlapping) markets. Given that empty nesters and young, childless professionals are at the forefront of the demand for alternatives to conventional development, it may be a shrewd strategy to locate walkable projects in areas that are populated by these demographic groups.

Although housing is not essential, most experts agree that a residential component greatly increases the viability of pedestrian-oriented developments—first because housing adds a human presence during evenings and weekends, when business districts are usually vacated, and second because it greatly increases pedestrian activity and generates market potential within a development.

Infill locations that are already surrounded by housing can bring foot traffic into the developments by creating pedestrian connections between the site and the surrounding neighborhoods. Indeed, adjacent land uses can become

Adjacent land uses should be connected with sidewalks and bike routes. RTKL Associates

a crucial asset for a project. In some circumstances, it may be prudent for a developer to control adjacent land uses through land assembly and purchase. The key to incorporating adjacent land uses into a development is to focus on how the uses are linked together. Connective sidewalks, streets, and bike routes should form an extensive network that, through its functionality, visual quality, and appeal, attracts people to the development.

A Growing Market

It is a fascinating time to be a real estate developer. There is a pent-up and growing market for creatively conceived walkable projects, as well as interest from various types of investors. To be successful, developers need to understand that today's built environment is very much a product of how real estate projects are financed: the focus has often been on short-term investment returns—which, in turn, has created an emphasis on lowering construction costs. The serial investment strategy, in which investors depend on financial returns from short-term cash flow that must be consistently reinvested, can thwart the production of higher-quality, longer-term products. This approach undermines the long-term investment power of real estate.

Pedestrian-oriented development creates environments that are more integrated, that relate to their surroundings, and that focus on the long-term life of their communities. Well-designed pedestrian-oriented developments can create viable, long-lasting, interesting, and sustainable places. They can generate significant profits for developers and financiers willing to invest for the long term.

Notes

1. Surface Transportation Policy Project, "Americans' Attitudes toward Walking and Creating Better Walking Communities," April 1, 2003; available at www.transact.org/report.asp?id=205.

2. National Association of Home Builders, "1999 Smart Growth Survey," cited in Dowell Myers and Elizabeth Gearin, "Current Preferences and Future Demand for Denser Residential Environments," *Housing Policy Debate* 12, no. 4 (2001): 638.

3. The figure of 9 percent is from the 1997 Mature Markets Study; the figure of 14 percent is from the 1996 National Association of Home Builders (NAHB) survey. These data are summarized in Myers and Gearin, "Current Preferences."

4. The figure of 37 percent is from the 1998 *Professional Builder* survey "What Buyers Want in New Homes"; the figure of 57 percent is from the 1996 National Association of Home Builders survey "What Buyers Want in New Homes." The data from both surveys are summarized and discussed in Myers and Gearin, "Current Preferences."

5. As summarized in Myers and Gearin, "Current Preferences."

6. Myers and Gearin, "Current Preferences."

7. Laurie Volk and Todd Zimmerman, "Confronting the Question of Market Demand for Urban Residential Development" (working paper, Fannie Mae Foundation, Washington, D.C., 2000).

8. National Association of Home Builders, Economics Group, *What 21st-Century Home Buyers Want* (Washington, D.C.: National Association of Home Builders, 2001).

9. National Association of Realtors, "Existing-Home Sales: Monthly Data for the U.S. and Regions"; available at www.realtor.org/Research.nsf/Pages/EHSdata.

10. Volk and Zimmerman, "Confronting the Question."

11. Emil Malizia and Jack Goodman, "Consumer Preferences for Residential Development Alternatives" (working paper 2000–02, Center for Urban and Regional Studies, University of North Carolina at Chapel Hill, 2000).

12. Nancy Graham Lawler, speaking at the Urban Land Institute/Joseph C. Canizaro Mayors' Forum, San Antonio, Tex., February 26–27, 2002.

13. Mark J. Eppli and Charles C. Tu, *Valuing the New Urbanism: The Impact of the New Urbanism on Prices of Single-Family Homes* (Washington, D.C.: Urban Land Institute, 1999).

14. Yan Song and Gerrit-Jan Knaap, "New Urbanism and Housing Values: A Disaggregate Assessment," *Journal of Urban Economics* 54, no. 2 (2003): 218–238.

15. PricewaterhouseCoopers and Lend Lease Real Estate Investments, *Emerging Trends in Real Estate 1999* (New York: PricewaterhouseCoopers and Lend Lease Real Estate Investments, 1999), 8.

16. Dolores Hayden, *Redesigning the American Dream: The Future of Housing, Work, and Family Life,* rev. ed. (New York: W.W. Norton, 2002).

17. Urban Land Institute, "Intown Housing: A Development Trend Fueled by America's Tendency toward More 'Hiving' and Less 'Cocooning,'" 2003 press release; available at www.uli.org/AM/Template.cfm?Section=Press_Releases1&template=/CM/HTMLDisplay.cfm&ContentID=21315.

18. Belinda Sward, "Where's the Money in Smart Growth Developments?" available at http://i.b5z.net/i/u/1455176/i/pdf/BS_GEDA_Smart_Growth_Presentation.pdf.

19. Joseph E. Gyourko and Witold Rybczynski, "Financing New Urbanism Projects: Obstacles and Solutions," *Housing Policy Debate* 11, no. 3 (2000).

20. Laurie Volk and Todd Zimmerman, "Development Dynamics," *Wharton Real Estate Review* 2, no. 2 (Fall 1998).

21. Charles Lockwood, "Raising the Bar," *Urban Land,* February 2003.

22. Hemson Consulting Ltd., *Conventional and Alternative Development Patterns; Phase II: Municipal Revenues* (Ottawa, Ont.: Canada Mortgage and Housing Corporation, 1997); cited in Myers and Gearin, "Current Preferences."

23. Gyourko and Rybczynski, "Financing New Urbanism Projects."

24. Christopher Leinberger, "Financing Progressive Development," *Capital Xchange* (May 2000); available at http://www.brookings.edu/es/urban/capitalxchange/Leinberger.PDF.

25. Donna Mitchell, "Mixed-Use Carries Risks, Some Warn," *Shopping Centers Today* 24, no. 8 (August 2003).

26. State of California Public Employees' Retirement System, "Real Estate Portfolio Performance Report, Quarter Ending June 30, 2003," www.calpers.ca.gov/whatshap/calendar/board/invest/200311/item09e-01.pdf (accessed 2004; no longer available online).

27. State of California Public Employees' Retirement System, "State of California Public Employees' Retirement System Statement of Investment Policy for California Urban Real Estate, April 14, 2003," www.calpers.ca.gov/invest/policies/pdfs/California-Urban-Real-Estate.pdf (accessed 2004; no longer available online).

Chapter 4

Public Sector Involvement

The public sector often plays a pivotal role in pedestrian-oriented development through land use regulation, planning, urban design, economic development, redevelopment, capital improvements spending, and investments in civic and public facilities. This involvement can serve as either an impediment or a stimulant. Regulatory influences include zoning, public review processes, and approval processes; financial assistance may take the form of land assembly, public improvements, incentives, and direct investment. In many cases, the public sector is the prime mover behind a project—assembling the land, creating a master plan, selecting a developer, investing in public improvements and public uses, championing the project before the public, and streamlining the approval process.

In fact, the increasing prominence and popularity of pedestrian-oriented developments can be traced, in large part, to the active support and involvement of the public sector. As the public sector becomes more aware of the benefits that walkable places bestow upon the community, more and more government entities have started looking for opportunities to encourage and develop pedestrian-oriented projects. If developers of such projects are to succeed, they must understand and appreciate the public sector's objectives and interests.

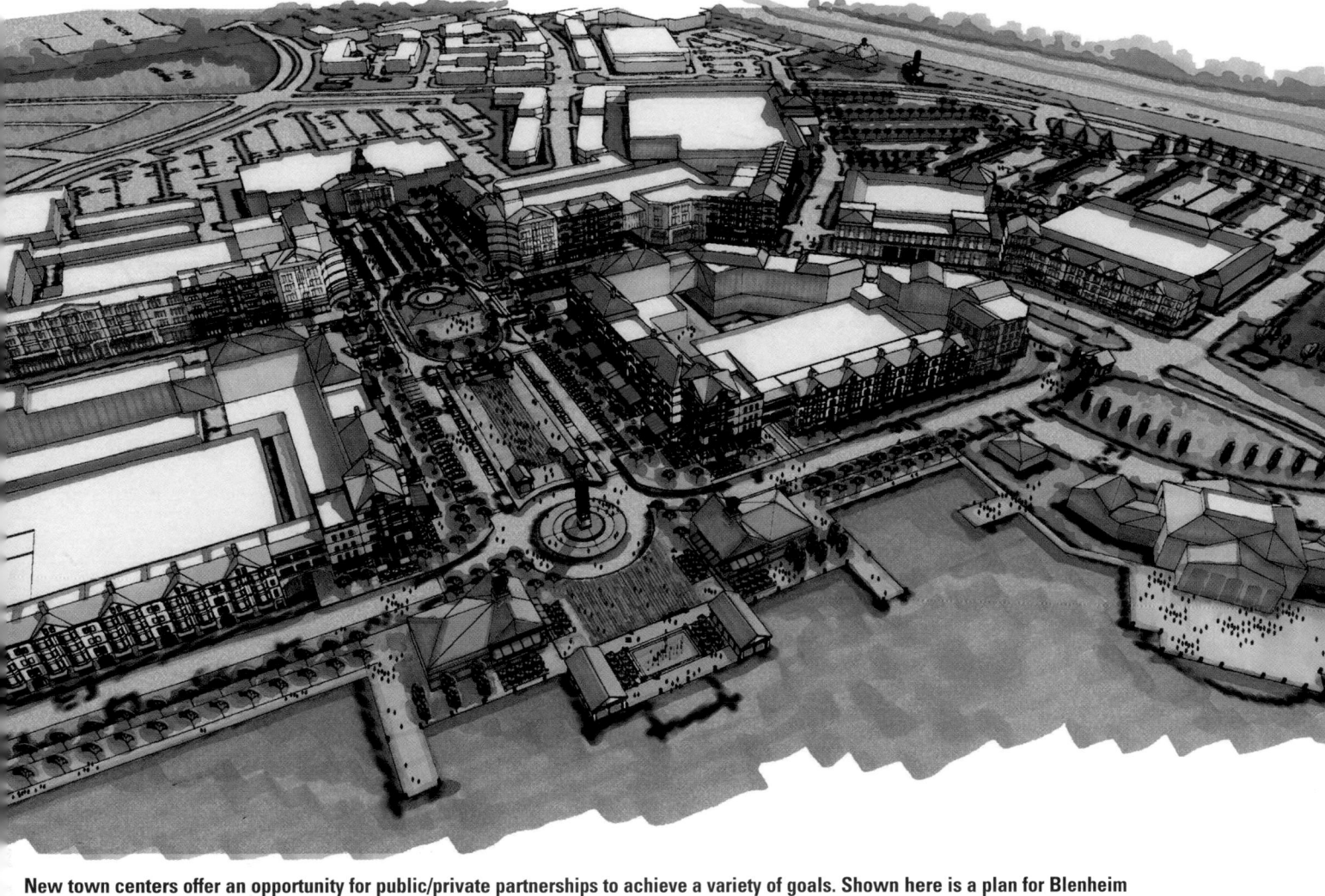

New town centers offer an opportunity for public/private partnerships to achieve a variety of goals. Shown here is a plan for Blenheim Park in Virginia Beach, Virginia. Shook Kelley/ Frank Quattrochi

Who Makes Up the Public Sector?

In his comprehensive book on public/private partnerships (PPPs), John Stainback lists the three main categories of public entities that have engaged in partnerships with real estate developers: governments, public school districts, and universities. With the enactment of the Military Housing Privatization Initiative (MHPI), in February 1996, the Department of Defense can be added to this list.[1]

The government category of public entities is especially inclusive, with entities ranging in size from the federal government to downtown business improvement districts (BIDs). It is well known that governments at all levels can participate in public/private partnerships. But quasi-governmental public authorities (such as airports, water and sewer districts, and ports) can become involved

in PPPs as well. Finally, special-purpose development corporations and BIDs are governmental entities that are usually created through partnerships and special taxing agreements with private businesses to achieve a wide variety of goals, including real estate development.

Two entities that have the potential to become important public partners are local school districts and public universities. School districts and universities often own underused land in desirable locations that have great economic development potential. These institutions are also committed to ensuring that the supply of state-of-the-art buildings for their students is commensurate with demand. Universities, in particular, have to provide a wide

The Village at the Naval Training Center

The U.S. Department of Defense (DoD) is facing a critical shortage of housing for its service members. There are two principal reasons for the shortage: first is the lack of affordable housing in many American cities; second is the substandard quality of military-owned housing.

Under the DoD's family-housing policy, service members must rely on the housing market within the communities where they are stationed. However, in many communities, most service members cannot find housing that is affordable to someone receiving a military salary. If there are no options available in the local housing market, the armed forces are supposed to supply housing. But of the 257,000 DoD family-housing units scattered around the globe, 50 percent need to be renovated or replaced. If the DoD used the same construction approach that was used to create much of the original housing stock, the cost would be $16 billion and the process would take 20 years.[1]

The Military Housing Privatization Initiative (MHPI) of 1996 was authorized to address this crisis. The MHPI encourages partnerships that rely on the strengths of the private sector and the vast resources of the military to create high-quality, affordable housing for service members. In one of the first public/private partnerships to result from the MHPI, two private development firms (Lincoln Property Company, of Dallas, Texas, and Clark Realty Capital, of Bethesda, Maryland) pooled their resources to form the Lincoln/Clark Public-Private Venture. The goal of the Lincoln/Clark Public-Private Venture is to provide high-quality, affordable rental housing for the Navy and Marine service members stationed in the San Diego area.

Only three miles (4.8 kilometers) from downtown San Diego, in the Point Loma community, the Village at the Naval Training Center is part of a larger redevelopment strategy for a 550-acre (223-hectare) decommissioned naval training center. Lincoln/Clark and the Department of the Navy worked together to build this 500-townhouse village according to new urbanist principles. Seven acres (three hectares) of the site have been set aside for a future elementary school, and the development includes a community center and recreational space. Nearby, the Navy Exchange already serves as a corner grocery store.

Torti Gallas and Partners, the firm that handled the architecture and urban design, based the concept of the project on the surrounding pedestrian-friendly context of historic prewar San Diego. In the design for the Village, alleys are located behind the

The award-winning Village at the Naval Training Center is a pedestrian-friendly community that provides affordable housing to military families. Torti Gallas and Partners

townhouses; this arrangement helps to transform the street into a social realm where neighbors can greet each other in a friendly, informal setting.

In 2002, the Village at the Naval Training Center won the Multifamily Executive Project of the Year; in 2003, it won the U.S. Environmental Protection Agency's National Award for Smart Growth in the built environment category. Because of the success of the partnership, in September 2003 the Navy selected Lincoln/Clark to build Phase II, which will involve the construction of 460 new townhouse units and the renovation of 1,000 existing units.—*J.S.*

Note

1. U.S. Department of Defense, Office of the Deputy Undersecretary of Defense, "Privatization 101"; available at www.acq.osd.mil/housing/about.htm.

range of building types, including housing, conference centers, bookstores, and sports stadiums. A recent study undertaken by the National Trust for Historic Preservation highlights the potential role of schools in the community-building process. As a result of this study, some school districts are rethinking their capital improvement programs and shifting their focus to the construction of more pedestrian-friendly school buildings with a stronger community emphasis.[2]

The MHPI has enabled the Department of Defense to engage in public/private partnerships with real estate developers and builders. The goals of the MHPI are to improve the quality of military housing and to address the shortage of affordable housing for service members. As of July 2005, 47 contracts had been awarded to private developers, 32 projects were pending solicitation, and 32 projects were being planned. (See feature box.)

The Public Sector's Interests in Pedestrian-Oriented Development

With so much governmental interest in public/private partnerships, the opportunities for developers are likely to increase. As PPPs become more common, it is important for developers to learn as much as they can about the public entities that they might partner with.

Developers can gain insight into a jurisdiction's values and goals by reading its comprehensive plan, which documents the jurisdiction's vision of its future. The degree of consistency between the comprehensive plan and the zoning code is a good indication of whether a jurisdiction has the political will to realize its own visions. Assuming that the zoning code and the comprehensive plan are in agreement, the comprehensive plan will provide an excellent overview of the zoning challenges a potential development might face. It is important for a developer to determine just how accommodating a jurisdiction is to pedestrian-oriented development because, as noted in chapter 3, lenders are more favorably disposed toward mixed-use and other nontraditional developments in jurisdictions that are supportive of alternative developments.

Fort Lauderdale has created a strand along the beach for walkers, bikers, and roller-bladers. This and other public investments have helped attract private development and redevelopment partnerships. EDSA

A developer must also understand the public sector's motives and interests in fostering pedestrian-oriented environments. First, as noted in chapter 1, more and more jurisdictions are recognizing the health benefits of walking. Public health departments at all levels of government are working with planning departments, economic development departments, and elected officials to promote walkable communities. Second, the creation of more attractive urban environments is often an important goal of public sector involvement in real estate development. Third, a number of overlapping agenda items—including smart growth, the need to increase transportation efficiency, and civic place-making efforts—are leading the public sector to place a stronger emphasis on pedestrian-oriented development. This emphasis will, of course, take many different forms, depending on the location and context of the site in question. Finally, many jurisdictions view walkable places as opportunities to spur economic development and increase tax revenues.

Suburban Place Making

In suburban or newly developing locales, the public sector's objectives are often about creating a sense of place, an identity, or a central focus for the community. Unlike single-use residential neighborhoods or commercial strips, pedestrian-oriented developments can help a community meet these objectives. Traffic congestion is a growing concern in many suburban areas, and many jurisdictions view pedestrian-friendly design as a key to mitigating some of the problems associated with automobile use.

Town centers are helping many suburban areas create a civic identity. In more mature, inner-ring suburban business districts, infill development is being used to create new, pedestrian-friendly environments with strong urban identities; examples include Downtown Silver Spring, Maryland; the Market Common, Clarendon, in Arlington, Virginia; and Centennial Lakes, in Edina, Minnesota. Other projects, such as City Heights Urban Village, in San Diego, have redeveloped or re-created existing main-street areas or transformed aging neighborhoods into attractive community focal points. Still others have combined redevelopment with suburban place making; examples include CityCenter Englewood, near Denver, and Paseo Colorado, in Pasadena, both of which involved the public sector in the redevelopment of defunct shopping malls. Several of these projects are described in detail in chapter 6.

Smart Growth and Mobility

Because walkability is largely determined by the number and variety of destinations that can be reached on foot, there is a close connection between mixed-use environments, transit-oriented developments, and pedestrian-friendly places. But the typical pattern of suburban growth at the fringes of metropolitan areas is not easily served by transit and does not encourage walking or biking. Many jurisdictions are finding that this development pattern—commonly known as *sprawl*—is not economically or environmentally sustainable. It consumes farmland and open space, generates long auto trips, and creates significant traffic congestion, air pollution, and other negative impacts. Some jurisdictions are addressing sprawl through regulatory tools that concentrate higher-density, mixed-use, pedestrian-friendly development around transit stations.

Mixed-use development is compatible with and supportive of both transit and walking. Because of their higher densities, significant mixed-use projects tend to generate substantial transit demand that can reach tens of thousands of trips per day. Mixed-use development also tends to spread trip demand throughout the day, because peak times for trip generation differ for each use. Thus, a mixed-use development within walking distance of a transit station can be a significant source of riders throughout the day.

Concentrating mixed-use development around transit stations in attractive urban settings is viewed as a smart growth strategy because it can increase densities at strategic locations, encourage walking and biking, reduce automobile use, reduce air pollution and traffic congestion, and alleviate some of the pressure to develop farmland and critical open space. Many exciting projects are now being built around transit stations in metro areas such as Washington, D.C. (Silver Spring, in Montgomery County, Maryland); Chicago (Arlington Heights); Atlanta (Atlantic Station and other proposed projects); Dallas (Mockingbird Station); San Francisco (Yerba Buena Center); and Portland, Oregon (Orenco Station). Federal, state, and local governments are all seeking to create more mixed-use and transit-oriented development.

Downtown Silver Spring, Maryland, has been revitalized as an 18-hour, mixed-use, transit-oriented development. RTKL Associates

Economic Development and Tax Revenues

The desire to foster economic development and increase tax revenues is another reason for a public entity to want to become involved in pedestrian-oriented development. Mixed-use, pedestrian-friendly projects can stimulate the economy, generate jobs, and increase the tax base. For example, a project that includes a hotel with conference facilities can attract convention attendees and tourists, creating jobs and new retail and hotel spending. New office space can attract office jobs to the area while also boosting the property tax base. And new retail space can increase retail employment, the property tax base, and sales tax revenues.

Well-planned pedestrian-oriented development can be an important value-added component for any of these projects. Pedestrian-supportive infrastructure encourages people to explore and linger in an area—and also creates memorable places that people want to return to or live in. Indeed, the demand for pedestrian-friendly environments

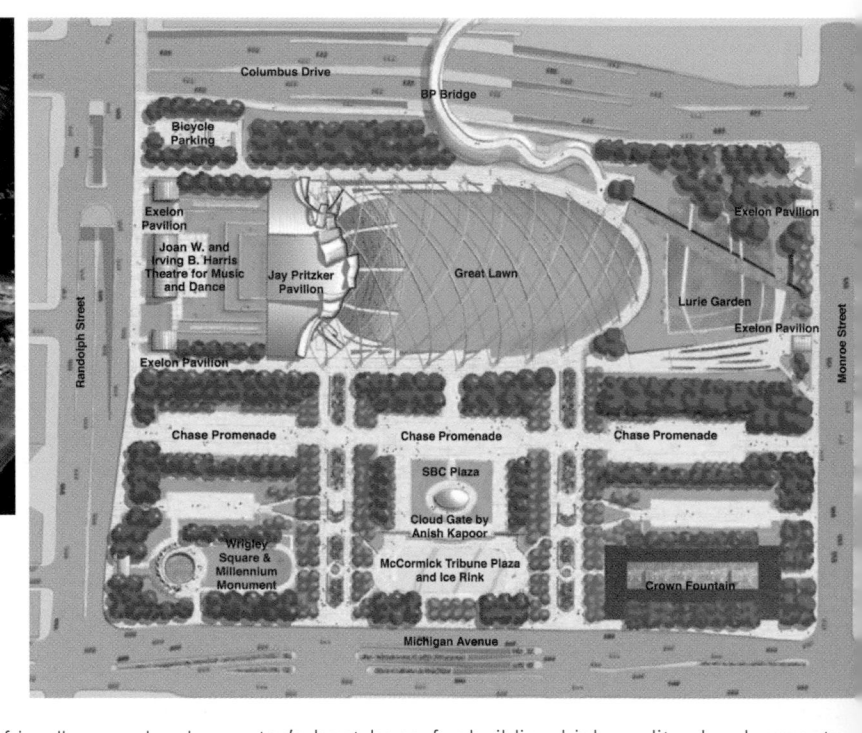

Completed in 2004, Chicago's Millennium Park was the result of a public/private collaboration that transformed a bleak railroad yard into a 24-acre (9.7-hectare) civic space. The project has spurred economic growth in the surrounding neighborhood. Millennium Park, Inc.

of all types is rising, and pedestrian-friendly new developments can be an economic boon for a jurisdiction. (See the feature box in chapter 3, "Town Centers Outperform Traditional Suburban Real Estate.") In blighted or underused areas, large-scale mixed-use properties can significantly increase the property tax base as well as the value of surrounding property.

Advantages and Disadvantages of Public Sector Partnerships

Public entities have a number of compelling reasons for wanting to build and promote walkable environments. Most public entities, however, lack the necessary resources or are not permitted by law to engage in certain aspects of real estate development on their own. Typically, the public sec-

tor's best hope for building high-quality developments comes from partnering with the private sector. There are compelling advantages for the private sector to work with the public sector, and some disadvantages as well. John Stainback has identified a number of advantages and disadvantages. While no such lists can be exhaustive, private developers should carefully consider Stainback's observations before entering into a partnership.

The advantages of PPPs include the following:

■ Most major PPPs are created to undertake high-profile, civic-oriented projects that can enhance the developer's image if the project is successful.

■ Government-owned real estate assets that have never been available in the commercial market are made available for development.

■ Many development partnerships include the long-term lease of a development site, eliminating the initial cost of land acquisition.

■ Government and university entities often share project costs with the developer, thereby reducing the private partner's investment.

■ Government and university entities have the ability to enhance cash flow if the pro forma indicates a shortfall.

■ A good public partner will develop a consensus among government participants and voters that facilitates the actions of the private partner.

■ Government entities have the power to streamline the approval process for design, construction, and operation.

■ Government and university entities often share the risks and responsibilities of PPP developments, thereby reducing the private partner's risks and responsibilities.

■ PPPs reduce investment risks.

The disadvantages of PPPs include the following:

■ The private partner must abide by the requirements of the request for qualifications (RFQ), the request for proposals (RFP), and the negotiation process.

■ The traditional process that private developers use to finance, design, and develop a typical project differs significantly from the process required to structure and implement a PPP.

■ The PPP development process can require significantly more time.

■ A consensus to proceed with the project is essential.

■ Political instability may undermine a PPP.

■ The expectations of the public partner must be in sync with the local market.

■ To undertake some projects, new legislation must be prepared and approved.[3]

Roles for the Public Sector

At the heart of any shared venture are agreements about the roles, risks, and returns. These "three Rs" are essential to the success of any public/private partnership. The responsibilities of each party must be balanced by the level of risk each party is willing to assume, as well as by the fair allocation of the returns generated by the project. Usually, parties that assume a greater share of the risk receive a greater share of the returns; and in many cases, those who assume greater risk have more responsibilities and discretionary power over the project.

The public sector's participation in pedestrian-friendly developments can take a variety of forms, from simple encouragement to active participation. Developers must familiarize themselves with these different forms so that they know what to expect from a public partner. Public sector entities can promote and support the creation of walkable places by the following means:

■ Providing zoning incentives, possibly including the creation of a mixed-use classification;

■ Streamlining the approval process and championing the project before citizens and various agencies;

■ Planning development areas such as mixed-use districts, traditional neighborhood developments, and transit-oriented developments, and creating land use and design guidelines to ensure that these districts are walkable;

■ Assembling land, outright purchase, or using powers of eminent domain;

■ Cleaning up brownfield sites for redevelopment;

■ Writing down land costs to make the project feasible;

■ Allowing tax abatements or offering tax incentives;

■ Providing public financing, including the use of general funds, tax increment funds, and state and federal funds;

■ Providing public infrastructure such as parking facilities, transit stations, and streetscape improvements;

■ Providing project components such as a convention center, city hall, civic center, library, performing arts center, or museum;

■ Developing a specific, pedestrian-oriented land use plan and program, and then using an RFP or an RFQ to develop that plan and program;

The appropriate role for the public sector depends, in part, on whether public participation is needed to make the project feasible, on the jurisdiction's sophistication and financial capability, on public objectives and needs, on the project's potential impact on the community, and on the costs and benefits of alternative actions.

Regulatory Process and Tools

Most conventional suburban development patterns grew from design criteria that inhibit pedestrian-friendly development. Overly wide streets, dangerous intersections, lack of sidewalks, large distances between destinations, and an overall orientation toward automobile transportation tend to discourage walking and bicycling as viable transportation alternatives. Most jurisdictions have land use regulations—such as single-use zoning, minimum building setbacks, and buffers between developments—that inhibit or prohibit pedestrian-oriented development. To encourage mixed-use development, the public sector must revise policies by taking actions such as the following:

■ Add mixed-use and other flexible and pedestrian-friendly categories to the zoning code;

■ Establish design guidelines that facilitate and encourage walking;

■ Modify and streamline the approval process for pedestrian-oriented projects, thus reducing the risk to developers;

■ Use public meetings and charrettes to build a vision and consensus for new walkable places in areas where they would be appropriate.

In some cases, jurisdictions should also establish minimums rather than maximums for building height, density, and floor/area ratio.

Most important, the public sector must champion mixed-use concepts and look for ways to facilitate the creation of places where walking and bicycling are viable transportation alternatives. Such efforts often involve a prominent offi-

■ Serving as master developer, actively directing the development plan and program, or both;

■ Creating comprehensive, areawide master plans that encourage walking and biking;

■ Assisting with marketing, promotion, and public relations;

■ Handling maintenance and upkeep of public spaces, including sidewalks.

Neighborhoods that include a mix of uses encourage greater pedestrian activity. Avalon Park, in central Florida, combines nearly 5,000 residential units of all types with 600,000 square feet (55,740 square meters) of commercial space in a pedestrian-friendly environment. John Bateman

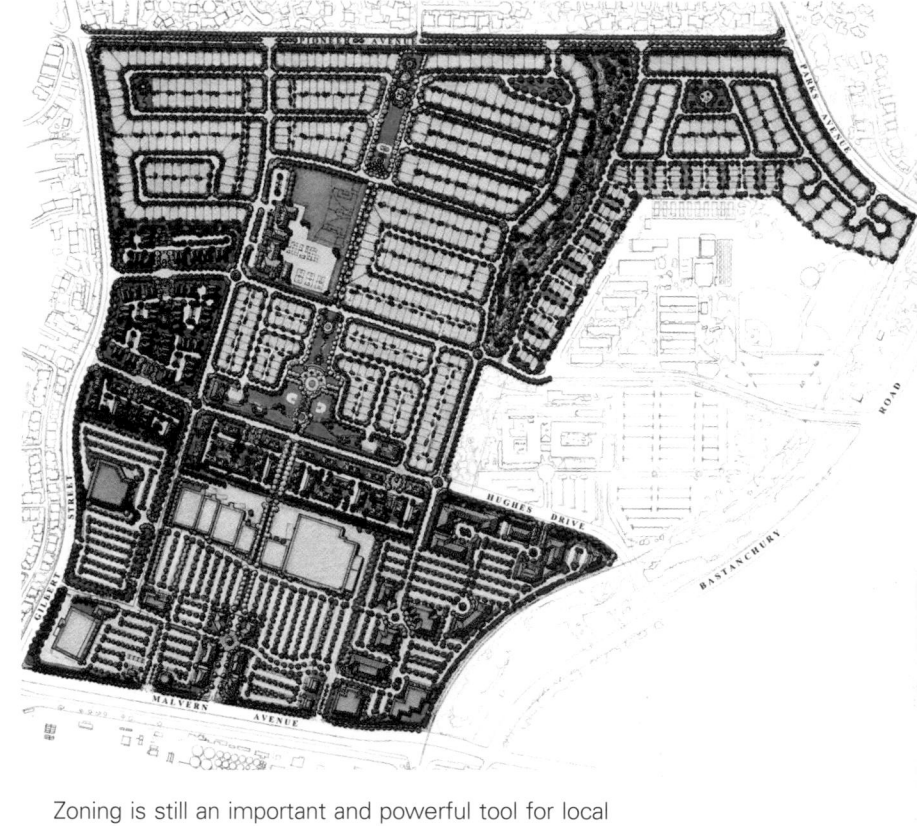

cial who is willing to strongly and consistently champion nontraditional projects before the public, and before the local legislative body.

Zoning

Historically, zoning has been used to segregate land uses, but the assumption that different uses should, in fact, be segregated has been called into question in recent decades. In the 1960s, Jane Jacobs, an urban theorist and early critic of conventional zoning, argued that cities need instead "a most intricate and close-grained diversity of uses that give each other constant mutual support, both economically and socially."[4] From a pedestrian perspective, the single-use districts created by conventional zoning limit the different types of destinations that are within walking distance and create less visually interesting experiences. And, although a single-use development can be pedestrian-oriented, it has limited ability to promote walking as an alternative form of transportation.

Zoning is still an important and powerful tool for local jurisdictions, and recent actions seek to remedy the deficiencies of traditional zoning in two ways: (1) creating regulations that support the well-planned integration of different land uses at a proper scale; and (2) creating incentives that encourage better design, more pedestrian amenities, affordable housing, and other public purposes. Numerous regulatory techniques can be used to accomplish these goals, including floating zones, overlay districts, performance zoning, special-purpose districts, and mixed-use zoning. Increasingly, special zoning ordinances are being used to encourage mixed-use development; these include mixed-use zoning ordinances, planned unit development (PUD) ordinances, traditional neighborhood development (TND) ordinances, and smart growth ordinances. Moreover, many jurisdictions are developing specific plans that delineate uses and design guidelines for specially designated areas.

Miami Beach: Urban Tropical Deco

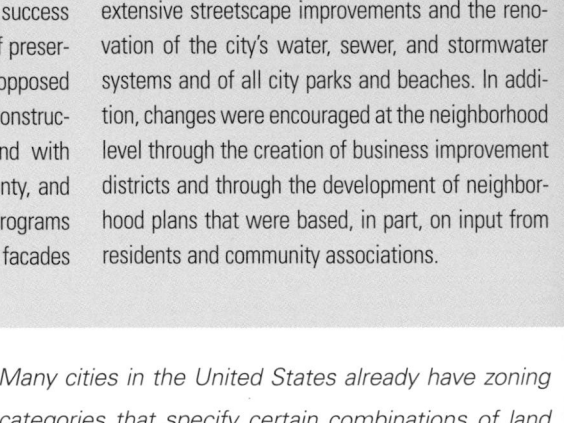

The late Italian fashion designer Gianni Versace called Miami Beach's South Beach a "global village"—an expression that captures both the cosmopolitan mix of people living in and visiting there, and the human scale and pedestrian-friendly nature of the architecture. Miami Beach—and South Beach in particular, with its urban village character—is often characterized as one of the urban success stories of the late 20th century.

During the 1930s, South Beach developed as a modest resort for middle-class tourists from the Northeast. Small two- and three-story buildings—most built as hotels or seasonal apartments, with no provision for parking—were constructed on 50- to 100-foot- (15- to 30-meter-) wide lots in the streamlined moderne, or art deco, style. After World War II, when larger resort properties were developed in Mid Beach and North Beach, South Beach declined. Mid Beach and North Beach reached their peak in the mid-1950s, when Morris Lapidus's landmark Fontainebleau and Eden Roc hotels were built. Overbuilding, the advent of jet travel, the development of competing resorts in the Caribbean, the failure to maintain existing properties, and an aging market resulted in another downturn in tourism.

By the late 1970s and early 1980s, Miami Beach had completed a precipitous decline: the resort economy was dead, the population was largely poor and elderly, and most properties had deteriorated dramatically. But a small band of preservationists, led by Barbara Baer Capitman, founder of the Miami Design Preservation League (MDPL), began a struggle for the recognition and protection of the historic architecture of South Beach. These preservationists appreciated the unique "tropical urban" environment of the area and recognized its potential; their efforts became the cornerstone of Miami Beach's renaissance.

The revitalization of South Beach was guided by a preservation and development plan, commissioned in 1980 by the MDPL, that (1) advocated the preservation and adaptive use of historic structures and (2) encouraged zoning changes to allow for new uses. Needed public improvements were identified—such as wide sidewalks on Ocean Drive and the renovation of Lummus Park—that would attract and accommodate cafés and pedestrian activity and create a public gathering place for the community. The plan viewed South Beach holistically: it was not sufficient merely to create a strip of hotels, restaurants, and bars to attract tourists. South Beach was perceived as a living, breathing community with residential, commercial, and tourist neighborhoods in close proximity.

During the 1980s, the MDPL created the Miami Beach Development Corporation (MBDC), a community development corporation, to serve as the economic development arm of the preservation movement. The MBDC understood that long-term success meant establishing the economic viability of preservation and small-scale development—as opposed to large-scale, neighborhood-altering new construction. Through education and advocacy, and with modest financial support from the city, county, and state governments, the MBDC sponsored programs to attract new business, restore commercial facades and storefronts, implement public improvements, create neighborhood associations and business improvement districts, initiate cultural activities, and provide affordable housing for area residents.

Thoughout the 1990s, the city government supported South Beach by expanding the historic district and by strengthening the powers of the city's design review board and the laws that protect historic structures. The city also embarked on a $500 million capital improvement program involving extensive streetscape improvements and the renovation of the city's water, sewer, and stormwater systems and of all city parks and beaches. In addition, changes were encouraged at the neighborhood level through the creation of business improvement districts and through the development of neighborhood plans that were based, in part, on input from residents and community associations.

Mixed-Use Zoning Ordinances. Mixed-use zones are different from most other techniques, such as PUD ordinances and special-purpose districts, primarily because they not only permit a mix of uses but also encourage or even require such mixing. The American Planning Association has stated:

Many cities in the United States already have zoning categories that specify certain combinations of land uses; for example, a community may permit multifamily housing in an office district. This "permissive" approach, however, is not likely to result in truly integrated uses. . . . If a community wishes to encourage a mixture of land uses, it must do more than permit residential uses: it must actively promote them.[5]

With its focus on pedestrians, Miami Beach provides a variety of environments for walking, biking, and jogging, from the wide, café-lined sidewalks of Ocean Drive to the boardwalk along the beach. Adrienne Schmitz

Public improvement projects were implemented citywide, including the renovation of the Lapidus-designed Lincoln Road Mall (one of America's first, and among its few, successful outdoor pedestrian malls), which again serves as the town center for Miami Beach. Public/private projects, such as the Loews Miami Beach Hotel, furthered the city's economic revitalization while respecting the scale of the neighborhood and the integrity of the historic architecture.

The city's efforts to target specific economic development initiatives and its support for emerging industries were major factors in the economic revitalization of Miami Beach, and South Beach in particular. For example, artists, cultural institutions, and nonprofit entities got things moving on Lincoln Road, attracting restaurants and retail businesses—a process that was enhanced by the renovation of Lincoln Road. Beginning in the mid-1990s, the city undertook a series of public/private partnerships, including the Loews and Royal Palm Crowne Plaza hotel projects, the Ballet Valet parking garage and retail project (see photo on page 73), and the development of office/retail buildings on city-owned parking lots to accommodate the growing media-related businesses.

The importance of parking cannot be overemphasized. The 636-space Ballet Valet parking garage was critical to the revitalization of Collins Avenue, a complementary street providing high-end retail and parking to those frequenting the adjacent Ocean Drive. New York developer Tony Goldman, the force behind the rebirth of Ocean Drive, persuaded the city of Miami Beach to purchase air rights over his property to construct the parking garage, which sits above a mix of renovated historic retail facades and new retail stores. More recently, the city, in a long-term deal, leased surface parking lots near Lincoln Road to a partnership headed by LNR Properties, an affiliate of Lennar Homes, to develop two office buildings with retail and surplus parking.

In the past, the economic health of Miami Beach depended on the national economy and regional domestic tourism, which made it vulnerable to fickle markets. Today, the city's tourism market is diverse, with about half of the 7 million annual visitors to Miami Beach coming from foreign locations, primarily Europe and South America.

New condominium products in Miami Beach are selling from a low of $400 per square foot ($4,306 per square meter) in North Beach to upwards of $1,000 per square foot ($10,764 per square meter) in South Beach; typical prices for new condominiums range from approximately $500,000 to over $2 million. Single-family homes in South Beach and Mid Beach begin at around $400,000, and waterfront homes in these areas cost from $2 million to more than $10 million. The city's nightlife and street scene continue to be a magnet for part-time residents, tourists, and the surrounding regional market of 5 million people.

During the 1980s, Miami Beach remained healthy despite a sluggish economy and real estate market because, with its lively, 24/7 pedestrian focus, it was different from most other tropical destinations. From 1980 to 2000, the city's median age dropped from 65 to 39, the number of people living below the poverty line dropped by 17 percent, and the number of households with incomes of at least $150,000 increased 135 percent. City revenues from tourism increased more than sixfold, and the value of all real property approximately quadrupled between the late 1980s and 2002. More than half of the 87,333 residents of Miami Beach are Hispanic, representing all countries in Central and South America as well as the Caribbean. The city continues to evolve while maintaining its essential character. This is what has kept Miami Beach fresh and interesting, and this is what should enable it to remain competitive during the uncertain economic times ahead.

Source: Adapted from Neisen Kasdin, "Miami Beach: Urban Tropical Deco," *Urban Land*, October 2002.

One of the earliest examples of a zoning ordinance that provided incentives for mixed-use development was a 1974 amendment to the Washington, D.C., zoning code. The amendment designated several areas as CR (commercial/residential) mixed-use districts and provided incentives and bonuses for the provision of various uses or amenities, including moderate-income housing, areas devoted to pedestrians or bicyclists, retail or service space contributing to the creation of evening activity centers, and preservation or enhancement of places or structures of historical importance. It was one of the first true mixed-use zoning ordinances in the United States.

Planned Unit Development Ordinances. PUD ordinances have been used for many years to allow more creative approaches to development, particularly in suburban communities. Often embodied as part of the local zoning ordinance, they increase flexibility in the design and siting of development. Developers have used the flexibility of PUD zoning to build pedestrian-oriented places in a wide range of settings. Many of the walkable town centers that have been developed in planned communities—such as Reston Town Center, in Reston, Virginia; and Valencia Town Center Drive, in Valencia, California—were developed under PUD ordinances.

PUD ordinances allow developers to arrange uses, density, and open space in an innovative plan, often allowing more intense development than would be permitted under conventional zoning. PUDs offer developers substantial advantages: higher densities, a more flexible design, savings in construction costs, and improved marketability. For example, because PUD zoning applies to large parcels rather than to individual lots, densities can be calculated by the overall parcel rather than by the lot, which makes it easier to cluster buildings. The greater flexibility of PUDs also allows for smoother integration of different land uses (commercial, residential, retail, etc.) and different project elements (such as transportation systems and open space).

For a community, a PUD ordinance can offer greater control over development, help preserve open space, and reduce the costs typically associated with sprawling development. Typically, the developer and the local planning board, working within broad legislative guidelines, develop a specific plan for a PUD. And, when properly devised, a PUD ordinance can be sufficiently flexible to create vibrant, pedestrian-friendly places.

Traditional Neighborhood Development and Smart Growth Ordinances.

More recent regulatory tools—TND and smart growth ordinances—are being adopted in many regions of the United States, often as overlay districts or as alternatives to more conventional zoning. These ordinances frequently focus on development standards for the larger community (especially for single-family housing), and include specific provisions that encourage a mix of uses and support their integration.

TND and smart growth ordinances are flexible in that they allow a variety of uses, but they are highly prescriptive about how these uses are arranged, designed, and developed. Generally much more prescriptive than PUD ordinances, TND and smart growth ordinances are used not simply to permit a mix of uses but to prescribe preferred urban design patterns.

Overlay Districts.

Local governments often use overlay zoning to gain greater control over development in areas that contain special features or conditions, such as historic buildings, wetlands, steep slopes, or downtown residential uses. Overlay zoning districts may be

Harbor Town, in Memphis, Tennessee, is one of the earliest TNDs. When it was started, Harbor Town violated existing planning and zoning ordinances but was permitted because the infrastructure remained private. Increasingly, localities allow—and even encourage—this type of development. Jim Hilliard Aerial Photography

The Addison Arts District, an outdoor arts and cultural district, is a focal point of activity for Addison, Texas. At a cost of $7.5 million, it has been a cost-effective generator of revenue for the town's hotels, retailers, and other businesses. Left: Sasaki Associates, Inc./Craig Kuhner, photographer. Below: Sasaki Associates

applied over one or more other districts. In Lenox Village, a 101-acre (41-hectare) new urbanist development on the outskirts of Nashville, the developers worked with planners from the city of Nashville to develop an urban design overlay district that would guide development. Both the developers and the city planners wanted to create a residential development that differed from the conventional suburban developments common in the region; but because the jurisdiction's zoning codes made no provision for such developments, the parties had to jointly create a code that would allow the high-density, pedestrian-friendly environment envisioned for the project.

Public Sector Master Plans. Cities are also creating their own master plans for publicly owned properties and hiring developers through an RFQ or RFP. In Addison, Texas, both the 1991 comprehensive plan and a more recent community-based visioning program, Vision 2020, recommended a higher-density, mixed-use residential neighborhood adjacent to Addison's Old Town. The purpose was to create a focal point and stronger population base for the town's commercial uses. In response, the developer, Post Properties, and the town undertook a series of steps (1) to formulate the program and design for Addison Circle, (2) to educate the public about the benefits of such a design, and (3) to establish the terms of the public/private partnership.

Eventually, the town and the developer hammered out a set of design and development standards that addressed issues such as density, lot coverage, exterior building materials, setbacks, and streetscape design; these standards were then codified in an approval for a planned development district. The developer also identified funding gaps that would need to be resolved in order to provide the infrastructure and level of quality the town and the developer wanted. The final agreement between the developer and the town of Addison committed the town to spending $9.5 million from its general fund over the life of the project: $5.5 million upfront for infrastructure, street, and open-space improvements, and $4 million during the second phase of development.

The Cap at Union Station

The Cap at Union Station is a $7.8 million retail development that reconnects downtown Columbus with the burgeoning Short North arts and entertainment district. Opened in October 2004, the project effectively heals part of a 40-year scar that was created by the construction of Interstate 670 (I-670), the city's inner-belt highway. Composed of three separate bridges—one for through-traffic over the highway, and one on each one of the first speculative retail projects built over a highway in the United States.

Historically, the area around the Cap was a vibrant commercial district and the site of the Columbus Union Depot. Designed by Daniel Burnham in 1897, it was the city's third train station and the hub for passenger rail traffic. However, urban renewal and the highway projects of the 1950s severed the northern neighbor- was physically and psychologically disconnected from downtown.

During the 1990s, urban pioneers rediscovered the Short North, and retailers, restaurants, galleries, and residents flocked to the new arts and entertainment district. To the south, the convention center was expanded in 1993, with a giant new wing designed by architect Peter Eisenman, and the city's last remaining public market, the North Market, was reborn. These commercially strengthened areas soon began to create enough synergy to make the Cap project not only imaginable but feasible.

Although the Cap was conceived in 1996, serious work on the project did not commence until 1999, when local developer Continental Real Estate Companies signed a memorandum of understanding with the city. Following the terms of the agreement, the city secured clear title to the air rights above the highway and obtained permission from the Ohio Department of Transportation (ODOT) and the Federal Highway Administration (FHWA) to construct the Cap platforms. Continental then entered into a ground lease of $1 per year for the platforms and constructed the buildings. In addition, the city receives 10 percent of the ongoing profits of the development, and if Continental sells the buildings, the city will receive 10 percent of the sale amount. Continental also agreed to reimburse the city for up to $75,000 in architectural fees for work that was necessary prior to the construction of the buildings on the Cap. The city spent $115,000 in preliminary architectural work to ensure that the Cap structures would be compatible with the highway design.

The Cap reconnects two neighborhoods through a series of bridges lined with retail buildings.

side, for the retail structures—the Cap provides 25,500 square feet (2,370 square meters) of leasable commercial space. The void caused by the highway—called an "engineered gash" by *New York Times* architecture critic Herbert Muschamp—has now been transformed into a seamless urban streetscape. While other cities, like Seattle and Kansas City, have erected convention centers over urban highways, the I-670 Cap is hoods and the North High Street commercial area from downtown. What is now known as I-670 cut underneath High Street with four lanes of freeway traffic, taking established neighborhoods with it and leaving a 200-foot- (61-meter-) wide gap in its wake. The emphasis on planning for automobiles hit its stride in 1976, when Union Depot was torn down to make way for the convention center. By this time, the Short North

sites, expensive environmental cleanup makes development infeasible without public involvement.

Land Assembly and Preparation. Local governments can facilitate development by alleviating problems associated with land acquisition. Under the power of eminent domain, local governments can take private land for public use, provided that the owner receives just com- pensation. Eminent domain can considerably reduce the time required to assemble and develop mixed-use sites; it also makes it possible to implement a large-scale redevelopment scheme under the guidance of one agency that controls the land. But eminent domain has become quite controversial. Alternatively, where market conditions are favorable, local governments can assemble land through fee simple acquisition, without the need for eminent domain.

Tenants were selected to provide day and evening activity, and the neighborhood does remain active for 22 hours each day.

As a part of the easement agreement, the city had to agree not to infringe on ODOT's ability to operate the interstate. For instance, ODOT can close down and evacuate the Cap in case of emergencies. ODOT also placed several design constraints on the Cap: no windows were permitted on the backs of the buildings, no access to the roofs or backs of the buildings was allowed, and lighted signs or advertisements visible to highway drivers were forbidden.

In addition to the upfront costs paid by the city, ODOT agreed to pay nearly $1.3 million for the construction of the Cap platforms. The city paid $325,000 to extend the necessary utilities across the bridge. The city also provided Continental with a ten-year, 100 percent tax abatement on the property. Before constructing the Cap buildings, Continental had to get design approval from the Downtown Commission, the Italian Village Commission, and the Victorian Village Commission.

Continental used existing financial relationships to obtain a $4.2 million conventional loan to finance the construction of the buildings. At the start of the project, Continental also secured $1.3 million in mezzanine debt and made an overall equity contribution of $500,000. However, in order to finance tenant improvements, Continental had to reorganize the financing scheme. The firm originally budgeted $650,000 for tenant improvements, but those costs eventually rose to $2.2 million. At that point, however, Continental had tenants in hand, and the capitalization rate had fallen from 10 to 7.5, allowing the company to secure a bridge loan with more favorable terms. Under the new financial scenario, Continental was able refinance the construction loan, finance the tenant improvements, and reduce the mezzanine debt to $300,000. Continental currently has a $7 million conventional loan, and its finance officials estimate that the firm will lock in at an interest rate of 5.5 percent.

Continental was able to achieve favorable loan terms because it had secured tenants willing to pay rents that were approximately 20 to 30 percent higher than those in the surrounding area. At $25 to $35 per square foot ($269 to $376 per square meter), the rents may be high—but, according to officials at Continental, tenants are willing to pay more for the cachet provided by the location.

Tenants for the Cap were selected to provide a day-to-night mix: two upscale restaurants, a coffee shop and wine bar, a clothing store, an apparel and gift shop, and a few smaller specialty food stores. By mixing retail space with restaurants and bars, Continental has been able to draw people in and then provide them with a reason to linger and shop. The coffee shop opens early and the bar stays open late, keeping the Cap—just like the surrounding Short North neighborhood—active for nearly 22 hours a day.

Though it was arduous, all of those involved say they believe that such a project is feasible elsewhere across the country. In fact, various highway caps are being considered in other places in Columbus, in order to knit back together the neighborhoods that surround the downtown. The current I-70/I-71 redevelopment plan for the downtown's southern and eastern sides, for example, offers opportunities for other caps. A retail cap may not work in every situation, but the I-670 Cap has provided a working model for future development in Columbus and beyond.

Source: Excerpted from Andrew Overbeck, "The Cap at Union Station," ULI Development Case Studies, available at www.casestudies.uli.org.

Brownfield cleanup is another way to create a viable site. Brownfield sites, which are often held by a single owner, may be economically worthless because the cleanup costs exceed the underlying land value. Often, the only way to bring such land back into use is for the local government to cover the costs of cleanup (usually with help from federal funds).

Other techniques to facilitate land assembly include land exchanges or swaps between the public and private sectors, and relocation assistance from the public sector for those who are occupying space in the property slotted for redevelopment.

Land Writedowns and Tax Incentives. In order to make a project feasible, the public sector must often write down the land that it owns—that is, sell the land for less than the government has invested in it, including acquisition, legal, infrastructure, and cleanup costs. The local packages are tailored to meet the needs of particular businesses and to provide adequate inducement for companies to locate in the zone and to hire workers from within the zone. Historic Westside Village, a 17.5-acre (seven-hectare) pedestrian-friendly, transit-oriented, mixed-use development in Atlanta, is a U.S. Department of Housing and Urban Development empowerment zone. Developed by the Harold A. Dawson Company, the project is designed to serve as a catalyst in the revitalization of a historic intown neighborhood. The development will include 200,000 square feet (18,580 square meters) of retail, including a grocery store; two 150,000-square-foot (13,940-square-meter) office buildings; 100 apartments; 200 for-sale loft and condo units; and 35 townhouses.

Providing Infrastructure Improvements

Provision of public infrastructure improvements is yet another form of public sector support for private development; improvements can include the construction or upgrading of public infrastructure, such as streets or roads; the creation of open space or parks; and the construction of public parking structures.

Tax increment financing (TIF) is a principal means of financing infrastructure improvements. Under TIF, a local government creates a TIF district, plans public improvements in that district, issues bonds to pay for the improvements, and pays off the bonds with monies derived from any increases in property or sales taxes in the district that result from the public improvements.

At the 138-acre (56-hectare) Atlantic Station project, in Atlanta, TIF is being used to pay off $110 million in revenue bonds; the bond money will be used to build streets, water and sewer lines, and other infrastructure, and to pay for environmental cleanup on the former industrial site. The tax-allocation district, administered by the Atlanta Development Authority, will remain in place until the bonds are paid off (in approximately 25 years) through the increased revenue stream. At CityPlace, $55

Stapleton, on the site of Denver's old airport, was the result of public and private entities working together. Adrienne Schmitz

government might also have to phase the sale of the land to the developer over time, to eliminate carrying costs for the developer.

To create tax incentives, the local government can (1) offer a simple tax abatement (that is, forgive the property tax altogether for a certain period of time), (2) freeze the tax for a certain period of time at a low rate, or (3) tie the tax rate to the project's income stream rather than to its assessed value.

Empowerment zones, which are used to encourage economic development and job growth in distressed areas, are another option. Businesses that locate in empowerment zones can take advantage of wage credits, tax deductions, bond financing, and reduced capital gains taxes. Incentive

Broadway Revisited

Developing mixed-use projects in small-city downtowns presents special challenges. Land values are too low to justify the construction of structured parking. Markets for downtown living are thin. Retail tenants are few and small, and may not be creditworthy. Most office tenants are unable to pay high enough rents to justify new construction. And hotels are typically leaving small-city downtowns, opting for more visible freeway locations.

After the construction of a regional mall outside Eugene, Oregon, the downtown department stores—Bon Marché, Sears, and Kaufman's—all closed, despite the fact that the city had transformed Broadway, its main retail street, into a pedestrian mall. After the functional demise of Broadway, the city initiated Broadway Place, a dense project that includes 170 market-rate rental apartments, 14,000 square feet (1,300 square meters) of street-level retail space, and offices that surround and are located above two 371-space public parking garages.

After the department stores closed, the city succeeded in luring Symantec, a computer software company, to relocate its headquarters in the rehabilitated Bon Marché store, which was adjacent to a parking lot that the city owned. But the company still needed more parking, so the city decided to build a garage and lease 550 spaces to Symantec, an arrangement that provided an income stream for the construction of the garage. The city then issued a request for proposals for developers to create an integrated project that would include mixed uses at the street level and above the garage. The city also opened up the pedestrian mall to traffic, hoping that the return of traffic and on-street parking would help to revitalize the downtown. (Symantec eventually left the downtown for Springfield, a suburb of Eugene.)

One benefit of developing in small-city downtowns is the lack of competition: only two proposals were received. The city chose Seattle-based Lorig Associates, LLC, and negotiated a joint-development commercial condominium agreement under which (1) the city would develop, own, and operate the two parking garages and provide the land for a $300,000 air rights payment, and (2) Lorig would develop, own, and man-

age the rental units and street-level retail space. The agreement also provides for income participation: after a 10 percent preferred return on equity to Lorig, the city receives 5 percent of net cash flow and 5 percent of net sales proceeds.

Broadway Place flanks both sides of the rebuilt retail street with mirror-image buildings. At the heart of each block is a three-level parking garage, half of which is set below grade. Shallow street-level retail spaces hide each garage from the street. Five landscaped courtyards, with views of downtown and the surrounding hills, lie on top of the podium and are lined with two-story dwellings, reinforcing the small-city residential character. The courtyards divide the dense, double-loaded layout and eliminate long corridors.

According to Lew Bowers, then project manager for the city, the fact that the city hired several different architects led to difficulties with coordination that, in turn, created cost overruns for the project. Both Bowers and Lorig executives Steve Bolliger and Harris Hoffman also noted that, if they had the project to do over again, they would have negotiated a turnkey agreement under which the city would have simply purchased the parking garage after the developer had completed it. However, they also agreed that the specificity required for such a contract might have precluded some innovative and pragmatic solutions to problems that were made possible by the close working relationship between city and developer.

In the end, Broadway Place cost $25 million—$12 million for the garages, which were funded by parking-revenue bonds and urban renewal funds, and $13 million for the housing and retail components, which were funded by equity from Lorig and local investors and debt from Seafirst/Bank of America.

Rents, designed to target the relatively affluent Eugene market, average about $1.12 per square foot ($12 per square meter), and range

from $550 for a 490-square-foot (46-square-meter) studio to $1,250 for a 1,115-square-foot (104-square-meter) corner unit with two bedrooms and two baths. Renters include young professionals, empty nesters, and graduate stu-

Broadway Place is a mixed-use main-street project in Eugene, Oregon. The project made use of public and private funds.

dents. Lease-up was slow, but average occupancy is now 94 to 96 percent. Lorig rents a block of 148 parking spaces (less than a 0.9-to-1 parking ratio) for $31 per space and re-rents them to tenants for $34—a 15 percent reduction from the $40 per month city parking rate.

Retail leasing has been less successful: about one-third of the space remains vacant. Corner retail has been the most successful, and includes Broadway Market, a shop offering a delicatessen, organic produce, and a wine bar; an upscale pizzeria; and a Savouré Teahouse. Interestingly, the departure of the 550-employee Symantec headquarters barely affected either the retail businesses or the apartment rentals.

Although the predevelopment phase took nearly three years in an inhospitable environment, and the development took nearly that long to mature into a profitable project, Broadway Place has pioneered a new model for mixed-use development in small downtowns that Lorig Associates, other developers, and other cities are adapting to their specific needs.

Source: Adapted from William P. Macht, "Broadway Revisited," *Urban Land*, March 2003.

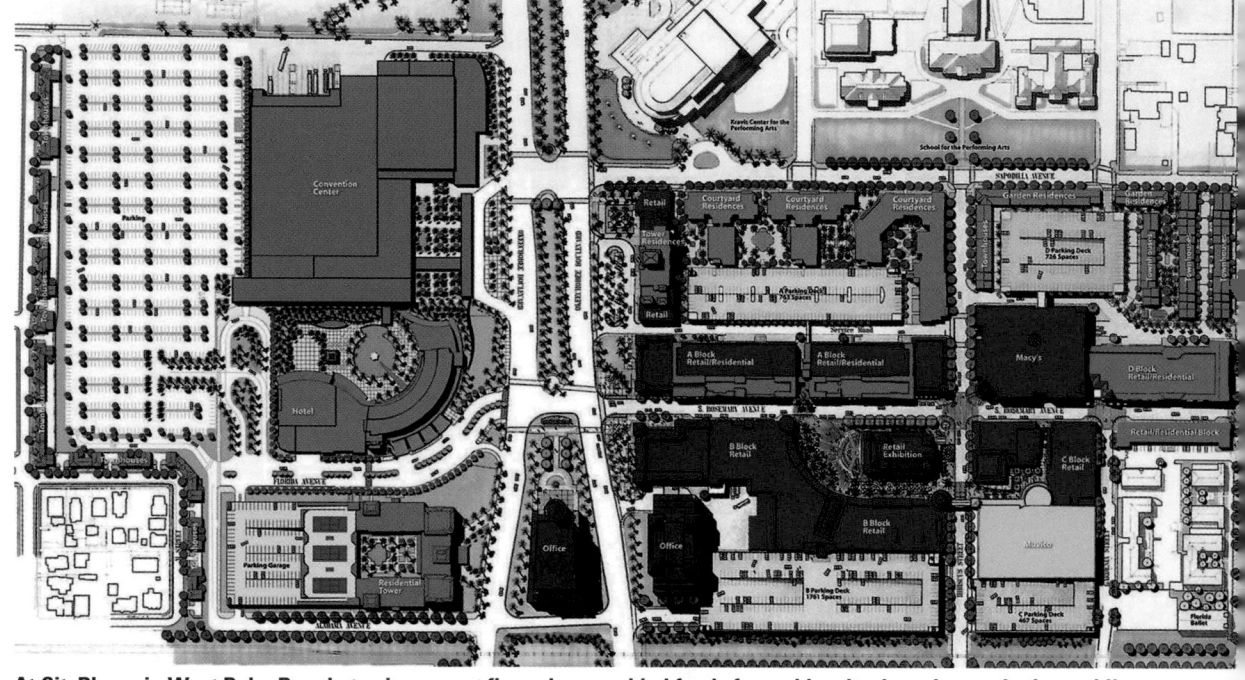

At CityPlace, in West Palm Beach, tax increment financing provided funds for parking, landscaping, and other public improvements. CityPlace Partners, L.P. Elkus/Manfredi Architects

million in tax increment financing funded 30 percent of the cost of constructing the parking deck; it also covered the costs of landscaping, fountains, artwork, lighting, and other public improvements.

A parking district that Montgomery County created in Bethesda, Maryland, was essential to the financial feasibility of Bethesda's commercial core—and, in particular, to the Bethesda Row project. Years ago, to support Bethesda's central business district, the county established a parking district and built a number of parking facilities; users paid for the spaces by the hour or the day. The facilities are partially supported by a surtax on property tax assessments for properties that do not provide their own parking, an arrangement that allows owners of smaller buildings to avoid having to provide their own on-site park-

ing and ensures that all the parking in the area is operated and managed efficiently. It was the construction of the 950-space garage at the center of the development site that made Bethesda Row possible. Nearly all the parking for the development is provided in the county-owned garage, on county-owned surface lots, or through metered on-street parking: 3,376 parking spaces are available within 500 feet (152 meters) of Bethesda Row.

Public Components, Ownership, and Financing

When the public sector has a very strong economic or civic interest in a prominent site, it may invest directly in a project, becoming a part owner. The public agency may participate in a number of ways: by granting the developer a ground lease, entering into a participating agreement, providing public financing, or constructing a major public facility such as a convention center, arena, museum, concert hall, city hall, or library. Other public financing may come from a range of sources, including industrial-revenue bonds, mortgage-revenue bonds, general-revenue bonds, federal grant programs, and state programs. Yerba Buena Center, in San Francisco, for example, includes numerous publicly owned components, starting with the Moscone Convention Center, the original impetus for the project. Other prominent examples of developments with significant public ownership include Smyrna Town Center, in Smyrna, Georgia; Fairview Village, near Portland, Oregon; Cathedral City Downtown, in California; and Cornelius Town Center, in North Carolina.

Public investment is generally directly tied to a much larger private investment; that is, the public investment is intended to leverage private investment. By requiring that public funds be leveraged, public agencies ensure that public investment (1) will generate known and immediate short-term benefits and (2) will be used to support projects that require small amounts of public assistance to become attractive private investments. In other words, leveraging protects governments from engaging in speculative or costly investments that may not yield significant private investment.

Public Development Entities

As is evident from previous examples, a local government may be the principal owner or master developer of a project. A variety of ownership structures can be used in such a case. Special development or redevelopment authorities, commissions, or corporations are frequently used to undertake large-scale mixed-use development. Such entities, which are generally empowered to use many of the tools described in earlier sections, have been used in both central city and suburban locations, taking the leadership role in creating vibrant mixed-use districts or communities. Numerous other public development entities may also be involved. Examples of such entities include redevelopment authorities, community development corporations, transit authorities, quasi-public development corporations, and city agencies.

Yerba Buena Center, in San Francisco, includes numerous publicly owned components, such as the Moscone Convention Center. The convention center is designed for maximum pedestrian access and is within a short walk of downtown hotels, restaurants, and cultural facilities. Roland Halbe

Smyrna Town Center, CityPlace, and the other examples noted earlier highlight the importance of strong public leadership in mixed-use development. Often, the best mixed-use projects are created, nurtured, and sustained by public development entities that are committed to the vision of a vibrant public realm—one that will play an important role in the civic life of the community.

Notes

1. John Stainback, *Public/Private Finance and Development: Methodology, Deal Structuring, Developer Solicitation* (New York: John Wiley & Sons, 2000).

2. Constance E. Beaumont and Elizabeth G. Pianca, *Why Johnny Can't Walk to School,* 2nd ed. (Washington, D.C.: National Trust for Historic Preservation, 2002).

3. Stainback, *Public/Private Finance.*

4. Jane Jacobs, *The Death and Life of Great American Cities* (New York: Random House, 1961), 14.

5. Teresa Zogby, "Mixed-Use Districts," *PAS Memo,* no. 79–11 (November 1979).

Healthy Trends

Since the mid-20th century, physical activity has largely been engineered out of people's daily lives. At work and at home, people are much more sedentary. Daily trips to work, to the store, and to school are mostly made by car. Because the built environment is often hostile to walkers and bikers, even trips of less than a mile (1.6 kilometers) are made by car.

Fortuitously, the public's desire for more walkable places has developed in conjunction with research findings that warn of the dangers associated with physical inactivity. As local governments become aware of the benefits of pedestrian-oriented development, many are working to foster walkable places. Among other techniques, local governments are using zoning codes and overlay districts to permit or encourage mixed-use and higher-density development. Nationwide, public/private partnerships are providing financing tools that benefit both the public sector and the developer. Given the growing consensus about the value of pedestrian-friendly places, government support of these places is likely to keep growing.

Downtown Los Angeles is being retrofitted for greater walkability and transit access. Grand Central Market is one of the key attractions for pedestrians. Carol M. Highsmith Photography, Inc.

The private sector has also shown increased interest in walkable places. Downtown development has been known to generate high economic returns. Town centers have shown higher returns than strip shopping centers, and homes in residential neighborhoods within mixed-use, walkable settings tend to sell for higher prices. In all kinds of locations, and among all real estate product types, pedestrian-oriented development is good business.

Urban Revitalizations

Scores of downtowns throughout the country are benefiting from renewed interest on the part of businesses and residents. Large and small cities alike have undertaken redevelopment projects designed to reinvigorate their urban cores, often by improving and expanding the pedes-

trian realm. Cities across the country, such as Seattle, Memphis, Atlanta, and Washington, D.C., are just a few places with urban neighborhoods that are being revitalized. These and other examples of downtown revitalization projects are described on the following pages.

Even Los Angeles, long associated with America's car culture, is being retrofitted for walkability and transit access. The multimodal transit system created by the Metropolitan Transit Agency of Los Angeles (Metro) includes a fleet of buses (with dedicated bus lanes) and the extensive Metro Rail system, which consists of four lines, more than 73 miles (117 kilometers) of track, and 63 stations. The rail system carries an average of nearly 240,000 riders each weekday and has been the impetus for many pedestrian-oriented projects that are reacquainting Los Angelenos with the pedestrian realm.

Complementing the expanding transit services are growing numbers of walkable, high-density places. Downtown Los Angeles may never become like New York, but more and more residents have the option of walking to nearby services or taking a high-frequency, high-capacity transit line. As the predominance of office space gives way to a wide mix of activity-generating uses, downtown Los Angeles is undergoing a major transformation.

Banking on the idea that downtown office workers will want to walk to work, Forest City Residential West is renovating the historic Subway Terminal Building, a 12-story beaux arts tower, built in 1925, that was a major hub on L.A.'s defunct streetcar line. Rechristened "Metro 417," the former office building began leasing its 277 luxury loft apartments in April 2005. Within walking distance of Metro 417, the new Walt Disney Concert Hall, designed by Frank Gehry, brings nightlife to the city's downtown. Working with developers selected through an RFP process, the city plans to add 3.2 million square feet (297,000 square meters) of new development near the concert hall; this construction will include office space, a hotel, entertainment space, and luxury residential projects.

San Francisco's ongoing revitalization includes dozens of residential, retail, and mixed-use projects and has extended the downtown core into the areas south of Market Street. The landmark Ferry Building now houses a farmers' market (often described as the best in the nation) and upscale restaurants and food shops, drawing tourists

San Francisco's Embarcadero is energized by the Port of San Francisco's renewal of the Ferry Building. The outdoor farmers' market draws tourists and locals alike. Richard Barnes, photographer

and shoppers to a once-dead part of the waterfront. A partnership between Forest City Enterprises and Westfield America combined the old Emporium Department Store with the adjacent San Francisco Centre mall to create a 1.5 million-square-foot (139,000-square-meter) urban mixed-use complex. Anchored by Nordstrom and Bloomingdale's, the new center connects the Union Square district with the Yerba Buena cultural district, generating activity between the two, and vastly expanding the pedestrian-focused portion of the city's downtown. All of these projects take advantage of San Francisco's excellent multimodal public transit system, which includes buses, trolleys, subways, and the famous cable cars.

An ambitious, long-term urban transformation is making downtown Denver one of the more vibrant and pedestrian-focused downtowns in the country. The centerpiece is the 16th Street Mall, one of the nation's few successful pedestrian malls. The mall draws tourists and local visitors alike, who stroll its 16-block length through the city's revitalized shopping, entertainment, and cultural district. A free shuttle bus runs the length of the mall, stopping at every corner.

At the mall's north end is the historic Lower Downtown (LoDo) district, where lofts, high-rise apartments, and other urban housing types have added to the district's nightlife in recent years. Just beyond LoDo is Riverfront Park, a major mixed-use development being undertaken by East-West Partners. The project will ultimately bring 2,500 residential units and 100,000 square feet (9,290 square meters) of retail space to the Denver riverfront.

Supporting the downtown's transformation is Denver's FasTracks program. Voted into effect in November 2004, this ballot initiative empowers the Denver Regional Transportation District to build 119 miles (191.5 kilometers) of light-rail and commuter-rail tracks, provide 18 miles (29 kilometers) of bus rapid transit, and expand bus service.

Once a steel mill site, now a mixed-use development, Southside Works is helping to revitalize the Southside neighborhood, near downtown Pittsburgh. Development Design Group, Inc./Walter Larrimore, photographer

Riverfront Park brings a sense of place to the edge of Denver's downtown.
© D.A. Horchner/Design Workshop

oped by the Soffer Organization, will have more than 610,000 square feet (56,670 square meters) of Class A office space, 164 multifamily housing units (84 lofts and 80 condominiums), and 300,000 square feet (27,870 square meters) of retail and entertainment uses, including a movie theater. Its location on the Monongahela River and the nearby walking and biking trails have attracted several major national tenants, including REI, which is an anchor store for the project.

The city of Pittsburgh has invested heavily in downtown projects, including two stadiums (both of which can be reached on foot) and a new downtown convention center. Southside Works, a brownfield reclamation project across the river from downtown, is transforming a 34-acre (14-hectare) former steel mill site into a pedestrian-friendly mixed-use development. The project, which is being devel-

New Towns Gain Town Centers

Since the 1960s, suburban "new towns" have provided housing in mixed-use settings. But something was missing: most of them did not have a downtown. Now, as these communities mature, they are creating town centers to provide walkable, urban-style focal points with office space, main-street shopping, and high-density housing.

REI Denver

In 1938, 25 climbers from the American Northwest joined together to create Recreational Equipment, Inc. (REI), a consumer cooperative, to supply themselves with climbing equipment. REI has since become one of the most well-known suppliers of specialty outdoor gear. The firm's progressive thinking is evident in its Denver flagship store, which opened in 2000. REI's innovative ideas and designs, coupled with Denver residents' love of the outdoors, allowed the store to be an almost instant success, attracting over 1 million visitors in the first year alone.

REI's determination to honor Denver's past is evident in its choice of location for the store: the historic Denver Tramway Building. From the early 1900s until 1950, the Tramway Building burned coal to power all of Denver's streetcars. After that, it served a number of uses until REI expressed interest in using the building for its new flagship store. The firm believed that this location and site would help establish the desired image for the store—in addition to enlarging market share and increasing profitability.

Since its opening, the store has become as much a tourist destination as a retail store. REI is truly an innovator in the retail industry: the store's interactive features include

■ An outdoor, 318-foot- (97-meter-) long mountain-bike test track that runs along hilly trails in front of the store;

■ A special darkroom where customers can compare bike lights and headlamps;

■ A 45-foot- (13.7-meter-) high indoor climbing wall with a separate boulder to allow customers to test climbing shoes;

■ An in-store test trail that simulates an assortment of natural conditions so that customers can test hiking boots;

■ A cold chamber where customers can test cold-weather gear in temperatures as low as -30 degrees.

Jerry Chevassus, REI's vice president of real estate, explains that these amenities are consistent with REI's philosophy: to ensure that customers buy the right equipment for the right use, REI believes in letting customers try the products before purchasing them.

Although REI could have built a sprawling new development on the edge of town, it chose to redevelop this historic property in lower downtown, at an estimated cost of $28 million. The site, located at the convergence of the North Platte River and Cherry Creek, near the Cherry Creek Bike Path, was a prime location for a store targeting active shoppers. As Gerhard Holtzendorf, district special events administrator for REI, explains, "Part of the reason REI located here was because there were miles of bike paths around us." The development team envisioned a store that could easily be reached by bike or on foot. Because the store is situated on the bike path, the team hoped that customers would use that transportation option.

REI actively promotes biking as a practical transportation option. To encourage employees to commute to work by bicycle, REI provides them with locker rooms equipped with showers. The firm also participates in the annual Bike to Work Day sponsored by the Colorado Department of Transportation. And, as REI envisioned, customers are indeed taking advantage of REI's location to bike to the store. "We have over 100 spots for bikes to park outside the store. We find them typically full on weekends or a nice summer day," Holtzendorf said. In fact, the number of customers who bike to the store is even greater than expected. "We completely underestimated the number of bicycle stands that we needed. After opening the store, we had to double the number of stands we had originally set up," explains Chevassus.

Through its location decision and continued support, REI has succeeded in encouraging customers to bike to the store. "We have been doing this for over 65 years, and we were amazed by the number of people who bike to the Denver store," Chevassus said.

The store has helped stimulate additional economic redevelopment in the area and new opportunities for growth in the urban core, including the expansion of Denver's downtown entertainment district, where community attractions are generating significant tourism revenues. Located in the area known as the Lower Downtown District, or LoDo, REI is within walking distance of the Downtown Denver Aquarium, Coors Field, the Pepsi Center, and Commons Park. In honor of its significant contribution to the creation of a unique, vibrant, and diverse downtown environment, REI was awarded the 2002 Downtown Denver Award.—**Erinn Dowling Torres**

At REI's flagship store, in Denver, customers can test canoes on the river. The store's location, on the Cherry Creek Bike Path, allows many customers to arrive by bike or on foot.

One of the oldest new towns, the Woodlands, near Houston, has begun construction of its urban-style town center, which will combine residential, retail, office, and hotel uses into a cohesive, 1,000-acre (405-hectare) downtown. Working with three design firms—Cooper Robertson, Street-Works, and Sasaki—the Woodlands Operating Company intends to create a pedestrian-centered environment featuring a riverwalk, town squares, and out-door cafés.

North of Dallas, in Plano, Texas, Legacy Town Center is evolving from a one-dimensional office park into a real downtown for Collin County. Today, Legacy is a 2,600-acre (1,052-hectare) office development with a 150-acre (61-hectare) mixed-use downtown where people can live, work, shop, and play.

In a similar vein, the city of Aurora, Colorado, an edge city east of Denver, is now building the downtown it never had: over $300 million worth of public and private projects are coming together to create a civic and commercial hub. Aurora City Place, developed by Miller Weingarten Realty, is a three-block-long mixed-use town center. Landscaped walkways encourage pedestrian traffic between the new center and an existing shopping mall. The civic compo-nent of Aurora's new downtown includes law courts, a library, a museum, and the city hall. About 500 residential units are included in the mix.

A partnership between Tarragon Development and the city of Kent, Washington, is embarking on a mixed-use urban center to complement Kent's mass-transit station. Kent Station will consist of over 500,000 square feet (46,450 square meters) of development, including residential units, offices, shops, a multiplex cinema, and a branch campus of Green River Community College. Tarragon also developed Saffron (see case study), in Sammamish, Washington.

Greyfield Redevelopment

Many suburban shopping malls built in the 1960s and 1970s are now aging and becoming obsolete. These failing malls, known as *greyfields,* offer the potential to be recon-figured into better-integrated, walkable, mixed-use districts.

Legacy Town Center, in Plano, Texas, was reconfigured from an office park to an active 18-hour downtown. RTKL Associates, Inc.

Redoing the Strip

Paseo Colorado transformed an enclosed shopping mall into a mixed-use place that reurbanized downtown Pasadena. RTKL Associates

As California seeks ways to provide more housing—especially affordable housing—for its growing population, local governments and the housing industry are becoming increasingly interested in converting rundown strip shopping centers into new mixed-use neighborhoods that include residences, shops, restaurants, entertainment, and offices.

According to Randy Jackson, principal of the Planning Center, a Costa Mesa firm specializing in land, community, and environmental planning, many California cities face two important planning issues: a critical shortage of affordable housing and the need to reinvent and revitalize aging urban areas. "We have to look back to our existing suburban areas, where infrastructure systems already exist, and we need to develop infill sites, intensify housing density, and revitalize our neighborhoods," Jackson maintains. "We need to dedicate ourselves to reinventing our suburban communities by committing to more efficient and creative use of land."

When successfully redeveloped, older strip shopping centers present an opportunity for communities to halt urban sprawl, reinforce community identity, and provide new housing, observes Melani Smith, director of government services for the Planning Center. "We're adding jobs, we're adding people, but at the same time, we're not building enough housing," she said. "We need a broader and more diverse selection of housing options beyond the single-family, detached home in suburbia."

A recent survey on land use conducted by the Public Policy Institute of California underscores the potential value of mixed-use urban neighborhoods as a source of new housing. According to the survey of more than 2,000 California residents, 47 percent of respondents said they would prefer a mixed-use neighborhood within walking distance of amenities such as shops, theaters, and restaurants.

Changing demographics, migration patterns, and family structures have created a large market for the higher-density housing of suburban villages, according to John Martin, principal of Martin & Associates, a Newport Beach, California–based strategic marketing firm. Martin notes that the state's ability to accommodate future housing demand depends on the ability of the homebuilding industry and the government to plan and build higher-density housing. "Builders have been building homes for families with children for more than four decades, but that market demographic has been changing dramatically from families to homeowners without children, and that change will continue through this decade and beyond," he said. "Along with changing demographics, planners and builders in California are facing the dual challenges of rapidly increasing housing costs and decreasing inventories of land for new residential development. We simply need to find new places, other than suburban environments, in which to build housing."

Analyzing the economics is crucial because cities need to maintain their tax bases, notes Jackson. When evaluating existing shopping-center sites to determine if they can be successfully redeveloped, cities, developers, and retail property owners look at the revenue generated per square foot. Jackson points out that "a good retail center should produce about $500 per square foot [$5,380 per square meter], but the marginal ones are doing only about $200 [$2,150 per square meter]. How can we use a mixed-use project to improve on these numbers, and what kind of commercial dollars can be captured? Along with understanding the site, answering these questions involves a solid understanding of a community's dynamics and demographics."

Underused mall sites, which are typically in prime locations, can be rendered more economically productive through development that capitalizes on built-in markets for higher-density housing and commercial facilities.

On the site of the old Town & Country Mall, in San Jose, California, Federal Realty Investment Trust developed Santana Row. Noted for its excellent design, this mixed-use, main-street project includes a boutique hotel, high-end shops and restaurants, and luxury rental apartments. Although Santana Row had a difficult start, including a disastrous $90 million fire during construction that gutted much of the residential and retail buildings and set back the opening by months, the completed project has ultimately been successful. The project was a learning experience for Federal Realty, which found that partnering with other development firms brought the diversity of experience that is necessary for such a complex project.

A first requirement for converting strip malls into mixed-use communities is finding sites that are large enough and priced low enough to be feasibly developed. Particularly in the early stages, developers need land at prices that offset the construction costs and risks associated with greyfield development. Jackson notes that the best locations are usually marginal sites where productivity and property values are in flux. There may even be sites in city neighborhoods, including vacant lots and lots containing abandoned buildings, that may be ideal for this type of project, although some may be hampered by legal problems, such as tax delinquency.

Shopping-center sites that are ideal for redevelopment range from two to 50 acres (0.8 to 20 hectares) in size. Developers can often acquire these sites at low cost, reducing their initial financial outlay and increasing their rate of return. Many of the sites already have the necessary components—infrastructure and transportation—that make them attractive for mixed-use development.

Planners and architects have developed prototypes for suburban villages that can be built on smaller sites, yielding a variety of housing options—from affordable apartments to luxury townhouses or condominiums. "These suburban villages don't have to be built on large shopping-center sites; there are smaller sites where they will work just as well," says Thomas Cox, senior principal with Thomas P. Cox: Architects, Inc., an architecture, planning, and urban design firm based in Irvine, California.

SEASONS at Ontario Gateway Plaza, in Ontario, California, is an example of a shopping center that was converted into a mixed-use community through a public/private partnership. Developed by LINC Housing Corporation, a nonprofit company that builds affordable housing in California, the project replaced a dilapidated 40-year-old shopping center. It combines retail and residential uses in a large-scale urban redevelopment plan. The revitalized property includes 80 units of affordable housing for seniors and 153,000 square feet (14,210 square meters) of retail shopping space.

An intricate network of partnerships and a complex financing structure may be necessary to convert shopping centers into mixed-use communities. For example, in the case of SEASONS at Ontario, Bank of America Community Development Bank provided nearly $3.17 million in construction financing for the residential component, and long-term financing was provided through the sale of $2.3 million in credit-enhanced tax-exempt bonds; Edison Capital Housing purchased $2.1 million in low-income housing tax credits. Overall, the project cost approximately $24 million, including $5 million in redevelopment funds, of which $1.5 million was for the commercial side and $3.5 million for the residential. The city purchased the land and leased it to LINC Housing, and also made a loan to the developer to be repaid by residual receipts from cash flow.

The residential component is an 80-unit, one- and two-bedroom apartment community located inside the "gateway" to the shopping center. The affordable apartments are home to active seniors (55 years of age and above) whose incomes are at or below 60 percent of the average yearly income for San Bernardino County.

The coming years will be challenging as California's real estate developers and builders look for new ways to house people, build businesses, accommodate traffic, and protect the state's environment. Focusing their creative energies and resources on transforming marginal shopping centers into vibrant suburban villages could be one solution.

Source: Adapted from Christine Rombouts, "Redoing the Strip," *Urban Land*, March 2003.

Winter Park Mall, in Winter Park, Florida, was a standard, 400,000-square-foot (37,160-square-meter) enclosed shopping mall located in a historic Orlando neighborhood. As the surrounding downtown became increasingly attractive, the mall suffered. In the late 1990s, the Don M. Castro Organization began converting the mall into a mixed-use village that is better integrated into its urban surroundings. Now called Winter Park Village, the 32-acre (13-hectare) project includes 400,000 square feet (37,160 square meters) of retail; 120,000 square feet (11,150 square meters) of second-level offices; a 20-screen movie theater; and 58 residential units.

In Lakewood, Colorado, Continuum Partners is creating Belmar, a new town center on the 100-acre (40-hectare) site of the old 800,000-square-foot (74,320-square-meter) Villa Italia mall. Belmar, which will give the city the downtown (and the identity) that it now lacks, emerged from a public process in which local residents photographed places they liked: the photos consistently showed walkable urban streetscapes. When completed, Belmar will include 1 million square feet (92,900 square meters) of office space, 1 million square feet (92,900 square meters) of retail, and about 1,300 residential units. Structured parking will be financed through a public/private partnership with the city.

Traditional Neighborhood Developments in Greenfields

Traditional neighborhood developments (TNDs) are one of the mainstays of pedestrian-oriented planning. TNDs are new communities, generally on greenfield sites, in which dense residential neighborhoods are organized around shopping districts, public squares, and other amenities, in such a way as to ensure that all components of the community are within a short walk of each other. Since the 1980s, the TND concept has had a growing impact on the design of residential communities, fostering an increasing emphasis on the pedestrian realm. Several hundred "pure" TNDs have been developed worldwide, and countless communities have borrowed some, but not all, of the elements of traditional neighborhood development. Some of the most established TNDs include Seaside and Celebration, both in Florida; the Kentlands, in Gaithersburg, Maryland; and Southern Village, in Chapel Hill, North Carolina. Seaside is the nucleus around which Water-Color, a new walkable community, is being developed (see case study).

Hedgewood Properties has been actively spreading walkable communities across the Atlanta suburbs. At Vickery, a 214-acre (98-hectare) community developed by Hedgewood and designed by Duany Plater-Zyberk & Company, residents of the 550 homes can walk to on-site

Santana Row, in San Jose, California, is a pedestrian-oriented district built on the site of the old Town & Country Mall. SB Architects

civic, recreational, and commercial amenities. One goal of the project design is to minimize the necessity of traveling off site to meet daily needs.

On a greenfield just outside of Nashville, Regent Development is creating Lenox Village, which is sited around a preserved hillside and a creek. The developer and the city of Nashville, with strong leadership and support from the mayor, have worked hard to make this 101-acre (41-hectare) mixed-use community a model for future pedestrian-oriented design in the region. The Lenox Village plan, designed by Looney Ricks Kiss, has won several awards.

Northern Virginia developers Preston Caruthers and Jim Epstein wanted to build a community where people could walk everywhere. They founded Belmont Bay, a 326-acre (132-hectare) community on a peninsula along the Potomac River. The development includes a mix of housing types, a town center, a golf course, and a promenade along a 158-slip marina. A hotel and convention center are proposed. The combination of pedestrian focus, amenities, and waterfront living makes for an active-living community.

Infill Communities

Like greyfield development, infill development can change the character and context of an area. Well-conceived mixed-use projects, like the Glen, in Glenview, Illinois, can bring new life to a neighborhood and transform an auto-oriented environment into a pedestrian-friendly realm. The growing demand for pedestrian-friendly places, the risks and costs of greenfield development, and ever-increasing traffic congestion are making infill projects more appealing to developers, retailers, residents, and consumers.

Opened in June 2005, Glenwood Park is a walkable urban infill project near downtown Atlanta. Charles Brewer, the founder and former chief executive officer of Mindspring.com, is the mastermind behind the project, which is the first development from Brewer's company, Green Street Properties. When completed, the 28-acre (11-hectare) site will feature 50 to 100 single-family homes, 50 to 90 townhouses, and 150 to 300 multifamily units, some of which are planned as accessory apartments. The commercial aspect of the plan includes 25,000 to 50,000 square feet (2,320 to 4,650 square meters) of office space and 98,000 to 114,000 square feet (9,190 to 10,590 square meters)

The developer's goal at Glenwood Park is to create a pedestrian-oriented district that helps to reinvigorate downtown Atlanta. Above: Walter Brown. Left: Loren Heyns, DreamStudio

of retail space. Also included are one large park and two smaller public squares. Streets will be narrow, to slow traffic, and will be lined with trees and wide sidewalks, fostering a pedestrian-oriented environment.

The site of the former Stapleton International Airport, in Denver, is one of the largest urban infill sites in the United States. Currently under development by Forest City Enterprises, Stapleton is planned as an urban-style, mixed-use community that will offer everything its residents need within walking or biking distance. To promote more active lifestyles and increase opportunities for walking and biking, the community has created the Active Living Partnership at Stapleton (ALPS), which focuses on transportation, land use, street designs, and policies that emphasize the connections between health and community design. The ALPS initiative is part of Active Living by Design, a national program of the Robert Wood Johnson Foundation that was established to create, enhance, and promote environments that make it safe and convenient for people to be more physically active. ALPS coordinates with the developer and local officials to ensure that Stapleton and the surrounding areas are designed with pedestrians in mind. One of ALPS's first projects was to improve the design of a major roadway so that it would be safer for pedestrians to cross from an apartment building to the grocery store.

At Playa Vista, a large urban infill project in Los Angeles, the vision is to create an urban, pedestrian-oriented lifestyle through a series of neighborhoods defined by squares and parks. Streets are pedestrian scale and organized in a traditional grid pattern. Restaurants and cafés border the parks, and a lively arts and entertainment district is being created alongside a lake with a boardwalk.

Inner-city revitalizations are also focusing on walkability. In Louisville, Kentucky, the Clarksdale HOPE VI revitalization project has teamed with ACTIVE Louisville, a coalition similar to ALPS that includes housing, transportation, and health agencies. One goal of the partnership is to ensure that the neighborhood revitalization incorporates design elements and programs that will promote active living. The partners will also create incentives for businesses and developers to promote active lifestyles and educate designers on ways to create active-living communities.

Stapleton is an urban-style, mixed-use community being developed on the Stapleton Airport site, in Denver. The community is working to encourage walking and biking for transportation. Dave McGraf, ProPix Photography

Housing for Seniors

In the past, housing for seniors was often relegated to the least expensive—and therefore most remote—locations. The result was that older people who could no longer drive were unable to get to the store or to visit family or friends. Failing health was compounded by isolation. Today, housing for seniors is more often integrated into places where residents can maintain their independence even after they give up driving.

While urban neighborhoods are typically seen as homes for hip young demographics, some cities and developers have recognized the value of drawing seniors to urban renewal districts. In Palmdale, California, for example, the city's downtown revitalization is anchored by a 300-unit housing complex for seniors.

Sunrise, one of the largest operators of housing for seniors, offers Sunrise at Sheepshead Bay, on a waterfront site adjacent to a shopping district in Brooklyn, New York. At Sheepshead Bay, the developer chose not to separate residents from commercial activity; instead, Sunrise strengthened and extended the pedestrian retail district by including commercial space and a restaurant on the first level of the residential building. HPD Cambridge, Inc., a St. Louis–based company that specializes in independent-living facilities for seniors, has developed properties throughout the country, many with ground-floor retail. HPD's goal is to help residents maintain independence. Its target market is seniors who are seeking convenient access for everyday needs and activities and who want to live in urban and suburban downtowns. The Gardens at Kentlands, a 212-unit rental-apartment community for seniors, is in the town center of the Kentlands, in Maryland, one of the first TNDs in the United States. The location offers all the conveniences of a thriving commer-

cial district. Most of the residents relocated from out of state to be closer to their children, who live nearby.

The Case Studies

All across America, walkable places are being developed. The case studies presented in this book come from many parts of the nation and represent many different contexts in which pedestrian-oriented developments can flourish. The case studies also attest to the challenges involved in creating walkable places, and to the range of solutions that are needed.

City Heights Urban Village, in San Diego, is a mixed-use development that was designed to become a catalyst for the redevelopment of one of San Diego's poorest neighborhoods. With over 52 languages spoken, City Heights is

New development at City Heights, in San Diego, has brought activity back to the neighborhood streets. Adrienne Schmitz

one of the most ethnically diverse neighborhoods in the country. The area was besieged by drugs and crime, had few retail facilities, and lacked many vital community services. The development of City Heights Urban Village brought many of the missing facilities and services—including a grocery store, an elementary school, a recreation center, and a police substation—to the neighborhood.

In City Heights, a pedestrian-oriented development succeeded in bringing street life back to a community: the sense of safety provided by the police presence, and the numerous walking destinations within the mixed-use project, have persuaded residents to "take back" their neighborhood and their streets. The project also brought economic revitalization to a neighborhood that sorely needed it.

In another ethnically diverse urban setting, the Market Common, Clarendon, a large-scale infill project in Arlington, Virginia, has helped to transform what was once the parking lot of a department store into a high-density residential and shopping complex that is well integrated into its surroundings. By focusing on high-quality design and pedestrian-friendly connections between destinations, the developer of the Market Common has created a thriving, 18-hour town center—and given the community lively public spaces in the process.

The project, which is within walking distance of the Clarendon Metro Station, a stop on Washington, D.C.'s regional transit system, has revitalized its portion of the Rosslyn-Ballston corridor. Spurred by the success of the Market Common, new pedestrian-oriented developments are springing up on the blocks surrounding the

Because of its pedestrian focus, the Grove, in Los Angeles, has been a popular and highly successful retail development. © RMA Photography, Inc.; Caruso Affiliated

project, making the neighborhood even more connected and walkable.

In greater Los Angeles, a region notorious for its lack of pedestrian-friendly infrastructure, new projects are showing that even car-loving Californians relish the chance to walk in vibrant urban environments. Paseo Colorado, a mixed-use greyfield redevelopment in Pasadena, has brought new life to a formerly fading urban district. The three-square-block urban village includes retail space, restaurants, entertainment uses, and housing. It replaced an enclosed mall that was built in the 1970s, making use of some of the original structure, including the underground parking garage. Paseo Colorado is a part of a larger plan that seeks to reestablish the pedestrian scale and atmosphere of Pasadena's original downtown.

The Grove, a new mixed-use retail and entertainment center in one of the more urban parts of Los Angeles, offers visitors easy pedestrian access to a number of different amenities and services, including restaurants, movie theaters, high-end shopping, and the historic Farmers Market. The project's carefully thought out design, which evokes the spirit of a revitalized downtown, creates a coherent visual and pedestrian connection between old and new uses—linking the Farmers Market, a cherished remnant of Los Angeles's past, and the Grove. Serving as both transportation and an attraction in itself, a trolley circulates between the Farmers Market and the Grove, further intensifying the sense of connectivity. The high level of pedestrian amenities and the linkage of multiple uses have made the Grove a major destination for walking in the Los Angeles region.

Centennial Lakes, in the city of Edina, Minnesota, a first-ring suburb of Minneapolis, is a mixed-use brownfield redevelopment project consisting of office buildings, multifamily residential units, shops, an eight-screen movie

On Florida's rapidly developing panhandle is WaterColor, a mixed-use, walkable community that builds on the success of Seaside. Adrienne Schmitz

theater, and a 15-acre (six-hectare) park, all surrounding a ten-acre (four-hectare) lake. This development is notable for two reasons: first for having given the suburban city of Edina a central focus, complete with multiple options for physical recreation; and second for the particular process that was used to develop the project.

Centennial Lakes is the product of a long-term relationship between the city, the developers, and the site's previous owner. Under the arrangement agreed to by these three parties, the city allowed the original owner of the property to hold the land tax free until favorable economic conditions enabled the developer to buy and build a portion of the site.

Like Centennial Lakes, Birkdale Village was developed to create a pedestrian-friendly central focus for a suburban area. Located in Huntersville, a rapidly developing suburb north of Charlotte, North Carolina, Birkdale Village is part of a concerted effort to manage growth within a new urbanist framework. In the 1990s, Huntersville and many of the surrounding towns adopted new urbanist development codes. Birkdale Village and the adjacent single-family development, the Greens at Birkdale, demonstrate that there is a healthy demand for walkable places even in suburbs that are largely characterized by single-family subdivisions. Both projects are success stories for the creation of pedestrian-friendly greenfield suburbs.

A visit to Florida's panhandle is in order for anyone who still doubts that people want more walkable environments—and that the demand for such environments can translate into extremely profitable development. Today, Florida's northwestern Gulf Coast is home to several pedestrian-oriented developments, all spawned in some way by Seaside, Florida. Since its opening, in 1981, Seaside has been the premier example of new urbanist design.

Wrapped around Seaside's northwestern edge sits a new development, WaterColor, a mixed-use, walkable development that builds on Seaside's fame, success, and

Baxter Village, in Fort Mill, South Carolina, is a pedestrian-oriented community where people can live, work, shop, and play.
Urban Design Associates

pedestrian character while remaining a distinct community. The two connected projects form a much larger pedestrian realm, with even greater opportunities for residents and vacationers to enjoy walking, biking, exploring, and shopping.

Some lenders are wary of financing mixed-use projects, particularly in greenfield locations, not only because of the higher infrastructure costs but because the potential markets in greenfield areas are generally not large enough to support the retail components of the development. Strip development, which is less infrastructure-intensive and often relies on standardized building forms, may be more appealing to lenders. But the developments of both Saffron and Baxter Village show not only that greenfield projects can be highly successful, but that they can provide a better land use alternative than strip development. As consultant Deborah Myerson has noted, "Don't underestimate the smaller efforts; recognize their cumulative success."[1]

Many people believe that Saffron, located in the recently incorporated city of Sammamish, Washington, will be the catalyst that spurs mixed-use, walkable development in this growing suburb of Seattle. In the 1980s and 1990s, when low property values and a beautiful natural setting created a housing boom, the city's unofficial downtown became an intersection lined with strip malls, one of which houses the city hall. Down the street is Saffron, a 4.4-acre (1.8-hectare) project that has set the standard for walkable places in the Seattle suburbs. Saffron has demonstrated that making walkable places is not just about building large, master-planned communities; well-designed smaller projects can also play a vital role.

As the regional economy has grown, the rural town of Fort Mill, South Carolina, south of Charlotte, has entered a period of suburbanization. Rapid growth looms large in this community's future. In an effort to control the impact of that growth, the Close family, which had owned land in the area for over 200 years, formed Clear Springs Development Company and allocated 6,200 acres (2,509 hectares) of land to open-space preservation and careful development, including Baxter Village. With a total of 1,325 residential units and 300,000 square feet (27,870 square meters) of commercial and civic space planned for this still-semirural area, Baxter Village is setting the tone for future developments.

Each of these case studies shows that people want to live, work, shop, and play in places that are pedestrian-friendly. Many other pedestrian-oriented developments are on the drawing boards, in the planning stages, or under construction. Pedestrian-oriented developments offer an alternative to the frustration of traffic congestion, to the rapid depletion of open space in suburban areas, and to the sense of isolation that comes from spending long hours in the car. Moreover, they may help to stem the obesity epidemic and curb chronic diseases related to physical inactivity.

For many of today's developers, the needs of the pedestrian are a new focus—and each of the case studies is therefore an ongoing experiment in the creation of a walkable place. Although all the projects described in the case studies are walkable, they vary in the degree to which they make walking a viable alternative. Some places, like Centennial Lakes and the Grove, will probably remain destinations that most visitors reach by car—but within which they walk from place to place. Other developments, like Birkdale Village, Baxter Village, City Heights, and the Market Common—thanks to their innovative designs, mix of uses, and pedestrian connectivity with their surroundings—are well poised to reduce automobile trips.

The development team for the Market Common, for example, paid close attention to the edges of the site. The project is already well situated within Arlington County's extensive, pedestrian-friendly sidewalk network, and is three blocks away from the Clarendon Metro Station; but the development also includes numerous pedestrian pathways that make the project porous and accessible from all angles. In addition, the sections of sidewalk that run adjacent to Market Commons properties offer a high-quality pedestrian environment, with planting strips, shade trees, and generous widths.

Because the designers eliminated blank building facades, the site is inviting and the streetscape is alive. The buildings on the site also mirror the uses on the opposing streets. The residential sides of the project are visually and functionally connected to the single-family houses on the opposite sides of the street, and the retail sections face other retail sections. The design extends the network of pedestrian-friendly amenities past the project's borders.

Likewise, the design of Saffron dares the surrounding areas to add to the pedestrian-friendly environment. In a similar fashion, the designers of City Heights established a template for pedestrian-focused development that will serve as a model for later development beyond the borders of City Heights.

The Glen combines many of the characteristics that make a place walkable. Developed on the site of the former Glenview Naval Air Station, the 1,100-acre project is anchored by a town center surrounded by offices, parks, walkable residential neighborhoods, and two golf courses. Metra commuter rail provides access to Chicago. John Herbst

The strong inward focus of the Grove, by comparison, establishes it as a car-free refuge from the auto-dominated environment of Los Angeles. Because at the time of its development, there were very few pedestrian amenities beyond the Grove's borders, and because there are a number of obstructions to pedestrian travel, the majority of visitors arrive, by necessity, by car. Unlike projects such as the Market Common, which offer opportunities to incorporate walking into one's daily routine, places like the Grove demonstrate that people need places to walk and to be social, that the sense of place is becoming an essential component to successful development, and that people are willing to drive in order to reach comfortable places to walk.

It is expected that the Grove's surroundings will become more pedestrian-friendly, as new development is designed to expand on the ambience set by the Grove. As Los Angeles County continues to expand its new light-rail system, jurisdictions located along the light-rail line are creating pedestrian-friendly, transit-oriented developments at many of the stops. Projects like the Grove, and Santa Monica's Third Street Promenade, are crucial for helping people to understand what walkable places in the Los Angeles area can look like. The more people understand the value and benefit of walkable places, the more likely they are to support new pedestrian-oriented developments.

The case studies included in this book were chosen for their potential to inspire the imagination. Without imagination, efforts to create pedestrian-friendly developments will not succeed. There is a growing demand for walkable places as businesses and residents look for alternatives to auto-dominated lifestyles. And the more people learn about

walking as a form of transportation—and as a source of numerous benefits, including improved physical and mental health, decreased traffic congestion, improved air quality, and an increased sense of social and civic connectedness—the more the demand for walkable places will continue to grow. Recent findings suggesting that walking as little as 30 extra minutes a day will be enough to stem the growing tide of obesity—which now claims thousands of lives a year—are adding further support to the quest for walkable places.

The outlook is increasingly optimistic. Changes in zoning regulations are making it easier to build pedestrian-oriented places. Consumer demand for such places is high, and the returns on existing pedestrian-oriented developments show that such projects can be very profitable. Slowly, real estate development patterns are becoming more pedestrian oriented. There is now a growing consensus among developers, businesses, retailers, gov-

ernment agencies, scientists, activists, and ordinary citizens that people need more opportunities to walk, bike, or otherwise be active on a daily basis. This consensus is a powerful indicator that more pedestrian-friendly environments are on the horizon.

At the core of this return to a more walkable pattern of living is a basic truth about the human race. Enrique Peñalosa, the former mayor of Bogotá, Colombia, expresses this truth quite eloquently, "God made us walking animals—pedestrians. As a fish needs to swim, a bird to fly, a deer to run, we need to walk, not in order to survive, but to be happy."[2]

Notes

1. Deborah Myerson, speaking at the Urban Land Institute/Joseph C. Canizaro Mayors' Forum, San Antonio, Texas, February 28, 2002.
2. Enrique Peñalosa, keynote address, Great Parks/Great Cities Conference, July 30, 2001.

Chapter 6

Case Studies

City Heights Urban Village

San Diego, California

City Heights Urban Village, a mixed-use redevelopment project in the Mid-City area of San Diego, is remarkable for its holistic approach to urban revitalization and for the public/private partnership that brought it to fruition. In just eight years, an eight-square-block area of rundown houses and businesses was transformed into a vital, walkable community center. As William Jones, chief executive officer of CityLink Investment Corporation and one of the Village's prime movers, notes with pride, City Heights now has "a heart."

Working with Price Charities; the San Diego Redevelopment Agency; the local school district, police department, parks and recreation department, and community college district; and several other public and private entities, the developer created a new hub of retail and community facilities that serves the entire City Heights area of San Diego. This "village," as its planners call it, has given the community a new focus and identity. But it has also netted highly tangible benefits, including accessible community facilities, new jobs, recreational facilities, educational opportunities, and housing.

The development team created a new hub of activity for City Heights. The public library and the Mid-City Continuing Education Center are at the core of the development. Martinez + Cutri

The Village's planners used a holistic approach. To illustrate this perspective, Price Charities created a graphic called the City Heights Wheel, which shows the many aspects of a healthy community—from safety and security to education, recreation, services, housing, and jobs—as slices of a pie. In keeping with the philosophy behind the City Heights Wheel, the Village includes a new police substation that also offers a gymnasium and community meeting rooms; a new public library; a community services center; a performance annex; a recreation center; a Head Start children's center; an elementary school and continuing-education facility; a retail center; an office building; and residential townhouses.

Architecturally, the "village" concept was realized through the creation of a concentrated, walkable precinct with strong pedestrian linkages, including the new Wightman Street Promenade—a widened, palm-lined street that ties together several of the land uses, offers a pleasant environment for walking, and provides additional on-street parking that would otherwise have been accommodated in a parking lot.

Site and Development Process

A community of 70,000, City Heights was developed in the early 20th century as a neighborhood of small, single-family homes. In the years after World War II, particularly

in San Diego. Along with these changes came crime and drugs. The situation declined to the point that the city council adopted a resolution declaring a state of emergency in City Heights. In 1992, city officials designated the wider City Heights area—some 2,000-plus acres (810 hectares)—as a redevelopment area.

The City Heights Urban Village project came into focus in the early

the 1960s through the 1980s, as middle-class residents and resources left the central city for the suburbs, City Heights began a sharp decline. Many of the single-family homes were redeveloped as six- to ten-unit apartment buildings, and the area became home to increasing concentrations of immigrant and lower-income families. By the 1980s, the area's population had tripled, but the availability of retail and community services had substantially declined from prewar levels. City Heights became one of the poorest—and, with 52 languages spoken, one of the most ethnically diverse—communities

National tenants were impressed by the City Heights master plan. The local residents wanted—and got—a Starbucks, which includes an outdoor seating area. Adrienne Schmitz

1990s. The precipitating factor was the closure of one of the last remaining supermarkets in the area. On separate but parallel paths, William Jones, of CityLink, and Sol Price, of Price Charities, both recognized the need for concentrated action—as well as the opportunities presented by the supermarket site and surrounding area. Jones had been convening focus groups of inner-city residents in various communities in order to better understand their needs. What he found was that residents wanted safety and security, and the same quality of services that other neighborhoods enjoyed. Jones says that "what all of these communities had in common is that they lacked a town center, a heart." Adding to the emerging concept of a mixed-use village was the city's interest in locating a

The continuing education center is operated by the San Diego Community College District. Courses focus on English literacy and job training. Martinez + Cutri

police substation on the supermarket site, and the school district's plans for a new elementary school nearby. "A need was felt, by all parties, for very bold action," notes Jim LoBue, City Heights community development coordinator for the San Diego Redevelopment Agency.

Backed by seed money and support from Price Charities, CityLink and its architect, Martinez + Cutri Corporation, developed a master plan that (1) addressed the articulated needs of the community and (2) made use of the opportunities presented by the 37.6-acre (15.2-hectare) area that included the old supermarket site. In 1994, on the basis of this physical plan and financing plans prepared by CityLink, the city granted development rights to the firm for an eight-square-block area. Ultimately, CityLink developed the retail center for its own portfolio, and undertook the site work and the development of the community facilities on behalf of the city.

Price Charities, a prime sponsor of the Village, contributed in many ways—providing planning funds, lending a portion of the funds needed to build the police substation, developing programs to aid in the restoration of City Heights, providing grants and subsidies for numerous City Heights endeavors, and directly developing the Village's six-story office building and residential townhouse community. The various programs and endeavors of Price Charities in City Heights have been brought together under an umbrella known as the City Heights Initiative.

Planning and Design

The master plan for City Heights Urban Village had multiple objectives:

■ To create a focal point for the community;

■ To provide retail and community services in a single, concentrated location accessible to all residents;

■ To provide a safe place for residents to congregate;

■ To provide an inviting physical environment for private investment.

To create a development site of suitable size to achieve these goals, the existing street grid was maintained, but several minor streets and alleys were closed off. University and Fairmount avenues, the primary thoroughfares through the site, were preserved and improved. Sidewalks were widened to ten or 12 feet (three or four meters) to provide generous and protected space for pedestrians, and were set off from the curb by a wide planting strip

The Black Box Theater, an indoor/outdoor facility, brings evening activity to the neighborhood. Martinez + Cutri

with shade trees. Wightman Street, which is perpendicular to Fairmount Avenue, was widened from 80 to 130 feet (24 to 40 meters) and transformed into a promenade that links many of the Village's facilities. The additional width is broken up by two double rows of diagonal parking and a central median planted with mature palm trees. The trees are set into a planting area of decomposed granite along an undulating sidewalk. In addition to providing parking, the promenade lends the Village the air of a small-town main street and focuses pedestrian movement toward the library's main entrance, at the corner of Wightman and Fairmount—in effect, forming the village square.

The combined Mid-City Police Substation and Mid-City Community Gymnasium, completed in 1996, was the first structure built in the Village. Price Charities lent funds for construction of this unique combination so that this essential building block could be built first, instilling confidence in the Village's prospects and anchoring the build-

ings to come. Given the city's capital funding schedule, construction of the police substation would have been delayed at least four years without this upfront support.

Instead of giving the police substation a defensive architectural character, the designers included large picture windows that give passersby a sense of security and provide "eyes on the street." In addition to the gymnasium, the structure contains a 2,900-square-foot (270-square-meter) community meeting space on the second floor. Not only does the police presence ensure that the gym will be a safe place for local youth, but it has also fostered interaction between neighborhood youth and the police, breaking down cultural barriers and lessening the tensions that often characterize relations between police and inner-city residents.

The second phase of Village construction consisted of the Rosa Parks Elementary School, completed in 1997. Consistent with the holistic approach that guided the development, the city of San Diego donated land adjacent to the school for playing fields, and the parks and recreation department entered into a joint-use agreement with the school district to allow public use of the fields after school hours and on weekends, creating a safe place for active play in the neighborhood. Enhancements to the baseball fields were donated by the San Diego Padres baseball team, which was recruited by CityLink's William Jones, and which has sponsored Little League ball fields in many San Diego–area locations.

Adjacent to the playing fields is a new recreation center that includes swimming pools, tennis courts, and other recreation facilities. Some observers, suggesting that inner-city residents don't swim or play tennis, questioned the provision of a swimming pool and tennis courts for this neighborhood. But Jones believed that it was important to change expectations, and his hunch proved correct: when the tennis courts opened, residents formed lines around the block to sign up for teams and lessons. Today, the neighborhood boasts competitive swimmers and tournament tennis players.

The City Heights International Village Celebration is a street fair that is held every June to showcase the diversity of the community and its businesses. Adrienne Schmitz

At the heart of the Village is the Weingart City Heights Library. Completed in 1998, the 15,000-square-foot (1,390-square-meter) library—with meeting rooms, an Internet technology center, and space for 60,000 books—has become a hub of neighborhood activity, logging more than 2,000 visitors per day. Some ten different funding sources, led by a $5.2 million grant from the Price family, went into

creating the library and the adjacent park and performance annex. The performance annex is a 3,000-square-foot (280-square-meter) "black-box" structure with roll-up doors that open onto the park. Operated by the library, the indoor/outdoor facility is part of the effort to bring life to the neighborhood during evenings and weekends, and has hosted a range of activities, including movie screenings, children's painting workshops, and performances by the San Diego Symphony and the Ballet Folklorico of Mexico.

Also adjacent to the library is the Mid-City Community Services Center, which includes four Head Start classrooms, the offices of the Town Council, and local branches of a variety of city agencies and service providers, enabling residents to pay water bills, obtain permits, and conduct other city business right in the neighborhood. Sponsored by the City Heights Initiative and funded by the city in conjunction with the San Diego Foundation, the Town Council was created to give residents an organized voice in community affairs.

Across from the library is the Mid-City Continuing Education Center, a three-story, 58,400-square-foot (5,430-square-meter) structure completed in 2000. Operated by the San Diego Community College District, the center focuses on English literacy and technical and job training. As with the public library, patronage of the facility—in this service-deficient part of the city—has exceeded expectations.

A new, community-focused shopping center and a six-story office building now front University Avenue, the neighborhood's traditional retail thoroughfare. The 108,900-square-foot (10,120-square-meter) retail center includes an Albertson's supermarket and a variety of national stores (Starbucks, McDonald's, and Subway,

The Weingart City Heights Library is a hub of neighborhood activity, logging more than 2,000 users per day. Martinez + Cutri

Colorful tiles adorn some of the buildings. Martinez + Cutri

among others). Although it was initially difficult to persuade creditworthy retailers to consider the crime-ridden and economically depressed City Heights area, tenants were ultimately swayed, according to William Jones, by the comprehensiveness of the master plan, the city's commitment to the project, the rapid implementation of the initial phases, and the prospect of locating within a $100 million master-planned community in the heart of one of San Diego's most populated areas. Ultimately, over 75 percent of the retail space was preleased before construction began, and 95 percent was leased before construction was completed. Nine months after opening, the center boasted a 100 percent occupancy rate, which it has maintained.

To facilitate movement from University Avenue into and through the Village, the supermarket was sited so that it was perpendicular to University Avenue. Smaller structures were developed fronting the street. Walkways between structures within the shopping center connect to other facilities in the Village, enabling shoppers to park once and conduct their business on foot.

The Office Center, which opened in 2002, is a 118,400-square-foot (11,000-square-meter) structure that houses office space for nonprofit agencies and service providers. Tenants include a street-level bank and two health clinics. The structure was developed by SDRC, a subsidiary of Price Charities, which financed the project internally. Joe LaBreche, SDRC's commercial development director, notes that because of poor soil conditions and escalating land costs in the later stages of development, the project was expensive to build. Rental rates are set so as to amortize the construction costs and provide a minimal (5 to 8 percent) return on investment. Rents for nonprofit tenants are not directly subsidized, but tenants can apply to Price Charities for operating grants.

SDRC developed the adjacent residential townhouses simultaneously with the office project. First priority was given to residents displaced by the construction of the Village, then to other residents of City Heights. Completed in the summer of 2003, the 116 units were initially intended as for-sale housing with subsidized mortgages. But because insurance could not be obtained for that construction option, the project was ultimately built as rental units. The units all have two or three bedrooms, and 34 are rented to low-income or very low-income households.

Development Team

The creation of City Heights Urban Village entailed cooperation among an unusually large number of public and private entities and the amalgamation of funds from many different sources. Although each building and each project had its own constellation of participants and funding sources, CityLink, Price Charities, and the San Diego Redevelopment Agency were all involved in every portion of the undertaking.

Incorporated in 1994, CityLink Investment Corporation is a San Diego–based, for-profit corporation that acquires, develops, and manages real estate ventures in selected urban communities. It was founded with startup capital from Price Charities and various corporations, foundations, and individuals. In March 1995, William Jones acquired 100 percent interest in the business.

Price Charities, headed by San Diego investor Sol Price, is the umbrella for several philanthropic entities inspired and funded by the Price family, which founded the Price Club retail chain. The work of Price Charities centers on community building in San Diego and Imperial counties, with a particular focus on City Heights. Price Charities sponsors the City Heights Initiative, which oversees educational programs; community development programs (including a community service program, a home loan program, and a fellowship program); and housing and commercial development initiatives.

Financing and Management

Land acquisition was spearheaded by the San Diego Redevelopment Agency. To acquire and clear the site of the retail center, the agency sold $15.9 million in tax-allocation bonds. The city then sold the land to CityLink for approximately $2.7 million. Construction of the retail center was financed through private lenders. Several other projects were funded in part by federal Community Development Block Grant (CDBG) funds. In an unusual display of community solidarity, city council members from adjoining districts agreed to pool their allocations of CDBG funds to support the City Heights Urban Village project.

Other funding sources included the San Diego Police Department, the parks and recreation department, the San Diego Unified School District, and the San Diego Community College District. The U.S. Department of Housing and Urban Development provided Economic Development Initiative funds and Section 108 grants. Rounding out the effort were funds donated by private corporations and businesses, such as the San Diego Padres baseball team.

Several management entities have evolved to coordinate and promote activities within the Village, including the Town Council, a merchants' association, and a business improvement district. In addition, representatives from CityLink, SDRC, and several city departments, including the police department, meet monthly to review issues facing the Village and to plan for upcoming events.

Site plan. Martinez + Cutri

Experience Gained

By several measures, City Heights Urban Village is a great success. The retail center is performing beyond expectations. Nine months after opening, the center boasted a 100 percent occupancy rate, which it has maintained since that time. When city planners expressed doubt that Starbucks was an appropriate tenant, residents argued that they wanted the same stores and services that other neighborhoods had—and that the area has succeeded in supporting. Residents also lobbied for greater density than the city initially wanted. Whereas in many neighbor-

hoods, NIMBY factions fight density and additional development, inner-city residents often welcome new development with open arms.

The office structure, built in a slow economic climate and limited market, achieved 76 percent occupancy in less than one year. From the municipal perspective, the tax increment for City Heights increased by $5.3 million since redevelopment began (based on an increase of approximately $530 million in districtwide property tax valuations).

According to the *City Heights Urban Village Fact Sheet*, crime decreased 39 percent between 1996 and 2000. While crime rates fell citywide during that period, in part because of a general improvement in the economy, decreases were substantially greater in the City Heights area. James LoBue, of the San Diego Redevelopment Agency, attributes the drop to the "multifaceted community revitalization efforts" in City Heights, including (1) the opening of the Mid-City Police Substation and the Mid-City Community Services Center, (2) increased resident involvement in neighborhood policing efforts, (3) enriched educational opportunities, and (4) increased investment sparked by the development of City Heights Urban Village and related improvements.

A visible result of these changes, notes CityLink's William Jones, is that people are out walking in the Village, both in the daytime and in the evenings—an uncommon sight just a few years ago. Echoing this observation, Robert Henderson, of TransWest Housing, which served as construction manager of the office and townhouse project, notes that kids, joggers, and families with strollers now take advantage of the communal village atmosphere.

An article in *San Diego Magazine* describes the scene: "Pedestrians are everywhere. A woman wearing traditional Vietnamese clothing and a pointed straw hat strolls down the street, winding her way between young men in baggy pants and shirts, Sudanese immigrants, and young Hispanic mothers with kids in tow."[1]

Among the conclusions that may be drawn regarding the City Heights Urban Village development are the following:

The success of the Village is largely attributable to the highly committed public and private partners of the project. LoBue notes that the project had "tremendous support up and down the chain of command," as well as a committed and savvy private developer and the generous support of a nonprofit sponsor. Another element that contributed to the project's success is the holistic approach embraced by all parties. The Village's planners provided a mix of uses, from child care and health services to recreation, retail, and education.

The concentration of uses within the Village benefits those who do not have cars. Residents can travel to the Village on foot and can take care of numerous errands, from paying bills to food shopping. In fact, the Village now attracts residents of outlying areas, who come by bus or automobile and conduct their business on foot. In the future, City Heights will be linked to downtown San Diego and to other parts of the city by TransNet, a proposed rapid-transit bus system.

The attention to the connective spaces that link the disparate facilities and the concentration on public safety and security have made the district a popular destination for pedestrians. Walking in City Heights Urban Village is safe and pleasant, qualities substantially lacking in the urban environment before the redevelopment. The wide, landscaped sidewalks; the linear, parklike Wightman Promenade; and the security and lighting improvements have brought out strollers and encouraged pedestrian activity for its own sake, in addition to encouraging patronage of the Village facilities.

Note

1. See www.sandiegomagazine.com/issues/may02.

City Heights Urban Village

San Diego, California

Land Use Information

Site area (acres/hectares)	37.6/15.2
Floor/area ratio	0.4

Land Use Plan

Use	Acres/Hectares	Percentage of Site
Building sites (including surface parking)	19.7/8.0	52.4
Streets	7.4/3.0	19.7
Landscaping, open space	10.5/4.2	27.9
Total[1]	37.6/15.2	100.0

1. Excludes elementary school.

Gross Building Area

Use	Square Feet/Square Meters
Private Facilities	
Office	118,400/11,000
Retail	108,900/10,120
Residential	140,800/13,080
Parking	145,700/13,540
Subtotal, private facilities	513,800/47,740
Public Facilities	
Police station	29,000/2,690
Gymnasium	10,000/930
Library	15,000/1,390
Performance annex and community services center	10,000/930
Recreation center	8,800/820
Continuing education center	58,400/5,430
Subtotal, public facilities	131,200/12,190
Total	645,000/59,930

Leasable Area

Use	Square Feet/Square Meters
Office	117,700/10,930
Retail	108,900/10,120

Office Information

Percent occupied	75
Number of tenants	15
Average tenant size	5,900 square feet (550 square meters)
Annual rents	$20–$26 per square foot ($215–$279 per square meter)
Average length of lease	5–10 years
Typical lease terms	NNN

Retail Information

Percentage of gross leasable area occupied: 100

Tenant Classification	Number of Stores	Leasable Area (Square Feet/ Square Meters)
General merchandise	4	15,200/1,410
Food service	6	14,400/1,340
Personal services	2	3,600/340
Recreation, community	1	4,500/420
Financial	1	4,700/440
Other (grocery, drugs)	1	66,300/6,160
Total	15	108,700/10,110

Residential Information

Unit Type	Number of Units	Market Rate Unit Size (Square Feet/ Square Meters)	Market Rate Number of Units	Market Rate Rent Range	Subsidized Number of Units	Subsidized Rent
A	70	1,280/119	65	$1,325–$1,375	5	$707
B	25	1,070/99			25	$707
C	12	960/89	10	$1,025–$1,075	2	$642
D	8	1,680/156	6	$1,575–$1,625	2	$757
E	1	830/77	1	$950		
Total	116		82		34	

Development Costs

	In Thousands
Police substation and gymnasium	$8,994
Wightman Street Promenade	3,670
Underground utility district	1,000
Retail center	33,400
Library, park, performance annex	14,744
Continuing education facility	8,559
Townhouses and Office Center	47,000
Total[2]	$117,367

2. Excludes elementary school.

Development Schedule

Site purchased	Multiple purchases, starting in 1994
Planning started	1994
Construction started	1995
Phase I completed	1996
Leasing started, office development	2002
Leasing started, townhouses	2003
Project completed	2003

City Heights Urban Village

Funding Sources

Total, all phases[1]	$117,367,000

Police Substation and Gymnasium

Substation

District One Community Development Block Grant (CDBG)	$25,000
District Two CDBG	300,000
District Seven CDBG	400,000
District One and Seven CDBG	152,000
District Three CDBG Section 108 loan	1,582,000
District Seven CDBG Section 108 loan	1,582,000
Citywide CDBG	1,000,000
Police department (general fund)	30,000
Interest earnings	275,000

Police Substation Expansion

District Three CDBG Section 108 loan	$618,000
District Seven CDBG Section 108 loan	400,000
Citywide CDBG Section 108 loan	1,982,000
Sale of land to San Diego Community College District[2]	459,000
Interest earnings	189,000
Total	$8,994,000

Wightman Street Promenade

Gas tax, TRANSNET bonds	$3,620,000
City of San Diego	50,000
Total	$3,670,000

Underground Utility District

Underground utility district funds	$1,000,000
Total	$1,000,000

Commercial Phase

Public phase (land assembly)

Tax-allocation bonds	$13,300,000
Land-sale proceeds[3]	2,700,000
Economic Development Initiative grant	400,000
City National Bank predevelopment loan	$800,000
City National Bank construction and permit loan	11,800,000
TRI/LISC equity	3,500,000
CityLink equity	900,000
Total	$33,400,000

Library, Park, and Performance Annex

Price family	$5,250,000
Economic Development Initiative grant	1,000,000
Section 108 loan	5,050,000
Community Development Block Grant float loan	2,200,000
San Diego Unified School District	309,000
Neighborhood House	291,700
Sale of old library	340,000
Parks and recreation department matching grant	73,900
San Diego Padres Foundation grant	80,600
Interest	148,300
Total	$14,743,500

Townhouses and Office Center

Housing set-aside funds	$5,115,000
Price Charities	41,885,000
Total	$47,000,000

1. Excludes elementary school.
2. The Community College District paid the San Diego Redevelopment Agency for the land early on, to allow the police substation to be completed on schedule.
3. Funded upfront by the developer, through a bridge loan from San Diego National Bank.

Development Team

Developer and Master Planner
CityLink Investment Corporation
San Diego, California
www.citylink.com

Architect and Master Planner
Martinez + Cutri Corporation
San Diego, California
www.mc-architects.com

Architect (Retail)
Fehlman, LaBarre Architecture and Planning
San Diego, California
www.fehlmanlabarre.com

Developer (Offices and Housing)
San Diego Revitalization Corporation
San Diego, California

Construction Manager (Offices and Housing)
TransWest Housing
San Diego, California

General Contractor
Sundt Construction Southern California
San Diego, California

Other Key Development Team Members
San Diego Redevelopment Agency
San Diego, California

Price Charities
San Diego, California

Paseo Colorado

Pasadena, California

Starting in 1940, with the completion of the Arroyo Seco Parkway, the first freeway on the West Coast, Pasadena transformed itself from a pedestrian-friendly town into an automobile-dependent community. Paseo Colorado is part of a coordinated citywide effort to return Pasadena to its walkable roots. Developed by TrizecHahn Development Corporation, with Post Properties, Inc., as the residential developer, the three-square-block "urban village" replaced an enclosed mall that had been built as part of a 1970s redevelopment effort. Both the old mall, Plaza Pasadena, and the new center, Paseo Colorado, were developed as public/private partnerships, with the city of Pasadena providing partial financing and other support.

The new center, Paseo Colorado, built on top of the Plaza Pasadena's two-level underground parking structure, mixes retail, restaurant, entertainment, and residential uses. The project includes 56 retail shops, a full-line Macy's department store, seven destination restaurants, six quick-service cafés, a health club, a day spa, a supermarket, a 14-screen cinema, and 387 rental housing units.

Paseo Colorado replaced an enclosed mall with an urban village, reconnecting the urban block pattern and restoring Pasadena's Civic Center as a vibrant, mixed-use district. Ehrenkrantz Eckstut & Kuhn Architects

Site

Paseo Colorado is located in Pasadena's Civic Center district; Old Pasadena lies to the west, and the Playhouse district and the post–World War II Lake Avenue retail area lie to the east. Garfield Avenue, the central focus of the Civic Center district, runs through Paseo Colorado, but access is limited to pedestrians. On the other side of Green Street, Paseo Colorado's southern border, is the Pasadena Civic Auditorium, which provides a southern terminus for Garfield Avenue. Next to the auditorium is the city hall, and on the other side of the city hall is the historic Central Library. These three beautiful buildings, all in the California Mediterranean architectural style, form a view corridor that was designed in 1925, at the height of the City Beautiful movement.

Within about a ten-minute walk of Paseo Colorado are two light-rail stations—the Memorial Park Station to the northwest and the Del Mar Station to the southwest. Both stations are on the Gold Line of the Los Angeles Metropolitan Transportation Authority.

The project faces Colorado Boulevard, a major retail thoroughfare linking Old Pasadena, the Civic Center district, the Playhouse district, and the Lake Avenue retail area. The design and siting of Paseo Colorado reflect the city's plan to transform Colorado Boulevard into an inviting pedestrian link that will encourage more people to walk to Pasadena's various attractions.

A series of plazas, courtyards, and walkways take advantage of Pasadena's ideal climate by providing a variety of outdoor spaces for dining, shopping, strolling, and mingling. Ehrenkrantz Eckstut & Kuhn Architects

Development Process and Financing

During the 1950s and 1960s, as retail shifted eastward, from Old Pasadena to Lake Street, many of the retail properties on Colorado Boulevard, which lay between these districts, began to decline. In the 1970s, in an attempt to revitalize Colorado Boulevard, the city pursued what was then a progressive idea: building an enclosed regional mall downtown. For the project that came to be known as Plaza Pasadena, the city acquired, through its redevelopment agency, 14.9 acres (six hectares) of land along Colorado Boulevard and the adjacent streets. As part of this effort, the city demolished 35 structures, some considered to be historic, relocated 122 businesses and households, constructed public improvements (including parking), and sold the air rights at a highly subsidized rate. The city also sold

$58 million in tax increment bonds to finance the redevelopment agency's expenditures.

The 600,000-square-foot (55,740-square-meter) Plaza Pasadena, which opened in 1980, was—in all respects except its location—a suburban mall. With three department store anchors (Broadway, May Company, and JCPenney), the mall was almost completely inward looking, leaving a two-block-long "dead zone" along Colorado Boulevard. Though built with the best of intentions, the mall was perhaps the worst possible intervention from an urbanistic point of view. In addition to destroying the pedestrian and retail continuity of Colorado Boulevard, the mall closed off Garfield Avenue, a key north-south street. Previously, the Garfield Avenue vista was terminated by the library at one end and by the civic auditorium at the other. In the Plaza Pasadena plan, this grand axis was replaced by the shopping center's glass entry wall. And in place of the beaux arts and Mediterranean-style structures that had preceded it, the new mall presented a mostly blank brick facade to the street.

The introduction of Plaza Pasadena into the downtown streetscape coincided with—and was to some extent responsible for—the growing historic preservation movement in Pasadena. During the 1980s and 1990s, Old Pasadena was brought back to life through the efforts of building owners and developers, and through substantial public investment in parking and other improvements. While Old Pasadena prospered, however, Plaza Pasadena began to decline. And while Old Pasadena's tax revenues steadily increased, Plaza Pasadena's tax contributions

A residential component is crucial for bringing activity in the evenings. Paseo Colorado includes 387 rental apartments above two levels of shops, theaters, and restaurants. Ehrenkrantz Eckstut & Kuhn Architects

withered as the center struggled to remain competitive. According to calculations prepared by Marsha Rood, the city's former development administrator, the city's $28.8 million investment in Old Pasadena netted between $400

and $500 million in private investment (a ratio of $14 of private investment for every $1 of city funds), whereas the city's $58 million investment in Plaza Pasadena netted only $40 million in private investment (a ratio of $2 of private investment for every $3 in city funds). In addition, the deadened streetscape along Colorado Boulevard was clearly an impediment to the regeneration of the Civic Center area and the Playhouse district just to the east.

In 1997, the city formed the Civic Center Task Force to address these and other issues. The task force formulated the following objectives for the Plaza Pasadena site:

■ Restore the city street grid, in particular the Garfield Avenue view corridor;

■ Reintroduce retail activity to Colorado Boulevard;

■ Provide for pedestrian circulation and gathering spaces;

■ Offer a mix of uses, including housing as well as retail.

TrizecHahn Development Corporation—which, through its forebear, the Hahn Company, had an ownership interest in Plaza Pasadena—participated in the Civic Center Task Force deliberations. TrizecHahn was both philosophically attuned to the objectives of the task force and economically inclined to accept the city's recommendations. In reference to Plaza Pasadena's advantageous location and 3,000-plus parking spaces, Jennifer Mares, general manager of Paseo Colorado, notes, "We were sitting on gold, but renovation for retail alone just didn't pencil out." To make the project work, TrizecHahn went in search of an experienced developer of urban housing, and ultimately selected Post Properties.

Paseo Colorado is part of the city's plan to transform Colorado Boulevard into a pedestrian-focused corridor connecting the Civic Center district, the Playhouse district, the Lake Avenue retail area, and two transit stations. Ehrenkrantz Eckstut & Kuhn Architects

Under the financing structure for the project, the city of Pasadena contributed $26 million, in the form of certificates of participation backed by the lease on the center's parking structures. TrizecHahn maintains an ownership interest in the air rights above the parking, and Post Properties owns the air rights above the two-level retail podium.

As noted earlier, the two levels of retail space were constructed on top of the concrete parking garage, maintaining to the greatest extent possible the same structural grid as the garage. The residential portion sits above the retail construction, on its own concrete base, which is raised four feet (1.2 meters) above the retail roof. This separation allowed utilities to be routed horizontally within the four-foot (1.2-meter) space above the retail ceiling.

Planning

Paseo Colorado is an "urban village" divided into several neighborhoods. The design, by Ehrenkrantz Eckstut & Kuhn Architects, responds to the urban context and to the mixed-use requirements. Inspired by Old Pasadena, Paseo Colorado has both street-fronting retail space, on Colorado Boulevard, and interior-block walkways lined with more intimately scaled shops. Construction entailed the demolition of everything above the subterranean parking structure except the Macy's department store.

While the old Plaza Pasadena was set back from the street, in a suburban approach to planning, Paseo Colorado is built right up to the street-facing property line. In a bit of good fortune, the blank brick facade of the Macy's store was set back sufficiently to allow for new shops (Starbucks and Juice It Up) to be built in front, thus continuing the facade line of Paseo Colorado and providing an additional increment of street activity.

Garfield Avenue, which runs north to south and is perpendicular to Colorado Boulevard, has been opened up once again, this time as Garfield Promenade, a 77-foot- (24-meter-) wide pedestrian walkway. Flanked by formal plantings and period light fixtures, the promenade restores the intent of the 1925 City Beautiful plan and reveals the previously hidden vista of the civic auditorium. Storefronts and freestanding kiosks activate the linear space, which is anchored by a mosaic-tiled fountain by artist Margaret Nielsen.

From Garfield Promenade, a grand stairway leads up to Fountain Court, a second-level plaza with destination restaurants and outdoor dining terraces. Most of Paseo Colorado's housing is located in a mid-rise block overlooking Fountain Court. Euclid Court, Macy's forecourt, provides access to underground parking and to the loft housing.

The Paseo, the interior midblock walkway, runs parallel to Colorado Boulevard and connects Garfield Promenade and Fountain Court, on the west, to Euclid Court and Macy's, on the east. The slightly curving walkway varies in width from 43 feet (13.1 meters) at Garfield Promenade to 18 feet (5.4 meters) at Fountain Court. The narrower portions of the Paseo create a more intimate space, and the curving plan invites exploration, as one end cannot be seen fully from the other.

Along with the dining establishments, a multiplex cinema anchors the second level of Paseo Colorado. The cinema has its own plaza fronting Colorado Boulevard, and two grand stairways lead up to the box office and theaters. Second-level walkways connect the multiplex to Paseo Colorado's food court and restaurants.

Three parking structures, with more than 3,000 parking spaces, serve Paseo Colorado. The largest is the two-level, below-grade structure. The remaining two structures, which were also part of the original development, are located across the side streets that border Paseo Colorado. Pedestrian bridges provide direct access from these two garages to the second level of Paseo Colorado. Funds provided by the city permitted substantial upgrades to the three garages, including new lighting, signage, elevators, and escalators. The garage underneath Paseo Colorado had to be strengthened for seismic protection and to support the weight of the new project.

The 387 Post Paseo Apartment Homes are grouped into two structures. The larger building, which includes 276 luxury apartments, overlooks Fountain Court. The second structure, which overlooks Euclid Court, contains 111 studio and two-bedroom units. Because of the articulated massing of the residential towers, RTKL Associates, Inc., the architect for the residential component, had to design more than 90 individual floor plans.

The residential units are well-appointed, with ten-foot (three-meter) ceilings, open floor plans, and balconies. The project features eight rooftop courtyards with amenities that include a swimming pool, barbeques, and an outdoor fireplace. The commercial facilities of Paseo Colorado constitute another amenity. Residents are within a short walk of the shops, restaurants, and cinema. An upscale supermarket, located at the street level, beneath the housing, includes a coffee bar, a sushi bar, and outdoor dining tables.

Design

The developers and designers of Paseo Colorado sought to re-create not only the more intimate scale of Old Pasadena, but also its textures and materials. Two detailed publications communicate to prospective commercial tenants the criteria for materials and design elements. The first, *Athens of the West: Pasadena Style*, details the Pasadena heritage, explains the design objectives for each of Paseo Colorado's "neighborhoods," and lists development standards for storefronts, signage, and similar elements. The second publication describes additional technical criteria and provides contact information for artists and artisans. It also describes TrizecHahn's philosophy and objectives: "The creative contributions of individual tenants are critical to Paseo Colorado's success in creating an environment where the visitor feels a tangible sense of place. Each merchant will be required to creatively alter or adopt predetermined design concepts to meet the specific existing conditions."

Stylistically, Paseo Colorado reflects Mediterranean motifs and materials, though in a more modern idiom. Facades are finished in smooth plaster and colored in various earth tones and pastels. Decorative lighting includes modern and art deco light standards; in the Paseo, Craftsman-style lanterns strung across the street provide a canopy of light. Custom-designed elements—ranging from stair railings to a tiled fountain with mosaic "postcards" of Pasadena—have been used throughout the project.

Site plan.
RTKL Associates

Operations

The relationship between the residential and commercial areas of Paseo Colorado has been carefully considered and controlled. Access to the three street-level residential lobbies is separate from access to the commercial areas. Parking is similarly segregated: residents have card keys that allow them to access the express lanes at the entries to the garage, and they park in a physically separate section on the lower level of the two-story underground structure. There are 494 assigned parking spaces for the 387 dwelling units, an allowance of 1.3 spaces per unit. For security reasons, the elevators that allow retail access do not allow access to the apartments. However, to facilitate residents' access to Paseo Colorado, stairs with electronically controlled gates lead from the lower level of the housing to Fountain Court and Euclid Court.

In mixed-use projects, the noise and other disruptions associated with loading docks can cause significant management problems. At Paseo Colorado, six loading docks, located on a side street, serve the development. Four of the docks are dedicated to the retail and restaurant portions of the project, and the remaining two are shared by the housing and the supermarket. These two bays are controlled by hours of use; the supermarket accepts deliveries in the early hours of the morning, and the apartments have access to the docks between 10:00 a.m. and 5:00 p.m.

Noise levels are controlled in several ways. The operating hours of restaurants with outdoor dining terraces end at midnight on weekdays and at 2 a.m. on weekends, and loud music is prohibited. Noise limitations are also written into the residential leases. The pool deck, which can sometimes be noisy, was placed away from Fountain Court, a more passive outdoor space.

Marketing and Management

Retail leasing for Paseo Colorado was complicated by the fact that the city of Pasadena had political and financial interests in the adjacent retail areas of Old Pasadena: the Playhouse district and Lake Street. The city's mandate to TrizecHahn was, in effect, to provide an active and successful mix of retailers without stealing from other Pasadena venues. The competition facing Paseo Colorado also included two successful regional malls in nearby communities. And there was yet another challenge: although

Old Pasadena in general was a proven success for retailers, the Paseo Colorado location had not, historically, been successful, and the urban village concept was somewhat new to the retail community. However, the developers of Paseo Colorado could look to four complementary market strengths to offset these constraints:

■ A large primary trade area of nearly 1 million people within a radius of 7.5 miles (12 kilometers);

■ A daytime office market within walking distance;

■ A visitor and tourist market, including visitors from the adjacent Pasadena Conference Center;

■ The planned on-site residential market and a growing nearby residential base.

By playing to these multiple markets, TrizecHahn succeeded in creating an active, mixed-use destination without duplicating (or stealing) tenants from nearby retail areas. Macy's, the one tenant that remained from the original mall, invested approximately $1 million in remodeling, converting the space from a discount outlet to a full-line store.

Jennifer Mares, of TrizecHahn, notes that one of the attractions of Paseo Colorado, to both retailers and patrons alike, is the "village experience." The developer is working to create a "marriage between retailers and residents"— the kind of friendly, first-name-basis relationship typical of a traditional village. To that end, community teas were held during the planning stages of the project, to acquaint people with the developer's concept.

Mares notes that since the project opened, in 2001, retail sales have exceeded expectations. Several tenants that are part of national chains have reported that their sales levels have placed them near the top for all U.S. outlets. The mixture of uses and market segments at Paseo Colorado appears to explain some of the success: according to Mares, the "professional crowd" supports the center Monday through Friday, and the "stroller crowd" and movie patrons round out the weekend. Sales are unexpectedly strong on Sundays, owing in part to the presence of a supermarket.

Experience Gained

Paseo Colorado's success can be attributed, in part, to the ways in which its design addresses the context, uses, and architectural styles of its surroundings. By adding to and enhancing the existing pedestrian fabric of downtown Pasadena, the developers benefited from the synergy created by walkable, mixed-use environments.

Dramatically changing public and private sector thinking about urban retail centers, Paseo Colorado has replaced the inward-focused mall that previously occupied the site with a mixed-use project that reintroduces streetfront retail; provides interior, midblock retail space; and restores the urban block pattern and the axial view originally intended for the site. The project's success is spurring proposals for the development of vacant, long-neglected adjacent parcels.

Despite substantial competition from nearby retail areas, Paseo Colorado seems to be forging a successful niche for itself through its mix of complementary uses. By tapping demand from several markets, the project remains activated seven days a week during daytime and evening operating hours.

Destination restaurants serve as successful anchors for the project. "People go for the food," notes TrizecHahn's Mares—but the lively, festive atmosphere encourages them to stay, and to come back later.

Second-floor commercial uses can be successful, but access is critical. At Paseo Colorado, several grand stairways and visible second-level plazas, as well as multiple elevators and escalators throughout the project, ensure easy access to second-level uses.

Paseo Colorado

Pasadena, California

Land Use Information

Site area (acres/hectares)	10.9/4.4
Floor/area ratio	0.86

Gross Building Area

Use	Square Feet/Square Meters
Retail and restaurants	644,900/59,910
Residential	397,200/36,900
Parking	1,284,500/119,330
Total	2,326,600/216,140

Retail Information

Percentage of leasable area occupied: 93

Tenant Classification	Number of Stores	Gross Leasable Area (Square Feet/ Square Meters)
Shops	56	208,400/19,360
Department store	1	152,500/14,170
Restaurants	13	68,500/6,360
Health club	1	24,400/2,270
Supermarket	1	37,000/3,440
Cinema	1	66,500/6,180
Total	73	557,300/51,780

Development Costs

Hard Costs	In Thousands
Site acquisition	$25,200
Demolition	3,600
Site work	1,150
Landscaping	1,200
Parking garages	7,100
Off-site improvements	2,000
Retail construction	49,770
Residential construction	75,000
Soft Costs	
Architecture and engineering	7,300
Project management	4,500
Marketing and leasing	26,550
Legal services	1,800
Taxes and insurance	980
Construction interest	8,200
Furniture, fixtures, and equipment	5,250
Other	2,100
Total	$221,700

Residential Information

Unit Type	Unit Size (Square Feet/ Square Meters)	Number of Units	Range of Initial Monthly Rents
Studio	510–833/47–77	126	$1,505–$2,325
1 bedroom	686–1,027/64–95	166	$1,780–$2,700
2 bedroom	986–1,434/92–133	95	$2,730–$4,290
Total		387	

Development Schedule

Planning started	June 1998
Sales and leasing started	March 1999
Site purchased	November 1999
Construction started	June 2000
Retail project completed	September 2001
Residential project completed	Spring 2002

Development Team

Master Developer
TrizecHahn Development Corporation
Los Angeles, California
www.trz.com

Residential Developer
Post Properties, Inc.
Atlanta, Georgia
www.postproperties.com

Architect
Ehrenkrantz Eckstut & Kuhn Architects
Los Angeles, California
www.eekarchitects.com

Residential Architect
RTKL Associates, Inc.
Los Angeles, California
www.rtkl.com

Paseo Colorado was the product of both public and private investment, and the results benefit both interests.
RTKL Associates

The Market Common, Clarendon

Arlington, Virginia

Thanks to its attention to walkability and place-making, and the shrewd business decisions made by its developer, McCaffery Interests, the Market Common, Clarendon, has created a new benchmark for pedestrian-friendly developments. Located in the Rosslyn-Ballston corridor in Arlington, Virginia, just southwest of Washington, D.C., this mixed-use project offers a vibrant urban environment on what was once a surface parking lot. While quite a bit of parking remains on the site (1,100 spaces, the majority of which are hidden from view in structured lots), the project also provides 101,300 square feet (9,410 square meters) of office space; 303,200 square feet (28,170 square meters) of retail; 87 residential townhouses; and 300 apartment units. In addition, two large parks and four smaller parks serve as outdoor space for the residents.

The Market Common, Clarendon, has been a catalyst for revitalizing a transit node and transforming it into a lively, pedestrian-focused neighborhood. Sisson Studios

Since its opening, in November 2001, the 13.9-acre (5.6-hectare) Market Common has led the way for other pedestrian-focused developments in the area. Within two years, 800 new residential units and 210,000 square feet (19,510 square meters) of Class A office space were under construction within a two-block radius of the Market Common.

The success of the Market Common derives, in large part, from the developer's dual commitment to creating high-quality pedestrian environments and to a unique development philosophy. Founded in 1991, McCaffery Interests firmly believes that there is a large market for walkable places, and the firm's success bears this out. All of the projects in the McCaffery portfolio (11 completed as of March 2005) create or emphasize connections to the urban street.

In conjunction with the firm's excellent pedestrian planning, the development philosophy of McCaffery Interests has been vital to its success. Each project is based on the "lowest and best use" for a site; in practical terms, this means that the firm eschews high-risk, large-scale projects in favor of lower-risk, small-scale projects that pay careful attention to the needs and demands of the markets surrounding their sites. With this philosophy, bigger is not always better.

For the Market Common, Clarendon, the developer's dual commitment to creating walkable places and finding the lowest and best use is visible throughout every aspect of the project. With six nationally known retail anchors (Ann Taylor Loft, Barnes & Noble, Chico's, the Container Store, Crate & Barrel, and Pottery Barn), the developer has tapped into an underserved community's demand for high-end goods and built a town center in the process.

Site and Development Process

The Market Common, Clarendon, is located on the Rosslyn-Ballston corridor, a three-mile- (4.8-kilometer-) long stretch of the Washington, D.C., Metrorail subway system. The five Metrorail stops in the Rosslyn-Ballston corridor were designed to spur redevelopment in an area filled with aging retail and office buildings and surrounded by single-family homes. As

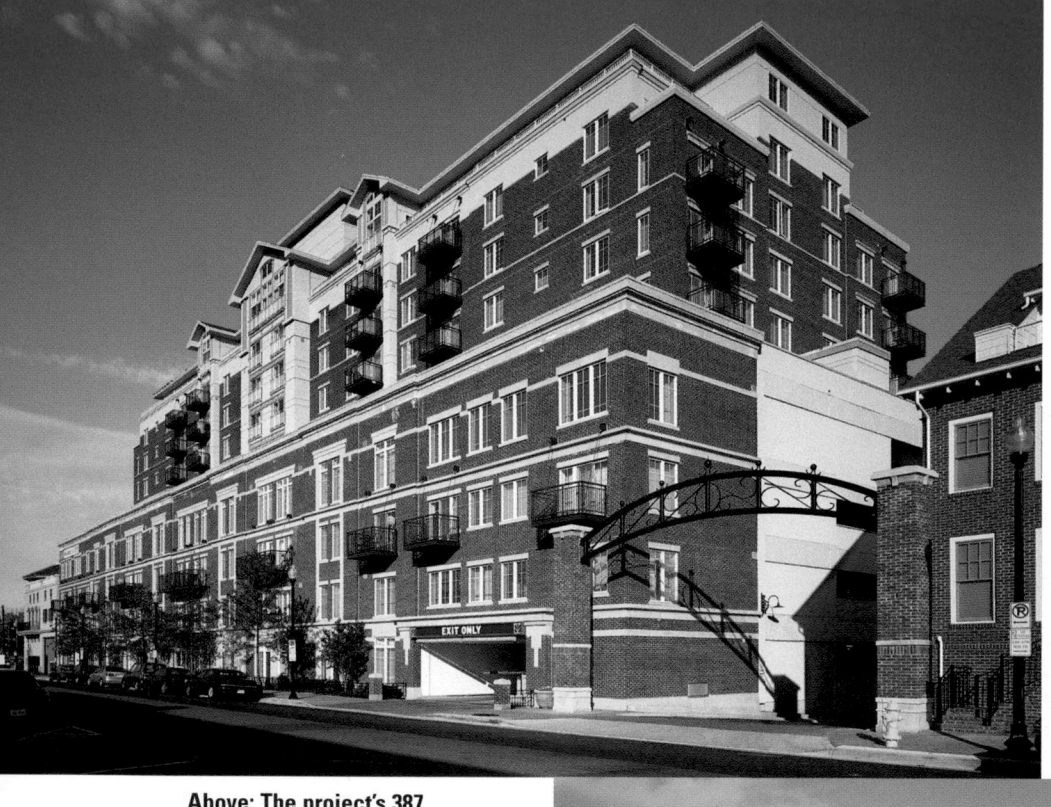

Above: The project's 387 residential units include 300 luxury rental apartments served by underground parking.

Right: A loop roadway runs through the center of the project and is lined with curbside parking for quick stops. Most parking is in garages located behind the shops.
Sisson Studios

planned, the Metrorail succeeded in revitalizing the corridor, transforming it into a vital growth center.

The Clarendon Metro Station area, for which the Market Common is named, is the central stop in the Rosslyn-Ballston corridor, but had been overshadowed for years by the Rosslyn Metro Station area, to the east, and the Ballston Metro Station area, to the west. Clarendon had little new development and an overabundance of surface parking lots. The original site of the Market Common was a 600-space surface parking lot for Sears garden and automotive centers. By the time McCaffery Interests came to the area, the two Sears buildings had been taken over by a Fresh Fields (now a Whole Foods Market) and the Clarendon Education Center, an adult-education center funded by Arlington County's public school district.

Before the development of the Market Common, Clarendon, there were few retail stores in the area, high-end or otherwise. However, the area had a thriving nightlife—numerous bars, restaurants, and dance clubs—and was especially known for its Vietnamese restaurants and businesses.

The demographics in Clarendon and for the Rosslyn-Ballston corridor as a whole indicated to the McCaffery team that there was a very large untapped market. The success of Fresh Fields provided hard evidence of a communitywide demand for conveniently located upscale shopping. Data compiled from the 2000 U.S. Census offered even more evidence. In 2001, almost 37,000 people—17,000 households—lived within a one-mile (1.6-kilometer) radius of the Market Common site. The median age was 35, the per-capita income $36,891, and the median household income $63,691.

The 13.9-acre (5.6-hectare) Market Common, Clarendon, development consists of one superblock (Phase I) and two smaller parcels (Phase II and Phase III). The Market Common Phase I, the largest and most readily identifiable piece of the project, consists of the retail component and 87 townhouses arranged around courtyards; the residential component wraps around the southern and eastern sides of the retail core. Directly across Clarendon Boulevard from Phase I is Phase II, which consists of two smaller blocks that originally held the Sears buildings. Phase II consisted of infrastructure improvements to the Fresh Fields store and a three-story expansion at the front of the Clarendon Education Center. In addition, the parking lot adjacent to the Clarendon Education Center was replaced by nine small retail spaces, and a small plaza was added to the front entrance of the office building. The Market Place, Clarendon, Phase III, occupies the block to the west of Phase II. This part of the development is home to Domicile Home (a home furnishings store) and two national restaurant chains (La Tasca Tapas and the Cheesecake Factory).

By 2003, following the success of Fresh Fields and of Phase I of the Market Common, several new construction projects were undertaken to transform the numerous surface parking lots to the west of the project into residential and office buildings. For example, on the lot to the west of Phase I and across the street from Phase III, construction has begun on a new, mixed-use building that will have retail and commercial uses on the ground floor and residential units above, thus continuing the pattern established by earlier phases.

The Market Common complex is spurring other investment in the area. Across from the Clarendon Metro Station, Wilson Boulevard, an aging, low-rise retail strip, is experiencing a renaissance. With their street-oriented storefronts and rear parking, the buildings on Wilson Boulevard are now leased by hip boutiques and restaurants—new businesses that are helping to bring life and pedestrian vitality to the area.

The rapid growth along the Rosslyn-Ballston corridor has been an increasing concern for residents of the single-family neighborhoods surrounding the Market Common. McCaffery Interests worked intensively to ensure that the needs of the surrounding community would be met, holding about 40 meetings over a six-month period prior to development. At the start of the project, the neighbors were uneasy about the fate of what was then no more than a giant parking lot situated too close to their homes. In particular, residents wanted to ensure that the new development would respect the design integrity of the adjacent neighborhood of single-family homes. The community had already been influential in preventing a Home Depot store from moving to the site; at the beginning of the development process, neighbors were prepared for a long fight with McCaffery Interests.

As they realized, however, that many of their design ideas were similar to those of the developer, nearby residents warmed up to the project. Both parties wanted the site to be integrated into the surrounding neighborhood, with multiple points of entrance and egress located throughout the project. Both sides also wanted the project to be built at a pedestrian-friendly scale, with thoughtful design and placement of amenities, and wanted high-quality, nationally known retailers for tenants.

Financing

McCaffery Interests put together a strong team to help finance the Market Common, working closely with RREEF and the Colorado Public Employees' Retirement Association (CoPERA). In this partnership, McCaffery Interests retained its role as lead developer, and RREEF provided the lease-up, marketing, and property management of the apartment units situated above the retail components. CoPERA's role was mainly to provide financing. Together, the three partners provided nearly 45 percent of the total cost as equity.

Construction financing came from Bank One, Fleet Bank, and PNC Bank. Because of RREEF's prestige and experience, and McCaffery's track record and solid relationships with national retailers, the major underwriting criterion for the loan was a request that the development team obtain letters of intent from five credit tenants who had agreed to lease space in the development. The five tenants were Ann Taylor Loft, Barnes & Noble, Chico's, the Container Store, Crate & Barrel, and Pottery Barn. With these five tenants, the Market Common was almost 50 percent preleased when construction began.

To minimize the risk that high interest rates would reduce the profitability of the project, the development team negotiated for a floating loan with a fixed ceiling and floor. While being unable to participate in record low inter-

A fountain and sculpture mark the main entrance to the Market Common, Clarendon. Sisson Studios

An inviting central green provides benches for shoppers to rest and a place for children to run and play. Sisson Studios

Planning and Design

The Clarendon Metro Station area presented an exciting opportunity for the development team. With large unmet demand for high-quality retail, proximity to a subway station, and a county government supportive of pedestrian-friendly design, conditions were favorable for building an exceptional place. To get ideas for the project, Daniel McCaffery, the firm's founder, visited successful pedestrian-friendly developments and town centers nationwide. Of those he visited, Mizner Park, in Boca Raton, Florida, was the main inspiration for the design of the Market Common, Clarendon.

The Market Common straddles both sides of Clarendon Boulevard. As noted earlier, it consists of one superblock (Phase I) and three smaller lots (Phase II and Phase III, also known as the Market Place, Clarendon). Most of the 13.9 acres (5.6 hectares) of the Market Common are located in Phase I. The central focus of the entire Market Common is a large, rectangular, landscaped courtyard in the center of Phase I. The courtyard includes a park with a bandstand shell, a small playground, a gazebo, and a fountain. At the front of the park is a garden with a water feature.

A one-way, two-lane street loops through the courtyard from Clarendon Boulevard. Both sides of the loop road are lined with parallel parking spaces; the entrance to the structured parking garage is along this loop as well.

est rates was a loss for the developers, the team believes that the greater interests of the project were best served by minimizing risk and maximizing predictability.

For the townhouse component of the Market Common, McCaffery Interests teamed with local housing developer Eakin/Youngentob. (The two firms had created a similar relationship for an earlier project, Friendship Centre, a mixed-use project in Chevy Chase, Maryland.) Following the master plan created by McCaffery, Eakin/Youngentob took on all responsibility for constructing the 87 townhouses. The 300 rental apartments were built and developed by McCaffery Interests.

The project has brought a wide range of large and small retailers, drawing shoppers from the neighborhood and beyond.
Adrienne Schmitz

The parallel parking adds to the urban character of the Market Common, provides convenient parking for quick stops, and helps calm traffic. The major retail component, with apartments overhead, encircles this street. Many of the larger stores occupy two levels, a configuration that was considered unworkable just a few years ago but that today is embraced by many retailers.

Shared parking minimizes the number of parking spaces required: about 1,000 structured parking spaces serve the entire development, including residents, shoppers, and others.

Anchor stores Pottery Barn and Crate & Barrel stand at opposite sides of the courtyard, marking the entrance and exit of the courtyard road. These two-story buildings help provide a transition between the one- and two-story buildings on Clarendon Boulevard and the taller buildings in the Market Common. They also extend the courtyard's vitality and pedestrian presence onto Clarendon Boulevard.

Not all the shops in the Market Common are along the courtyard. The Container Store, a nationally known anchor tenant, is situated next to Crate & Barrel but faces Clarendon Boulevard rather than the courtyard. Next to the Container Store is a health club. At the corner of North

Fillmore Street (the western boundary of Phase I) and Clarendon Boulevard is the restaurant Harry's Tap Room.

On the opposite side of the boulevard is Phase II, which consists of nine shops and restaurants situated where there was once a small surface parking lot. The construction of these shops added further street presence along Clarendon Boulevard. Two levels of parking sit atop the Phase II stores. Placing the garage above the street level allows storefronts to line the sidewalk along the entire block, an important design strategy for pedestrian-focused development.

On the next block is the Market Place, Clarendon (Phase III), where McCaffery Interests has transformed a low-rise, auto-dominated area into a vibrant, pedestrian-focused urban environment. The building presents a bold, two-story facade, and outdoor dining spills out onto the sidewalk. The Cheesecake Factory and La Tasca, two national chain restaurants, occupy prominent sites at each corner.

Small, well-placed developments, such as Phase II and the Market Place, can build on the success and synergy of much larger pedestrian-oriented projects. (Phase II includes 29,500 square feet [2,740 square meters], and the Market Place includes 22,500 square feet [2,090 square meters].) And, if small projects offer appealing routes and interesting destinations, they can not only take advantage of the foot traffic generated by larger projects but can also contribute to it. One notable design strategy

that helps create synergy between Phase I and the two smaller phases is the use of strong architecture at the street corners, which helps intensify the sense of place and forms visual connections between streets. These corners present interesting destinations that not only draw people from other parts of the Market Common but also bring people into the development.

Once a strong network of attractive destinations along interesting and safe routes has been established, even less walkable places can become major pedestrian destinations. The Whole Foods Market, at the northeastern corner of the project, has a strong automobile focus, and pedestrians must walk through a surface parking lot to get to the entrance. Nevertheless, the market reports that between 8,000 and 10,000 of the 30,000 to 32,000 shoppers who visit each day arrive by foot or bicycle.

The development team paid careful attention to finding the right combination of uses. Because the team believed that a strong residential component would create more street life and give both the project and the

Townhouses border the two sides of the project that face existing residential neighborhoods, helping to knit the new development to an older community. Sisson Studios

A small park lines the rear of the project and provides an attractive setting for the townhouses along that side. Adrienne Schmitz

surrounding commercial district a greater sense of vitality, the team chose to include much more residential space than office space. Indeed, the street presence created by the residential component adds to the overall experience of being at the Market Common. With thriving restaurants, book signings at Barnes & Noble, and residents buying after-dinner snacks at the Whole Foods Market, the area is active long after the office-dominated areas nearby have shut down. By comparison, the streets at the nearby Courthouse Metro Station area are empty in the evenings: the inward focus of the high-rise office towers and their related ground-floor retail, combined with underground parking, minimize the number of pedestrians in the area. Visitors park in the buildings, take the elevators up, and never need or want to venture out into the street. As the Market Common demonstrates, careful mixing of restaurants and residential, office, and retail space, along with a pedestrian-focused approach to design, can extend the operating hours of businesses and provide a sense of safety and security for the surrounding community.

Housing was integrated into the project with great care and consideration. The 300 apartment units above the courtyard are a mixture of studios and one-, two-, and three-bedroom units. To help create a greater sense of openness in the courtyard and visually distinguish the apartments from the retail, the units are stepped back from the retail facade. The result is a comfortable balance between openness and enclosure. The windows and balconies, functioning as "eyes on the street," create a sense of safety, further strengthening the feeling of comfort.

The 87 townhouses that flank the southern and eastern boundaries of the project were likewise planned with great care, and help to knit the project into the neighborhood. The 30 townhouses on the eastern edge are arranged in three courtyard groupings of ten townhouses each. Between the courtyard groupings are parking alleys that provide access to the individual townhouse garages.

Twenty-one of the townhouses line the southern edge of the Market Common. The alley behind these townhouses contains two loading docks that serve the needs of the retailers; all the garages attached to the townhouses also open onto this alley. With a width of 35 feet (11 meters), the alley provides more than enough space for shipping trucks to maneuver and drop off goods to the retailers. Despite the alley's width, a sense of enclosure makes it feel small, and hidden from the rest of the development.

Situating the garages in rear alleyways creates two separate realms, one for cars and one for pedestrians. The sidewalks and streets in front of the townhouses are more inviting to pedestrians, more visually pleasing, and more conducive to spontaneous social gatherings than they would be if the garages faced the streets and sidewalks.

The south-facing townhouses look out onto a one-acre (0.4-hectare) public park that was mandated by Arlington County. To help distinguish the public space of the park from the private space of the townhouses, the houses and their front lawns are elevated above the park by a couple of feet. This ingenious design allows residents to enjoy the park but defines the boundaries of their personal space and creates a greater sense of security.

The placement of the townhouses at Market Common creates a transition zone from the lower densities of the adjacent neighborhoods of single-family homes to the higher densities of the project. Pedestrian paths lead from these townhouses to the main courtyard, increasing the permeability of the Market Common and allowing neighboring residents to enter the development without having to walk around the outer edges of the project.

Different architectural firms were hired to design the various aspects of the project. The townhouses were developed by Eakin/Youngentob and designed by the Lessard Architectural Group. Antunovich Associates designed the rest of Phase I. McCaffery Interests also allowed some of the anchor tenants to hire their own architects. Street exposure can be a very effective form of marketing and brand identification for retailers, and the development team has learned, through experience, that retail tenants are eager to take advantage of that exposure. By giving retailers a high degree of architectural autonomy, the development team not only helped support their marketing and branding efforts, but also created a rich and varied environment within a master-planned development.

Although there are varying architectural styles, the development retains visual cohesiveness. For example, the brick used to pave the sidewalks is the same as the brick used in the buildings. In addition, the brick sidewalks subtly tie together all the aspects of the development and provide a contrast to the sidewalks of the surrounding areas, which are paved with standard concrete.

Also crucial to the overall coherence of the project was the involvement of residential developer Eakin/Youngentob in the public participation process. The collaboration between McCaffery Interests, Eakin/Youngentob, and the public helped all parties form a common vision for the final outcome of the project.

Construction

Integrating the infrastructure and utility services for mixed-used projects often creates challenges for developers. McCaffery Interests, aware of the potential risks, planned and budgeted accordingly. For example, the larger retailers did not want the air-conditioning and plumbing systems from the residential units above them to be run through their spaces. To address this and other issues, the development team engaged in careful negotiations with retail tenants and developed some clever engineering solutions. In the completed development, two of the largest stores (Barnes & Noble and the Container Store) have independent plumbing and heating, ventilating, and air-conditioning systems. The rest of the retailers share systems with the residential units.

Parking was another challenge. Residents of the surrounding community expressed concerns about parking; and, like many jurisdictions, Arlington County requires new developments to meet very specific parking ratios based on land use. Without shared parking, about 1,600 parking spaces would have been required for the project. Instead, the development team persuaded the county that since the spaces would be occupied by different groups of users at different times of day, shared parking would work. (For example, during the workday, many of the residential parking spaces are empty.) Only 1,100 parking spaces were built, and the development team believed that parking was overbuilt.

Management, Tenants, and Performance

Management and marketing were handled differently for each component of the Market Common, Clarendon. As developer/builder for the townhouse component, Eakin/

Youngentob was responsible for marketing and selling the units. Because of RREEF's long history of working with multifamily projects, it took the lead in managing and leasing the rental apartments. McCaffery Interests, relying on its network of relationships with nationally known retailers, secured tenants for the retail component.

The development team had very little trouble leasing the retail space. As retailers discover the benefits of pedestrian-friendly design, demand for such retail space is increasing. In addition to the marketing advantages that are created when storefronts face the street, streetfront locations offer lower maintenance fees than locations in enclosed malls. The common-area maintenance fee at the Market Common, for example, is about $4 per square foot ($43 per square meter), versus $10 to $40 per square foot ($108 to $430 per square meter) for indoor shopping malls.

Hard work and careful attention to pedestrian-oriented design have yielded exceptional market performance. Shopping centers of similar size, with similar target markets, generally experience a tenant turnover rate of 10 percent per year. After the first two years of operation, however, only one retail tenant—Imaginarium—had left the Market Common, and that was because the entire chain went out of business. The overall success of Phase I boosted the projected rents of Phase II by 40 to 50 percent. And rents in the surrounding area have doubled, in part because of the presence of the Market Common.

Experience Gained

That the Market Common, Clarendon, has succeeded in fostering pedestrian activity is readily visible to the casual observer. The sidewalks are lively and interesting places—with neighbors walking their dogs, residents walking to the Whole Foods Market, shoppers exploring the shops and the surrounding neighborhood, children playing on the playground in the courtyard, and salespeople in front of the Orvis store demonstrating proper fly-casting techniques.

Part of the success of the Market Common stems from McCaffery's firm commitment to the creation of a pedestrian-oriented place that would fully engage its sur-

Aerial view of site. Sisson Studios

roundings—a commitment that is evident in many aspects of the development. On the basis of its previous experience building walkable places, the development team knew that people want inviting, safe, and interesting places to walk. The Market Common provides this kind of environment. To maximize visual interest, create a feeling of safety, and integrate the project into the surrounding neighborhood, the design team refused to allow any blank walls or empty facades in the development. In place of blank walls are storefronts, townhouses, windows, and balconies, all of which interact with the streetscape.

The development team also paid close attention to the walking routes in and around the project; through visually appealing facades and well-thought-out urban design and landscaping, these routes bring people into the project and keep them coming back to shop and dine. And multiple routes into the project allow visitors to gain easy entrance from many different directions.

While many developers and urban theorists focus on how to appeal to shoppers and homebuyers, McCaffery Interests has also focused on making pedestrian-friendly environments appeal to retail tenants. The firm has demonstrated that streetfronts can strengthen tenants' brand identity and marketing, and lower their common-area maintenance costs.

Taking advantage of the existing pedestrian network, the developers enhanced it with interesting architecture and design, and added new routes to the network. They have created a unique destination with a heightened sense of place, that people can conveniently reach by foot, by transit, or by car.

The Market Common, Clarendon

Development Team

Developer
McCaffery Interests
Chicago, Illinois
www.mccafferyinterests.com

Development Partner
RREEF
Chicago, Illinois
www.rreef.com

Architect, Planner, and Landscape Architect
Antunovich Associates
Chicago, Illinois
www.antunovich.com

General Contractors
Plant Construction
San Francisco, California
www.plantco.com

Hensel-Phelps
Chantilly, Virginia
www.henselphelps.com

Residential Developer
Eakin/Youngentob Associates
Bethesda, Maryland
www.eya.com

Financing Arrangements
Downey Engebretson
Minneapolis, Minnesota
www.downeyengebretson.com

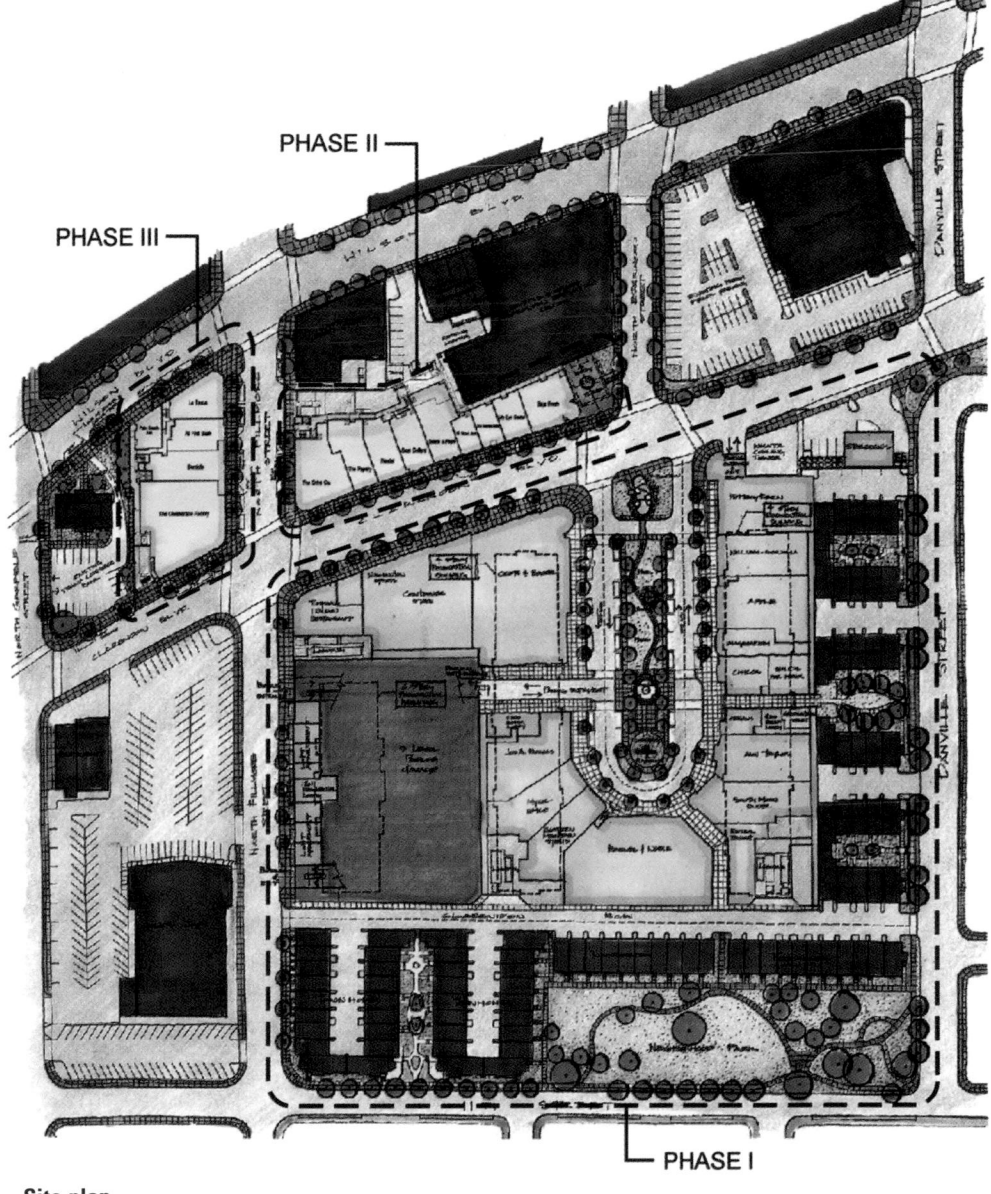

PHASE III

PHASE II

PHASE I

Site plan.

The Grove

Los Angeles, California

The Grove is an open-air, mixed-use, 575,000-square-foot (53,420-square-meter) retail and entertainment center adjacent to the historic Farmers Market in Los Angeles. Within a year of its completion, in 2002, the center had posted patronage levels that exceeded those of Disneyland, in nearby Orange County. The Grove is patronized by neighborhood and area residents as well as by tourists. It receives nearly 20 million visitors annually.

What drives the Grove is the synergy between its entertainment-focused uses—a 14-theater cineplex, a range of unique sit-down restaurants, a three-level Barnes & Noble bookstore, and a complement of major retailers—and its outdoor, architecturally friendly, and communal environment. The Grove offers the heavyweight anchor of the 70-shop Farmers Market on one end and a flagship Nordstrom on the other; at its center is a 3,000-seat cinema, complete with a revolving blade sign and a marquee.

The view down First Street. Facades are varied to reflect the feel of a small town, and to give each retailer its own identity. While most of the facades are period-style, some retailers chose modern designs, in keeping with their corporate and marketing preferences. © 2003 Caruso Affiliated Holdings/RMA Photography, Inc.

Architecturally, the Grove is designed to evoke a small-town past. According to Rick Caruso, chief executive officer of Caruso Affiliated Holdings, the developer of the Grove, the design was guided by a story line about "an old downtown that has come back to life." First Street, the circulation spine of the Grove, is a traditional street, complete with a crowned roadbed, raised sidewalks, and two- and three-story buildings in the styles prevalent locally in the 1930s and 1940s. The street winds around a wide town green that has its own lake and bridge, and is traversed at ten-minute intervals by a double-decker trolley.

Site and Development Process

The Grove's 17.5 acres (seven hectares), which formerly housed surface parking lots, a nursery, and a bank, are situated in the middle of one of Los Angeles's most densely developed and affluent areas and within the broad halo of the world-famous Farmers Market. Developers had eyed the site for many years; although it had been entitled for the development of a 1 million-square-foot (92,900-square-meter) regional shopping center, no developer had been able to overcome neighborhood opposition to such a large undertaking.

First Street, between the green and the Farmers Market, is interrupted by a triumphal column topped by a winged statue entitled *The Spirit of Los Angeles*, **evoking the public art that marks many European plazas.** © 2003 Caruso Affiliated Holdings/RMA Photography, Inc.

Early in the process, Caruso and his team held community meetings to discuss neighborhood concerns, such as the scale of the project, the types of uses, and the amount of traffic that would be generated. To minimize the potential impact of traffic on the adjacent community, the team made several adjustments to the project design and planned operations. After discussions with neighborhood residents, and taking into account the earlier battles associated with the site, Caruso offered an enticing deal:

■ A project approximately half the size of the previously entitled project;

■ A promise to preserve the Farmers Market and the nearby historic Gilmore Adobe, an early California hacienda;

■ A more neighborhood-oriented mix of uses, including restaurants and a bookstore;

■ An outdoor setting in the spirit of the adjacent Farmers Market.

In addition, Caruso offered a solid track record of developing successful, neighborhood-oriented, open-air retail centers in the more outlying areas of Los Angeles. Ultimately, the development received the unanimous support of the planning commission and city council.

Development rights to the site were acquired by Caruso Affiliated Holdings through a long-term ground lease from the Gilmore family, owners of the adjacent Farmers Market. Equity financing was provided by Caruso Affiliated Holdings from internal sources, and a construction loan was obtained from a consortium consisting of Bank of America, PNC Bank, and Union Bank. Permanent financing was subsequently obtained from Lehman Brothers Bank.

Developer

Founded in 1980, Caruso Affiliated Holdings is a developer of neighborhood and regional shopping centers, primarily in Southern California. The philosophy of the firm, in Rick Caruso's words, is to create town centers "where friends and family can gather, shop, dine, and enjoy spending time together." In keeping with that philosophy, the firm focuses on creating active public spaces within the context of its retail centers. As part of this focus, Caruso Affiliated Holdings invests significant energy and capital in landscaping, architectural detailing, and amenities for pedestrians, and works to develop tenant mixes that include a substantial dining and entertainment component. A measure of the success of this approach is that 90 percent or more of each project is typically pre-leased before the start of construction. The firm's business plan is to create unique, high-quality centers, which it holds for the long term in its own portfolio.

Planning and Design

The focus of the Grove's site plan is the pedestrian-only First Street, which runs from the Farmers Market, on the west end, to a new valet-parking area and dropoff at the east end, a distance of more than a quarter of a mile (0.4 kilometers). From building face to building face, the street is 60 feet (18 meters) wide, and consists of a 28-foot- (nine-meter-) wide roadbed, with a 16-foot- (five-meter-) wide sidewalk on each side. The street bends around a one-acre (0.4-hectare) green, the focal point of the project. The green is broken up into three areas, with a lake on one end, several kiosks on the other, and a lawn in the middle. The lake, which features "dancing" fountains computer-choreographed to music, is ringed by a stone balustrade and crossed by an old-fashioned bridge; both the balustrade and the bridge are popular places for people

The town green with its lake, provides a central open space for events, ambling, and people watching. © 2003 Caruso Affiliated Holdings/RMA Photography, Inc.

The Grove's urban design re-creates the character of pedestrian-oriented city blocks. Buildings are tall enough to enclose the streets, giving them an intimate ambience that could not be produced with single-story buildings.
© 2003 Caruso Affiliated Holdings/RMA Photography, Inc.

watching or for viewing the fountains. The lawn is used as a play area for children and for outdoor seating for programmed performances and activities. The kiosks offer ice cream, hot dogs, juice, and coffee, and are the only fast food at the Grove.

The green is the Grove's "100 percent corner"—its most active and visible place. Most of the Grove's patrons park in the 3,500-car garage on the northern edge of the site; after passing through a narrow, restaurant-lined walkway, visitors emerge on the green. The cineplex, with its broad marquee and animated sign, commands attention from across the green, as does the streetscape, a mix of period and contemporary facades.

The straight portion of First Street that runs between the green and the Farmers Market is interrupted by a triumphal column topped by a winged statue entitled *The Spirit of Los Angeles*. Dave Williams, senior vice president of architecture for Caruso Affiliated Holdings, notes that the sculpture is meant to "encourage people to pause and linger." It also provides a focal point for the end of Bow Street—a 25-foot- (eight-meter-) wide street that is intended to evoke the narrow lanes and alleyways of European cities. Besides offering additional boutiques, Bow Street provides access to the freestanding restaurants that are adjacent to the historic Gilmore Adobe.

Both the location and the site design of the Grove encourage pedestrian activity. Unlike most malls, which are surrounded by acres of open parking lots, the Grove is adjacent to relatively dense residential neighborhoods; in fact, a substantial contingent of patrons walk to the project. The approximately 10,000 dwelling units that are located within walking distance of the Grove include about 1,600 new apartments; the Grove appears to be a strong attraction for potential renters. According to the Grove's developers, joggers and walkers of all ages make the circuit around the green and up and down the quarter-mile- (0.4- kilometer) long First Street throughout the day and evening. The project's street design allows for different types of pedestrian activity: the roadway is generally used for "through" pedestrian traffic, and the sidewalks are for the slower-paced pedestrians who are window-shopping or out for a stroll.

A seven-level structure, with access from the three city streets that surround the Grove, provides parking for the development. Because the Farmers Market relies on its adjacent surface parking lots, a system of separate parking validations is used to keep the surface parking available to Farmers Market patrons. The arrangement ensures that shoppers can carry heavy purchases to their cars and that those who just want a cup of coffee can get in and out quickly and easily.

The Grove prides itself on offering a higher level of amenities than a typical shopping center, and this aspect of the development is readily apparent upon arrival. Visitors traveling by car can use the valet dropoff, which looks and functions much like a hotel roundabout. Alternatively, visitors can use the parking garage and descend by escalator to an elegant outdoor "lobby" with a concierge station that offers services ranging from store information to restaurant and theater reservations. Rick Caruso notes that even the security staff is trained to provide customer service. (According to Caruso, all Grove personnel are trained by the same firm that trains staff for the Ritz-Carlton hotels.)

The Grove's streetscape, designed by Elkus/Manfredi Architects Ltd., of Boston, is intended to be nostalgic, echoing the architectural styles prevalent in Los Angeles in the 1930s and 1940s. The two- to three-story store-fronts are highly detailed, with period windows, trim, balconies, and awnings. These architectural details, along with the irregularity of the facade widths and alignments, combine to evoke the richness of gradual, building-by-building development.

While all the facades were initially designed by Caruso Affiliated Holdings and Elkus/Manfredi Architects, retailers were given leeway to modify or redesign the facades to

Located at the end of the green, this three-story, multitenant building, designed to resemble a London train station, terminates the vista along First Street and provides enclosure to the green. © 2003 Caruso Affiliated Holdings/RMA Photography, Inc.

suit their corporate or marketing image. Several retailers, including Apple Computers, Crate & Barrel, and Gap, opted for more modern building facades; Apple, for example, offers as its public face a simple and refined composition of glass and stainless-steel panels. Rick Caruso, who retained rights to final design approval, encouraged the mix of modern and period styles because it helped create the sense of a town that had grown over time.

The image of the Grove as a town, rather than a development, was further bolstered by the developer's substantial investment in mature landscaping and custom-designed street lighting. To provide shade for pedestrians and to create a sense of permanence, Caruso Affiliated Holdings installed a number of specimen trees, including mature magnolia trees, a 50-year-old jacaranda, and 45-foot- (14-meter-) tall palm trees.

In contrast to the storefronts along First Street, the facades that face Third Street, a preexisting collector street for the area, are primarily false fronts, with limited window displays and some surface articulation and lighting—but, with the exception of Nordstrom, no retail entries. Although in the early design stages the development team considered making Third Street more active, Caruso's Dave Williams notes that the decision to turn inward was based on two principal considerations. First, since the surrounding Third Street development pattern consisted mainly of foundering strip malls, outward-facing storefronts would not have looked out on a very appealing visual prospect. Second, prospective Grove tenants wanted to face the internal main street: "Retailers thought First Street would have the energy," notes Williams. Initially, Nordstrom also

Bow Street, a narrow offshoot of First Street, is lined with boutiques and restaurants, and designed with the character of European lanes. Besides offering additional boutiques, Bow Street provides access to the freestanding restaurants that are adjacent to the historic Gilmore Adobe. © 2003 Caruso Affiliated Holdings/RMA Photography, Inc.

wanted its sole entrance to be from inside the Grove, but Caruso persuaded the store that a Third Street entrance would help to bring in the many residents of nearby apartments, who would arrive on foot and spend money in Nordstrom on their way into the Grove proper. While it is not known how many pedestrians enter the Grove through Nordstrom, Caruso reports that foot traffic from the nearby apartments has been substantial, and has been of great benefit to both Nordstrom and the Grove. Between the Grove and the Farmers Market is a transition element, housing restaurants and shops, that was developed by the management of the Farmers Market and designed by Santa Monica–based Koning-Eizenberg Architecture. Caruso worked with the Farmers Market and its designers to achieve a seamless connection among all the elements, which are tied together by the design of First Street and by the trolley right-of-way.

The First Street Trolley serves as both a tourist attraction and a mode of transportation. Williams notes that it also has a larger purpose: though the distance traversed is relatively short, the trolley makes "a real physical connection" to the Farmers Market. In traditional fashion, the trolley runs on steel wheels and inground tracks; but it is powered by a clean, state-of-the-art magnetic-induction battery system that was pioneered in Germany and made its American debut at the Grove.

Tenants

In addition to the three largest tenants—Nordstrom, Pacific Theatres, and Barnes & Noble—the Grove has approximately 50 shops and restaurants. Retail tenants are mostly national firms, ranging from Abercrombie & Fitch to Banana Republic to specialty stores such as Apple Computers and NIKEGoddess. In an unusual move for mall retailers, the developer required all retail tenants to lease two levels; this approach yielded a more urban shopping environment and increased the density and energy of the development.

Food is an integral part of the marketing plan for the Grove. As of 2005, there were eight restaurants at the Grove, a mix of one-of-a-kind establishments and regional and national chains. Unlike most malls, the Grove has no food court, and the restaurants are not the usual low-budget chains. Instead, the restaurants are destination restaurants—branches of upscale and mid-priced eateries not generally located in malls and not extensively represented in the local market. Most of the restaurants provide outdoor seating (some on balconies above the street), which further strengthens the see-and-be-seen ambience of the Grove and keeps the streetscape continuously active and interesting.

Children stop to experience the statuary. © 2003 Caruso Affiliated Holdings/RMA Photography, Inc.

The restaurants have a synergistic relationship with the movie theaters: they not only reinforce the theaters' destination appeal, but also gain patronage from the movie-going crowd. On busy weekends, the 14-screen Pacific Theatres at the Grove, with its monumental lobby and its stadium seating, has logged attendance of more than 10,000 patrons per day. Caruso Affiliated Holdings sold the cinema complex to its operator, Pacific Theatres, for approximately $30 million, or $2.1 million per screen. According to *The Hollywood Reporter,* the per-screen price set a new record—one that was justified, however, by the extraordinarily high gross sales per auditorium. Rick Caruso credits the "one-stop entertainment experience of dinner and

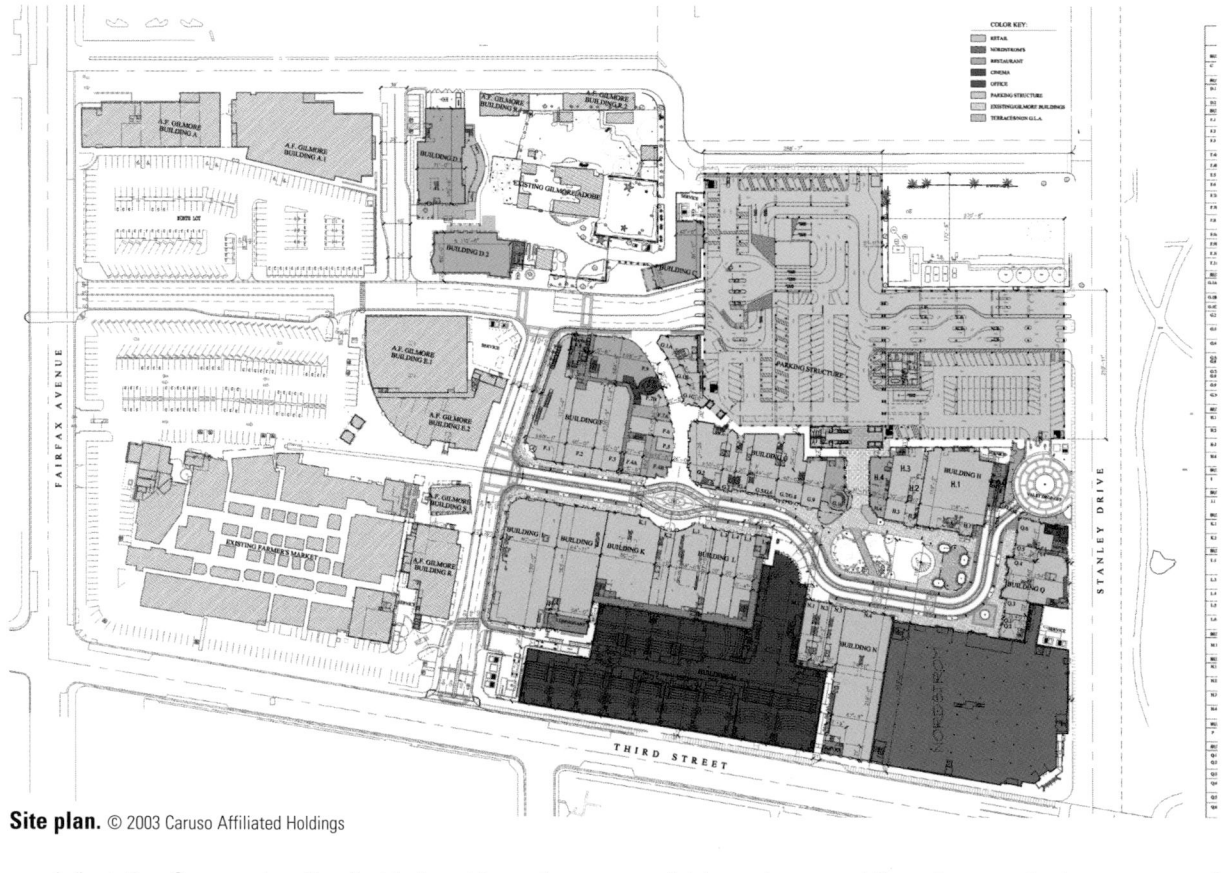

Site plan. © 2003 Caruso Affiliated Holdings

movie" at the Grove, plus the "added ambience" created by the town green and the retail component, for this achievement.

A strong link in the entertainment chain at the Grove is the 38,000-square-foot (3,530-square-meter) Barnes & Noble bookstore. In an arrangement that is unusual for low-rise Los Angeles, the store is laid out on three floors, which are accessed by means of an escalator situated in an atrium. With a 3,500-square-foot (330-square-meter) mezzanine and only 7,000 square feet (650 square meters)

available on the ground floor, the store had to put most of its retail space on the third floor, above the adjacent buildings. As Caruso's Dave Williams notes, "The bookstore is a great amenity for the movie theaters," allowing people to pass the time pleasantly while waiting for a movie.

A wealth of statistics collected by the Grove reveal the synergy among the uses and the success of the concept. The center is 100 percent occupied and has a waiting list of potential tenants. Sales for most tenants are running well ahead of expectations: average sales are over $600 per square foot ($6,460 per square meter), and are over $1,000 per square foot ($10,800 per square meter) for some restaurants. The Grove draws from 78 zip codes and has an average conversion rate (percentage of visitors who spend money at the mall) of 92 percent; the national rate is about 50 percent.[1] Moreover, the average amount spent per visit is roughly twice the national average. These numbers indicate that the Grove has not sacrificed sales by offering visitors a higher level of amenities; in fact, the project is doing even better.

The Grove has had a positive impact on the Farmers Market as well. The market has extended its operating hours and has significantly more business overall than it did before the Grove joined it. Thanks to easy pedestrian and trolley access via First Street, many Grove patrons dine at the more casual and less expensive Farmers Market while shopping at the Grove, and evening patrons of the Grove have added a strong and previously nonexistent source of market shoppers. Finally, the presence of the Grove has strengthened the destination appeal of the Farmers Market for tourists.

Experience Gained

The mix of entertainment and shopping at the Grove appears to be a powerful draw that is well tuned to the increasing amount of time and money spent on leisure-time activities. In 2003, the Grove drew about 18 million visitors.

For pedestrians, the Grove offers a sizable yet protected environment—a place to be active, outdoors, and safe. The open-air design, including First Street and the town green, encourages strolling. At the same time, the bounded interior creates a feeling of safety and security. Finally, the many different seating areas—benches, dining terraces, and balconies—and the high quality of the landscaping, fountains, and other site details add up to a strong sense of place: an environment that is welcoming, lively, and visually appealing.

Note
1. Roger Vincent, "Caruso Is at the Center of Open-Air Movement," Los Angeles Times, January 1, 2004, C1–C2.

The Grove

Los Angeles, California

Land Use Information

Site area (acres/hectares)	17.5/7
Gross leasable area (square feet/square meters)	575,000/53,420
Total parking spaces	3,500 (all structured)

Land Use Plan

Use	Acres/ Hectares	Percentage of Site
Buildings	7.00/2.8	40.0
Parking structures	3.75/1.5	21.4
Paved areas (surface parking, roads)	3.00/1.2	17.1
Landscaped areas	3.75/1.5	21.4
Total	17.5/7.0	100.0

Tenant Information

Classification	Number of Stores	Gross Leasable Area (Square Feet/ Square Meters)
General merchandise	1	121,900/11,320
Food	8	58,000/5,390
Clothing and accessories	21	137,900/12,810
Shoes	1	5,800/540
Home furnishings	5	35,200/3,270
Home appliances, music	1	6,000/560
Movie theater	1	83,300/7,740
Hobby, special interest	2	65,900/6,120
Gifts, specialty	2	11,800/1,100
Jewelry	3	8,500/790
Personal services	1	7,200/670
Offices	3	40,300/3,740
Total	49	581,800/54,050

Major Tenants

Tenant Name	Space Occupied (Square Feet/ Square Meters)
Apple Computers	6,000/560
Banana Republic	28,400/2,640
Barnes & Noble	41,900/3,890
Crate & Barrel	24,500/2,280
FAO Schwarz	24,400/2,270
Gap	25,100/2,330
Nordstrom	121,900/11,320
Pacific Theatres	83,300/7,740

Development Costs

Hard Costs	In Thousands
Site acquisition cost (ground lease)	$5,000
Site improvement costs (on and off site)	20,000
Construction costs[1]	100,000
Subtotal, hard costs	$125,000

Soft Costs	
Architecture and engineering fees	$15,000
Legal and accounting fees	2,000
Taxes and insurance	1,000
Title fees	12,000
Other	5,000
Subtotal, soft costs	$35,000
Total	$160,000

1. Excluding tenant improvements.

Development Schedule

Site acquired	July 1997
Planning started	July 1997
Leasing started	April 1998
Approvals obtained	May 2000
Construction started	December 2000
Project opened	March 15, 2002

Development Team

Developer
Caruso Affiliated Holdings
Santa Monica, California
www.carusoaffiliated.com

Design Architect
Elkus/Manfredi Architects Ltd.
Boston, Massachusetts
www.elkus-manfredi.com

Architect of Record
Langdon Wilson
Los Angeles, California
www.langdonwilson.com

Cinema Architect
Perkowitz + Ruth Architects, Inc.
Newport Beach, California
www.prarchitects.com

Landscape Architect
Lifescapes International, Inc.
Newport Beach, California
www.lifescapesintl.com

General Contractor
The Whiting-Turner Contracting Company
Irvine, California
www.whiting-turner.com

Leasing Company
AFC Commercial Real Estate Group, Inc.
Westlake Village, California

Centennial Lakes

Edina, Minnesota

Centennial Lakes, in Edina, Minnesota, a first-ring suburb about ten miles (16 kilometers) southwest of Minneapolis, is unusual among infill projects for two reasons. First, at about 100 acres (40 hectares), it is large for an inner-ring infill site; properties of sufficient size for such redevelopment are hard to come by. Second, the project's pedestrian focus is unusual within such strongly automobile-oriented surroundings.

Centennial Lakes includes a mix of office, residential, entertainment, and retail uses, all interconnected by a large, pedestrian-oriented public park that offers walking trails, a lake, and a range of recreational uses. The project's economic success derives, in large part, from the park: without it, most of the uses would share little more than a common boundary. But by designing the park as the focal point of the site plan, the planners created an amenity that adds aesthetic and monetary value to the project.

Centennial Lakes has become a popular place for walking, biking, and other activities for residents of the entire region.
United Properties

Centennial Lakes includes five Class A office buildings totaling 940,000 square feet (87,330 square meters); a 106,000-square-foot (9,850-square-meter) medical office building; 250 residential condominium units; 96 luxury townhouses; an eight-screen, 39,000-square-foot (3,620-square-meter) movie theater; a 220,000-square-foot (20,440-square-meter) retail center; and a 25-acre (ten-hectare) city park.

Site

The Centennial Lakes property is surrounded by a variety of automobile-dominated retail, residential, and office uses. France Avenue, a six-lane, north-south arterial corridor, forms the western border of Centennial Lakes. Southdale, the first enclosed mall in the United States, lies one mile (1.6 kilometers) to the north, along France Avenue, and an interchange with Interstate 494 is one half-mile (0.8 kilometers) to the south. Much of the land between Centennial Lakes and Southdale is occupied by retail uses. To the south and east of Centennial Lakes, residential and office uses predominate. One nearby development, Edinborough, is another notable mixed-use project that opened in the late 1980s. In fact, it was the public/private cooperation during Edinborough's development process that set the bar for Centennial Lakes.

Centennial Lakes is unusual for its pedestrian focus in such automobile-oriented surroundings. The project includes a mix of office, residential, entertainment, and retail uses, all interconnected by a public park. United Properties

Centennial Lakes is divided into three parts: north, central, and south. The 25-acre (ten-hectare) park, which features a ten-acre (four-hectare) lake, meanders through all three parts. A 1.5-mile (2.4-kilometer) walking trail rambles along the lake's edge. The park also includes a mini-golf course, an amphitheater, a lawn-bowling green, and extensive landscaping. Centennial Lakes Park is owned and operated by the city of Edina.

Pedestrian access to the site from the west is limited by France Avenue, a busy roadway. Access from the east is slightly better, but the vast majority of the pedestrians at Centennial Lakes arrive by vehicle or live there.

The site plan for Centennial Lakes was based on thoughtful consideration of the surroundings. Office, entertainment, and retail uses are sited on the west, along France Avenue, and residential uses are to the east, adjacent to the surrounding residential uses.

Development Process

A substantial portion of the 100-acre (40-hectare) site was formerly used as a gravel pit. In 1986, when the owners of the Hedberg Gravel Pit put up the property for sale, the offer generated interest from developers around the country. The city of Edina, however, had a number of requirements for the last large piece of developable commercial land within its borders: the city wanted a public park and moderate-income housing to be part of the mix of uses for the site; it also needed a stormwater retention system large enough to handle 34 acre-feet (41,940 cubic meters) of water from a 100-year rainfall.

United Properties, which came forward with a master plan for a mixed-use development that would balance the city's desires with the realities of the market, was chosen as the master developer for the site. United Properties is a Twin Cities–based brokerage, property management, and development firm that employs approximately 400 people and owns approximately 5 million square feet

(464,500 square meters) of commercial real estate, with another 25 million square feet (2.3 million square meters) under management contracts.

Because United Properties specializes in office and industrial properties, several other developers with additional expertise were involved in the Centennial Lakes project. BRW, Inc. (now URS Corporation) served as master planner; Larry Laukka, now of Laukka-Jarvis, Inc., developed the residential portion; Gabbert & Beck developed the retail center; and Eagle Enterprises developed the medical office building.

The city of Edina approved the plan for Centennial Lakes in 1988. A planned unit development zoning code—essentially written after the plan was finished—accommodates the variety of uses planned for the site.

Much of the project was financed by the sale of general-obligation bonds supported by two 25-year tax increment financing (TIF) districts, the first established in 1977 and the second in 1987. The bonds will be repaid by 2014,

when the second district is set to expire. The TIF plan financed the acquisition of the park and the construction of all the improvements within, including the Centrum Building, a social hall on the site. It also paid for the street and utility improvements for the entire project, and for land acquisition and site improvement for the condominium project.

Planning and Design

Centennial Lakes Park serves both functional and aesthetic purposes. The key element of the project, it gives the entire community a public gathering space: an attractive

Centennial Lakes Park serves both functional and aesthetic purposes. In addition to providing attractive views and recreation for residents and workers, the lake is a stormwater retention facility for the entire southeastern quarter of the city. United Properties

Condominium residents enjoy lake views and recreational amenities, including a putting green. Sam Newberg

Because of the trail network, it is possible to navigate the entire site on foot without crossing a street. The trails pass under the two east-west roads that bisect the development. Each use at Centennial Lakes is well integrated with the park, providing access and views for visitors, residents, and workers.

Most of the recreational uses are located in the central portion of the site, near the Centrum Building, a 7,000-square-foot (650-square-meter) social hall that can be rented for banquets, receptions, and other events, and that also serves as a warming house for ice skaters. Outdoor facilities surrounding the building include a mini-golf course with grass greens (as opposed to the more common artificial turf), an amphitheater for musical and theatrical performances, and a lawn-bowling green. Paths run for 1.5 miles (2.4 kilometers) around the lake, providing an attractive and convenient place for walking, jogging, and biking. In the summer, remote-control sailboating is a popular activity; paddleboats are also available for rent. In the winter, a Zamboni grooms most of the lake for ice skaters.

Most of the design challenges BRW faced at Centennial Lakes related to the park, and how to best take advantage of access and views. Although a view of the park is considered a plus for residential and office buildings, the physical layout of Centennial Lakes Plaza, the shopping center, posed a challenge. The center backs up to the park, which created two problems: first, truck access is usually at the backs of stores, but it would not have been desirable for park patrons to be exposed to a steady stream of truck traffic or a view of the loading docks. BRW solved this problem by siting the truck access at the side of the building's lower level and creating a shared truck dock and common corridor within each retail building. Second, the blank wall of the retail center faced the park. This problem was largely mitigated by landscaping: a mix of evergreen and deciduous trees conceals the tall back wall of the retail center. (Some of the restaurants at Centennial Lakes Plaza do overlook the park, taking advantage of the views.)

body of water with recreational uses around its perimeter. It also links the different land uses together in a way that sets the project apart from other development in the area. The lake, which receives stormwater from the entire southeastern quarter of the city of Edina, is a creative response to the area's stormwater retention needs. By controlling drainage at the southwest corner of the lake, the city can maintain a relatively consistent water level even during dry spells, and thereby improve the lake's appearance and value as an amenity.

The developers could have created a more typical stormwater retention pond, with a smaller surface area, but the difference in water levels would have been much greater in the event of heavy precipitation. (This difference between high and low water levels is called bounce. In the case of Centennial Lakes, the large surface area of the lake results in a lower bounce: a 100-year rainfall, for example, would result in only a three-foot [0.9-meter] rise in the water level.)

With its variety of recreational uses, Centennial Lakes Park is very popular, even during the cold Minnesota winters, among area residents and the employees of the businesses that occupy the development. The outdoor public spaces are heavily used by the lunchtime office crowd, as well as by workers from other nearby office buildings.

Construction and Financing

A complex, multiphase development, Centennial Lakes took 13 years to build, beginning in 1988 and ending in 2000. Most development began in 1988 or shortly thereafter and was completed by 1992. The Coventry townhouses and Centennial Lakes Office Park were begun in the mid-1990s and finished by 2000.

Financing was the most complex aspect of the Centennial Lakes project. When the development first began, in the late 1980s, market conditions, including a weak office market, made it impossible to build all the components at once. In addition, United Properties did not have sufficient resources to acquire the entire site unless it could generate income from every use.

Thus, in a complex arrangement, United Properties obtained a contract for deed from the owners of the Hedberg Gravel Pit, then assigned the contract to the city of Edina. This approach enabled United Properties to purchase and develop each portion of the site as the market allowed. As an incentive from the city, the owners were allowed to hold the property tax free while awaiting payment from United Properties for each portion of the site. In effect, the city acted as intermediary, allowing the buyer to develop portions of the site according to market demand, and promising the owners that they would incur no penalty by waiting for payment for the property. In 1988, United Properties acquired a substantial portion of the site for $12 million, enabling the firm to begin development and allowing the city of Edina to begin work on the park.

The city contribution to the development totaled approximately $40 million, including $11 million for park improvements and amenities. Another portion of the city funds for the project went to support the construction of moderately priced housing. Through a program run by the city, income-qualified buyers of units at the Village Homes at Centennial Lakes were offered a second-mortgage arrangement that essentially provided an upfront discount of up to $20,000 on each unit. The second mortgages were held by the city at a 5 percent interest rate (market interest rates at the time were over 10 percent), and payoff was required when the resident sold. Approximately 100 of the 250 original buyers of the Village Homes units took advantage of the second-mortgage program.

Since the opening of the Village Homes at Centennial Lakes, prices have increased dramatically, and sellers have been able to pay off their second mortgages with ease. The second-mortgage program has been tremendously successful, and the city of Edina continues to distribute the pool of money in the program to other housing projects.

Marketing

The long-term economic success of Centennial Lakes has surpassed the developers' expectations. Success can be attributed to a number of factors:

■ The project's location within the Twin Cities metropolitan area;

■ The project's proximity to downtown Minneapolis, which is ten miles (16 kilometers) to the northeast, and to the Minneapolis–St. Paul Airport, which is five miles (eight kilometers) to the east;

■ The project's proximity to a large employment base in the southwestern Twin Cities area;

■ The built-in park and other public amenities, which draw visitors from a large area.

The lake, path, and other recreational facilities are very attractive amenities for office workers. Sam Newberg

Sales and leasing in all portions of Centennial Lakes reflect its success. Leased properties have attained higher rents and occupancy rates than have competitive properties in the area, and prices for the residential units have increased dramatically since opening.

Both residential projects at Centennial Lakes have drawn buyers from all over the Twin Cities, not only because of the project's recreational amenities and pedestrian orientation, but also because residents can walk to shopping, entertainment, and employment. Coventry townhouses, which had initial sales prices between $195,000 and $310,000, are now selling for nearly $600,000. Homes overlooking the lake command even higher prices.

A large percentage of buyers are from the southwestern region of the metropolitan area. Many buyers of the luxury townhouses at Coventry have lived outside Minnesota and returned; some own one or more other properties, and simply wanted a maintenance-free unit in a premier location for the months they spend in the Twin Cities.

At the Village Homes at Centennial Lakes, buyers are singles or couples ranging in age from the late 20s to the late 60s; at Coventry, the age range is from the late 20s to the 70s. The age range at the Village Homes was as expected, but the developers were expecting mostly empty nesters at Coventry, and were surprised by the number of young buyers. Over the years, a few households have included preschool children, but none of school age.

Since their construction, between 1995 and 2000, the five office buildings at Centennial Lakes Office Park have performed better, in terms of both rents and occupancy rates, than competitive properties. Even during the economic downturn that began in late 2000, vacancy rates at Centennial Lakes were half the average rate for the rest of the southwestern metropolitan area. For example, in late 2003, vacancy rates at Centennial Lakes were around 8 percent, whereas rates in the overall southwestern metropolitan area were between 16 and 18 percent. Rents at the Centennial Lakes office park are approximately $1 to

$3 per square foot ($11 to $32 per square meter) higher than rents for competitors' space. Tenant retention has also been greater than at other office properties, and firms with offices at Centennial Lakes have an advantage in employee recruiting that is attributable, in part, to the project's amenities.

Despite significant competition in southeastern Edina, including Southdale and the Galleria (another nearby enclosed shopping center), Centennial Lakes Plaza has generally remained fully occupied since its construction. In addition, the retail center shows average sales of about $300 per square foot ($3,229 per square meter); the nationwide average for recently built community shopping centers is about $200 per square foot ($2,153 per square meter).

Management

Centennial Lakes Park, the crown jewel of Edina's park system, is managed and maintained by the city through a variety of funding sources. Under an innovative agreement with the developer, the city is responsible for park maintenance and operations, but about half the park's operating budget comes from association fees paid by the office and retail tenants, residents, and theater. Office tenants, for example, pay $0.20 per square foot ($2.15 per square meter) per year toward park maintenance; residents' fees are $15 per month, and are paid directly to the city of Edina. Other income sources include the Centrum Building's snack bar concessions, putting-green fees, equipment-rental fees, and fees from the rental of the Centrum Building. The remaining 20 percent of the $1.5 million annual budget is provided by the city of Edina, partly through a trust fund.

Throughout Centennial Lakes, parking is shared: visitors using the recreational facilities can park in the office, retail, or theater parking lots. This arrangement works relatively well because peak parking demand varies for the different uses. At the medical office and theater, for example, which share a surface parking lot and structured parking, peak hours of use do not overlap.

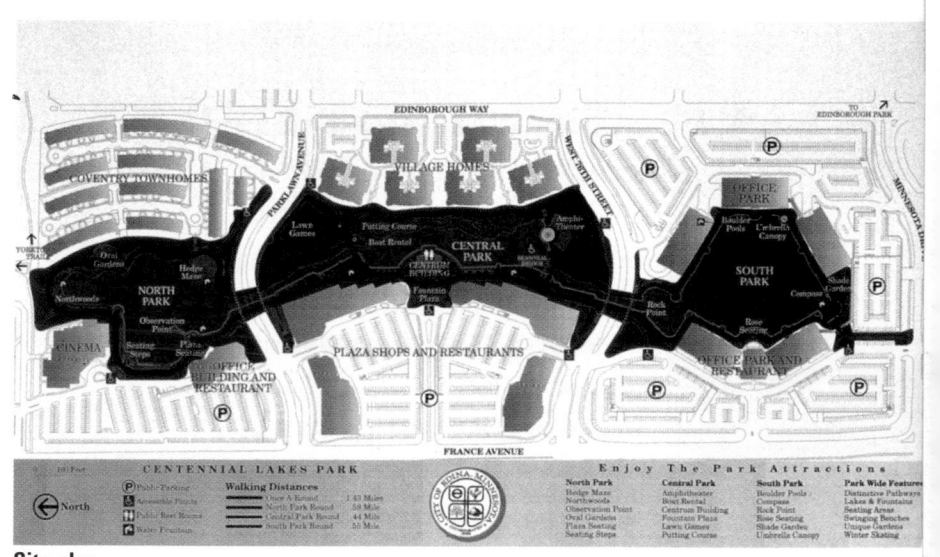

Site plan.

Experience Gained

Centennial Lakes is a vibrant, self-contained, pedestrian-oriented development. Thanks largely to the project's well-planned park, which interconnects all the uses on the site, the development is more economically successful—in terms of sales prices, rents, and occupancy rates—than competitive projects, and very likely more successful than a typical, separate-use suburban design would have been.

Centennial Lakes serves as a reminder that large, complex projects often require public and private cooperation. Few developers can purchase large sites outright for mixed-use development and hold them until the market is right for each use. The city of Edina was proactive about what it wanted to see on the site. City officials' willingness to work with the development team was critical to the project's chances of success, and the city's flexibility has paid off.

Birkdale Village

Huntersville, North Carolina

Birkdale Village was envisioned as a village-style, mixed-use town center that would serve the northern portion of Mecklenburg County, a rapidly suburbanizing area north of Charlotte, North Carolina. The 52-acre (21-hectare) pedestrian-oriented project includes a highly efficient mix of retail, office, and residential uses. Birkdale Village features a traditional grid street system with attractive open spaces, angled and parallel parking, and residential and mixed-use buildings oriented toward the project's interior. Additional parking is on decks located behind the buildings. The project's pedestrian connections and scale add to its bustling urban feel. It was the first project to be developed under the mixed-use new urbanist planning codes developed for Huntersville, the town in which Birkdale Village is located.

Building residential units over main-street retail is an increasingly popular way to achieve greater density and mix uses in order to create an active urban village.
Crosland and Pappas Properties

In northern Mecklenburg County, suburban developments and golf-course communities are quickly replacing farmland. As the population has continued to grow, residents have expressed concerns about the lack of any real community or sense of place. Pappas Properties, LLC, and Crosland, Inc., kept these concerns in mind as they developed Birkdale Village. The center offers 233,000 square feet (21,650 square meters) of street-level retail; 54,000 square feet (5,020 square meters) of office space; 320 residential units (81 percent of which are above the retail space); and a 16-screen, 53,000-square-foot (4,920-square-meter) movie theater, all surrounding a town green where residents and visitors gather for community events.

The joint venture between Pappas Properties and Crosland builds on the partners' understanding of the local market. The principals of Pappas Properties have over 20 years of development experience; among their past projects is Phillips Place, in downtown Charlotte, which was one of the first projects in the nation to reflect the recent trend toward open-air, pedestrian-oriented "lifestyle centers." Pappas had also worked with the town of Huntersville on the approval of Birkdale, a golf-course community, and the Greens at Birkdale, a new urbanist residential

Clustering restaurants around the central green brings activity both day and night to the project's main street. The green provides an attractive setting for diners and passersby. Crosland and Pappas Properties

community. Crosland has 66 years of experience managing construction and developing residential, office, and commercial projects, which it applied to the task of creating a seamless project.

Patterned on a New England coastal town, Birkdale Village is a welcoming home for residents and a shopping and entertainment destination for visitors. With 81 percent of the residential units located above retail space, special attention—reflecting the needs of all users—had to be given to parking, signage, lighting, noise, and street access.

Site Description

Pappas Properties and Crosland acquired the 52-acre (21-hectare) former equine farm from Forest City Enterprises, Inc., a nationally recognized master developer based in Cleveland, Ohio. Located 15 minutes from downtown Charlotte, the site is well connected to the region. Sam Furr Road, a major east-west thoroughfare, runs along the southern and western sides of the property, providing easy access to the interstate highway system. The property is bounded by an office park on the east and by the Greens at Birkdale on the north. Two golf-course communities and a regional shopping center are nearby. To ensure connectivity and easy access, the site plan includes a grid street system, sidewalks, and a pedestrian path and bridge that link Birkdale Village to the office park and the Greens at Birkdale.

Development Process

During the mid-1990s, Huntersville and other nearby towns adopted new development codes designed to manage the area's explosive growth by encouraging mixed-use development and the new urbanism. Birkdale Village was the first large-scale, mixed-use development ushered through Huntersville's new approval process. Because the greenfield site was originally designated for retail development, major rezoning was required to achieve the use designation and density that would support the economics of the project. Although a residential density of 14 dwelling units per acre (35 per hectare) is not in itself unusual in the suburbs, the configuration of mixed-use development is. The fact that the residential units are located over the retail component and are in close proximity to entertainment, offices, and public space resulted in a far more bustling, urban-style village center than is typically found in such regions.

By carefully combining a variety of components, the developer created an active urban environment with a strong sense of place. Along the main corridor, the retail and residential buildings line ten-foot- (three-meter-) wide sidewalks; the project also offers parallel and angled street parking and a wide, grassy median, which runs the length of the main street. The open space acts as a visual divider between lanes, is a traffic-calming device, and provides a connection between the pedestrian spaces and the built environment. In the center of the development, the village green serves as a community gathering place and as the site of many outdoor activities and events. During the summer, young and old alike gather at the splash fountain. Numerous outdoor seating areas allow residents and shoppers to enjoy being a part of—and watching—the active street life.

By clustering retail and entertainment uses along the main street, the developers facilitated continuous foot traffic. The clusters are located near the intersections of the main street and the three cross streets. The blocks between these intersections are approximately 400 feet (122 meters) in length.

Along the central green are retail facilities and destination restaurants. From the green, a restaurant patron may choose to walk to the east, to the entertainment cluster that includes the movie theatre and small retail shops, or to the west, where the fashion and home-furnishings stores are located. Birkdale Village also includes big-box retailers, such as Dick's Sporting Goods and Barnes & Noble. To help maintain the pedestrian orientation of the main street and to provide the big-box retailers with maximum exposure to the auto traffic on Sam Furr Road, the developers

The architecture of Birkdale Village is based on that of New England villages. Buildings incorporate high-pitched roofs and are faced with brick and clapboard siding. Crosland and Pappas Properties sited the big-box stores one block south of the main street, still within walking distance of the main-street shops.

Because the retail space in Phase I had to be 50 percent leased before the construction of the mixed-use buildings could begin, demand for the retail space dictated the timing for the completion of the infrastructure and the residential units. For nearly the first six months of the project, however, the movie theater was the only leased and open tenant. The developers became con-

cerned that unfilled leases could delay the completion and lease-up of the residential units, so they adjusted the building design to minimize the effect on residents of continued construction being undertaken by retail tenants. For example, to lessen construction noise, the developers increased the thickness of the concrete walls between the retail and the residential units beyond code requirements. To accommodate future electrical and plumbing needs, the developers incorporated open shafts into the design of the retail space.

The slow retail lease-up of Phase I proved short-lived. Midway through Phase I, several national retail chains became interested in locating at Birkdale Village. Because of this unexpectedly high interest, Phase II—which had already been permitted and designed as an all-residential phase—had to be redesigned to accommodate more

A strong mix of national and regional retailers in an appealing setting brings shoppers from a ten-mile (16-kilometer) radius. Crosland and Pappas Properties

mixed-use buildings. The original plan for Phase II called for lower density and for more stand-alone apartment buildings. The redesign added 56,000 square feet (5,200 square meters) of retail space and 74 apartment units, all located above the retail space.

To keep Phase II on track and facilitate the redesign of the upper-floor residential units, the developers' design team worked closely with the retail tenants' architects. The highly individualized retail spaces yielded 45 different floor plans for the residential units. The Phase II buildings, located along the cross streets that intersect the main street, are double-loaded buildings designed to provide retail tenants with 80 feet (24 meters) of merchandising depth. The residential units share a central hallway, with one set of units facing the main street and the other facing the inside parking court. The units located along the main street are just one unit deep, with living spaces that face the main street and bedrooms at the rear of the

Centrally located open space adds to the pedestrian activity in Birkdale Village. Children enjoy the splash fountain at the village green. Crosland and Pappas Properties

building. Although this through-building design has been successful from a residential perspective, the shallow layout limits the retailers' merchandising depth.

The 45 different residential floor plans lend a custom element that attracts renters; in fact, residential rents (which range from $600 for a one-bedroom apartment to $1,750 for a three-bedroom apartment) are 20 percent above those elsewhere in the area. Demand for the main-street residential units has been brisk, with renters paying a premium of 15 to 30 percent for units with balconies and main-street views. Early on, the developers underestimated the premium that renters were willing to pay; however, as the rental units turn over, prices are being increased to better reflect the strong demand.

Giving renters an overview of available floor plans has proven to be a challenge. Typically, a renter visiting an apartment community will receive three or four floor plans from which to choose an apartment, but Birkdale Village has so many floor plans that management must first narrow the selection by identifying the size and location that best fit the prospective tenant's budget.

For renters who do not want to live over retail, other options are available. The upper floors of the community clubhouse offer apartment flats, and ground-level townhouses with upper-level flats are located one street north of the main street.

The developers carefully managed road and infrastructure construction to minimize its impact on open retail

Wide sidewalks in front of the shops and along the central median foster pedestrian activity and interaction. The walkway from the parking area provides a safe and comfortable connection to the village center. Crosland and Pappas Properties

stores and occupied residential units. A soft job market that developed while construction was underway made it possible to hire additional construction workers, which allowed the developers to speed up construction without going over budget.

Because the retail, residential, and office elements were completed so rapidly, the project benefited from the resulting synergy. The residential and office occupants provide a captive market for the retail, while the retail serves as a desirable amenity for the office and residential tenants. The synergy is most visible in the evenings, when residents are home from work and the stores and restaurants are in full swing. The location of the residential units above retail adds to the bustle. Eager to be a part of the vibrant street life, residents go out to the restaurants, the shops, or the movie theater—or just to walk their dogs. On pleasant evenings, residents sit on their balconies and enjoy the activity below.

timing was a concern throughout the phased development process. Nevertheless, its unique mix of retail, residential, and office uses and pedestrian-oriented design enabled Birkdale Village to achieve rents in all components that are significantly above market averages.

The urban character of the village is apparent on a summer evening as residents and other patrons enjoy restaurants, shops, and the movie theater. Crosland and Pappas Properties

Financing

Financed as a 50/50 joint venture between Wachovia Bank and Bank of America, Birkdale Village was substantially completed in September 2003 without the use of any public funds or investment tax credits. Both Crosland and Pappas provided substantial guarantees to secure financing. Given the faltering local office and apartment market,

The importance of the national retailers' interest in Birkdale Village should not be understated. Although the presence of these retailers brought higher costs (because they required more tenant improvements), it also reassured lenders that the project would succeed. The national

The management hosts seasonal events—such as Easter egg hunts, 4th of July parades, and Christmas festivities—to promote the businesses at Birkdale Village. Courtesy of Crosland and Pappas Properties

retailers signed longer leases than local tenants would have, and also enabled the developers to collect higher rents than they could otherwise have charged to local tenants: premiums were in the range of $5 to $8 per square foot ($54 to $86 per square meter).

Retailers such as Banana Republic, Gap, and Victoria's Secret, which ordinarily locate only in regional malls, provide an added amenity for residents and attract shoppers from a wider market area. The developers note, however, that it took longer than expected to recruit suitable restaurant tenants, which they view as key to creating a successful lifestyle center. Since the completion of the project, residents can enjoy a variety of local and national restaurants. Although 40 percent of the national retail tenants occupy 65 percent of the gross leasable area, the developer works to maintain a unique product mix by attracting local businesses: restaurants; gift and specialty stores; clothing and jewelry stores; and service retailers, including a copy center and a hair salon. The local merchants that have come to Birkdale Village are high-quality, "best of breed" businesses; the pull of the national retailers is so strong that there has been no need to subsidize local retailers' rents.

In May 2003, Pappas Properties and Crosland recaptured their investment, receiving more than a 20 percent profit when they sold their majority interest in Birkdale Village to Inland Retail Real Estate Trust, Inc., of Northbrook, Illinois. Both Pappas and Crosland retain property management responsibilities and minority interest in the property. Crosland manages the residential and office units, and Pappas manages and markets the retail space.

Planning and Design

Creating a sense of place was the driving force behind the planning and design of Birkdale Village. The design and development team collaborated to incorporate appealing architectural elements from the past into a format that would be successful for today's retailers, residents, and office tenants. From the very beginning of the Birkdale project, the team—which included experts in office, retail, and residential uses, as well as members with experience and expertise in construction, leasing, property management, marketing, and event planning—convened weekly to determine how best to integrate the uses. The consensus decision-making process employed by the group took extra time; but according to the developer, it created a much better product, which ultimately fueled the strong demand for the retail and residential units. The approach also enabled the team to focus on the details, such as connecting the village to the larger community and attending to the differing and sometimes conflicting needs of residents and retailers.

To evoke the character of a traditional community, the design team patterned Birkdale Village on a traditional Nantucket village, where the buildings generally have two to three stories, the first floor is occupied by retail, and the upper floors are filled by office or residential tenants. Because of the need for a larger retail footprint, the buildings at Birkdale Village are much larger in scale than those of a historic village, and the design team had to carefully program the pedestrian experience. Familiar village elements—including buildings styled after a bank, a hotel, and a bed and breakfast—were used to vary the streetscape and to provide visual appeal for pedestrians.

Easy pedestrian and vehicular access to the village center shops was essential. The team solved the potential conflict between residential and commercial needs for access and parking by locating public parking on the bottom floors of parking decks, which provides shoppers with direct access to stores; the upper, gated parking levels are reserved for residents, who can walk directly from their cars to their front doors. Residents who live above street-level retail also have stair access to their units from the ground level of the main street.

On-street parallel and diagonal parking create easy access to personal services and store clusters. When on-street parking is not available, patrons can use the four centrally located parking garages, which have entrances along the main street and are tucked in behind the retail stores.

To better accommodate pedestrian needs, the design team studied how pedestrians would move through the village—where they would park, when they would stop to rest, when they would unload their packages, and how they would interact with other pedestrians. To provide a pleasant street experience, the designers minimized the distances between parking, sidewalks, crosswalks, public gathering spaces, and outdoor seating. The manageable block length of 400 feet (122 meters) allows pedestrians to move between shops without being overwhelmed by the scale of the buildings. To make the transition from the street to the sidewalk easier for pedestrians with disabilities and those pushing strollers, extra curb cuts were added to the sidewalks.

The design team also tackled another issue: the efficient loading and circulation of vehicles. Loading zones for retail shops are located at the rear of the shops, in the parking decks. To better accommodate shoppers loading and unloading their cars, sidewalks were placed along the center median, in front of the angled parking. Clearly marked directional and parking signs located throughout the village facilitate vehicular and pedestrian traffic.

A traditional grid street pattern connects Birkdale Village to the surrounding neighborhood. Wide sidewalks along the connecting streets and a pedestrian pathway allow residents from the Greens at Birkdale easy access

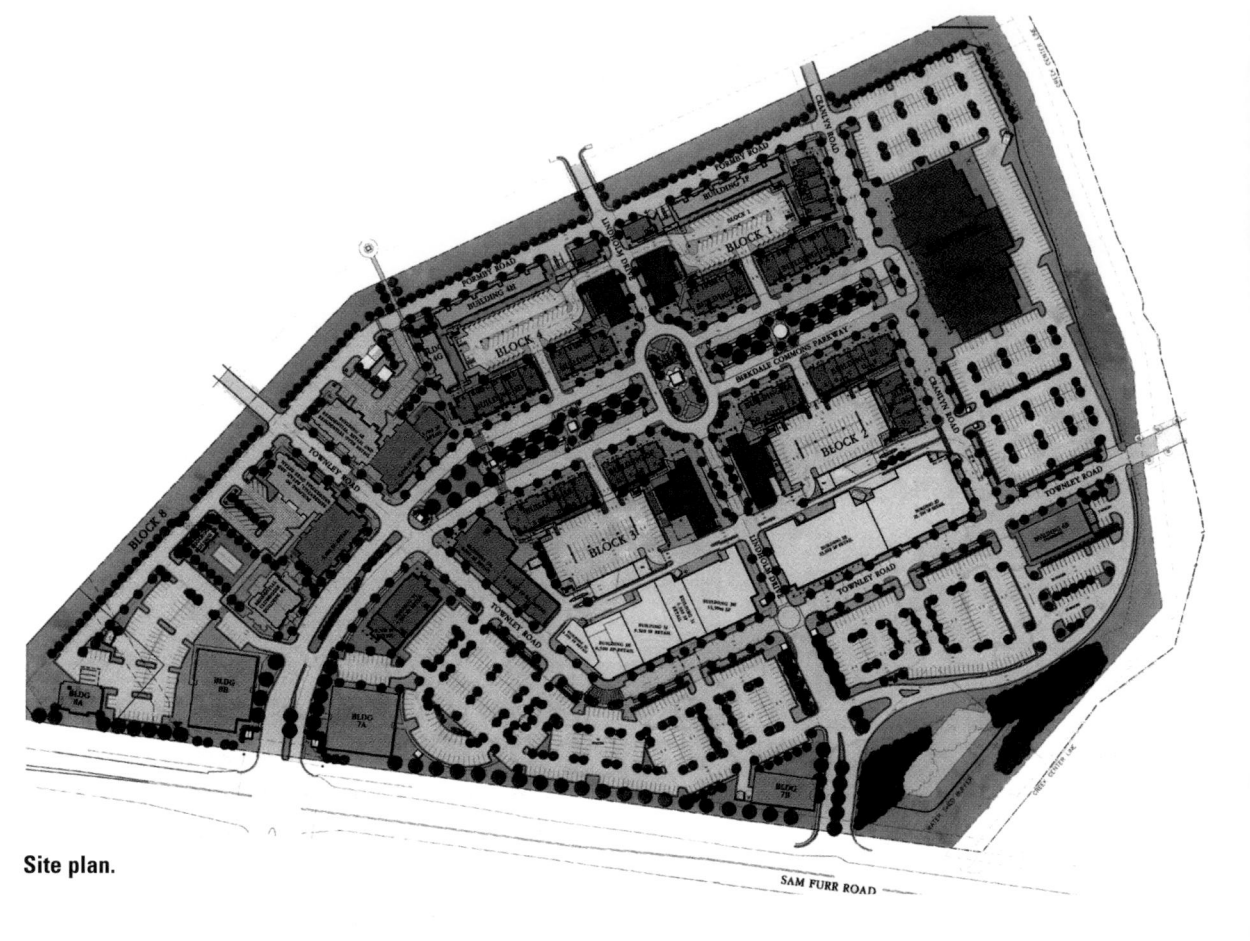

Site plan.

to the village center. During weekday lunch hours, workers from the neighboring office park take advantage of the pedestrian bridge, located near the movie theater, to visit the village restaurants and shops. The developer notes that much of the movement between Birkdale Village and the surrounding community is still largely vehicular, but the pedestrian connections provide additional options and add to the village ambience.

Management and Marketing

Just as coordination was key to the successful development of Birkdale Village, ongoing collaboration between Pappas and Crosland ensures that shopping, living, and working in Birkdale Village continue to be enjoyable. Working together, the two firms arrange security, land-

scaping, maintenance, and trash collection to provide an appropriate level of service without disturbing residents or retail tenants. Even small details, such as sidewalk sweeping, must be scheduled so as not to create excessive noise or interfere with store operations.

Marketing efforts support Birkdale Village's image as a destination community. Crosland and Pappas collaborate on marketing, with the marketing director at Pappas taking the lead on social programs and special events. Birkdale's location provides it with a unique market niche for both retail and residential uses: there is no regional mall nearby, and there are few opportunities for renters to live in an active, mixed-use environment. Over 138,000 people live within ten miles (16 kilometers) of the village, and the opportunity to enjoy a regional shopping experience in an active, outdoor, pedestrian setting draws shoppers from throughout the region.

The promotional material created for Birkdale Village is designed to attract a wide range of residents and visitors by branding the experiences and activities that the community offers: the images show people working, relaxing, shopping, and dining, all within the village setting.

Marketing for the residential units targets empty nesters, young professionals, and renters-by-choice who want to take advantage of the amenities, such as the movie theater, restaurants, shops, and the 24-hour fitness facility, all of which are within walking distance. The marketing efforts that focus on community- and family-oriented activities are designed to attract young families and active individuals to the village.

A full-time marketing director oversees a newsletter for residents, fosters networking among merchants, and arranges signature events such as a Christmas-tree lighting, a Fourth of July parade, and a Halloween festival. Finally, all residents are given a Live It Up card, which offers discounts on merchandise and services from participating Birkdale Village shops.

Experience Gained

In a mixed-use project, synergy comes from the interaction among each of the pieces. Residents view the shops, entertainment facilities, and restaurants as amenities. To meet residents' expectations and to activate the street, at the early stages, it is important to open as many restaurants as possible in conjunction with the residential component.

So that mixed-use buildings can be completed quickly, and so that conflict between construction and completed residential and retail uses can be minimized, it is essential to create a construction staging and sequencing plan before work begins. By phasing the project, the developer obtained interim income to support construction of the final phase.

The creation of a safe and welcoming destination entails higher construction costs: a mixed-use project requires more landscaping, signage, and lighting than an auto-oriented project would. Landscaping and streetscaping help pedestrians feel connected to the built environment. Signage direct visitors to parking and helps maintain the traffic flow. Street-level lighting must be bright enough to create the perception of safety and support retail presentation, but not so bright as to disturb residents who live above the stores. The developers of Birkdale Village set the street-light fixture height at 11 feet (3.4 meters) and reduced the bulb wattage to minimize the amount of light streaming into the residential units. To ensure adequate illumination for pedestrians, they increased the number of light fixtures along the street and sidewalks.

Birkdale Village

Huntersville, North Carolina

Land Use Information

Site area (acres/hectares)	52/21
Number of mixed-use buildings	18
Number of apartment buildings	3
Number of residential units	320
Total number of parking spaces	1,354

Gross Leasable Area

Use	Square Feet/Square Meters
Office	54,000/5,020
Retail	233,000/21,650
Entertainment	53,000/4,920
Total	340,000/31,590

Residential Information

Floor area (square feet/square meters)	650–2,700/60–250
Range of initial rental prices	$650–$2,000

Unit Type	Number of Units
1 bedroom	98
1 bedroom + loft	56
1 bedroom + den	17
2 bedroom	108
2-bedroom townhouse	19
3-bedroom townhouse	22

Development Costs

Site acquisition	$7,000,000
Site improvements	11,700,000
Construction	55,000,000
Soft costs	8,800,000
Total cost	$82,500,000

Retail Information

Percentage of gross leasable area occupied	95
Annual rents (per square foot/square meter)	$21–$23/$226–$248

Tenant Classification	Number of Stores	Gross Leasable Area (Square Feet/Square Meters)
Food service	11	47,800/4,440
Clothing, accessories	15	60,900/5,660
Shoes	3	4,100/380
Home furnishings	5	22,300/2,070
Books and music	1	23,000/2,140
Hobby, special interest	5	37,500/3,480
Gifts, specialty	6	10,200/950
Jewelry	2	2,200/200
Personal services	7	11,200/1,040
Pharmacy	1	15,000/1,390
Entertainment	1	53,300/4,950
Total	57	287,500/26,700

Development Schedule

Site purchased	1997
Planning started	1997
Leasing started	1999
Construction started	2000
Phase I completed	2001
Project completed	2003

Development Team

Developers/Owners
Crosland, Inc.
Charlotte, North Carolina
www.crosland.com

Pappas Properties, LLC
Charlotte, North Carolina
www.pappaspropertiesllc.com

Master Planner and Architect
Shook Kelley
Charlotte, North Carolina
www.shookkelley.com

Architect
The Housing Studio P.A.
Charlotte, North Carolina
www.housingstudio.com

Landscape Architect
LandDesign
Charlotte, North Carolina
www.landdesign.com

Owner
Inland Retail Real Estate Trust, Inc.
Oak Brook, Illinois
www.inlandgroup.com

Saffron

Sammamish, Washington

A small, intensively designed urban village within Seattle's suburban fringe, Saffron is a pedestrian environment within an entirely automobile-dependent context. This upscale residential and commercial development, built without a public partner, is the first mixed-use project ever permitted in an unincorporated part of King County, a jurisdiction that includes the city of Seattle and several of its suburbs.

Saffron has set new design standards in an area filled with generic, builder-generated housing. Bold, energetic architecture and generously furnished outdoor spaces make the small development an eye-catching, inviting place to visit or live. It is both a successful residential community and a destination for area shoppers.

Saffron's main entrance is marked by signage that serves as a design element visible from the roadways.
Tarragon Development

The project consists of 99 apartment units situated above 49,714 square feet (4,619 square meters) of ground-level retail, restaurants, and professional services offices, all located on one 4.4-acre (1.8-hectare) block. The block is divided by a street-and-sidewalk grid that extends the axes of an abutting arterial and a through-way in a neighboring strip mall. On-site parking accommodates 333 cars: there are 133 surface spaces, and 200 spaces in a 66,000-square-foot (6,131-square-meter) underground parking structure. The parking structure, an important element of the project, made it possible to create a more pedestrian-friendly design that would not be overwhelmed by surface parking.

Saffron addresses an underserved market for rental housing at the eastern edge of the rapidly urbanizing Puget Sound area. Located very near a major high-technology employment center, it was designed with the mobile young professional in mind. The development capitalizes on its market position by offering amenities that include high-speed wiring in all residential units and electrical outlets for laptop computers in outdoor public areas.

Site

Located 30 miles (48 kilometers) east of Seattle, on the Sammamish Plateau, Saffron is a 20-minute drive from Microsoft's main campus in Redmond. The plateau, a 40-square-mile (103.6-square-kilometer) area of land east of

Outdoor restaurant seating brings the flavor of the city to Saffron. The development is the beginning of a more urban, pedestrian-friendly environment in the midst of suburban sprawl. Tarragon Development

tions, especially near the bordering highways: Interstate 90 on the south, and Route 202—a state highway that leads to Redmond—on the north.

Because the Sammamish Plateau is inside the Puget Sound regional urban growth boundary (a growth-planning measure created by the state to preserve rural and natural-resource lands outside such boundaries), there are few development restrictions, and growth has proceeded rapidly since 1990, when the boundary was set.

Before the incorporation of the city of Sammamish, in 1999, the county, in an effort to encourage more dense commercial development, had designated the intersection of 228th Avenue Northeast and Northeast 8th Street for commercial development, and had followed up by rezoning the intersection from residential to office mixed-use. The intersection, which sees about 31,550 cars per day, is both the center of the plateau and the most active intersection in what is now the city of Sammamish. Saffron, located on the northeast corner of the intersection, is bounded on the north and west by multifamily residential development.

In the early 1990s, at about the same time as the intersection was upzoned, the county expanded its library system by constructing a new branch at the northwest corner of the intersection. A large commercial strip development that dates from the 1980s—rustic, lap-sided storefronts surrounding a large parking lot—occupies the southeast corner of the intersection. The offices of the new city of Sammamish are housed in one of the storefronts. Another commercial strip occupies the southwest corner of the intersection.

Seattle, was named after Lake Sammamish, a large lake that borders the plateau on the west. As of 1999, when leasing began at Saffron, the estimated average household income within a three-mile (4.8-kilometer) radius of the Saffron site was $120,000.

The area is characterized by planned communities and large and small tracts of housing built in the 1980s. In between these developments are pockets of underused farmland and ranch land that date from the original settlement of the area, in the 1870s. Large, single-family estates take up the lakefront and part of the plateau. Strip commercial development has taken over at some intersec-

Because it was at a busy corner in an area undergoing rapid commercial development, the Saffron site was passed over for residential development. Until it was upzoned to mixed use, in the early 1990s, the gently sloping site lay neglected, collecting refuse.

Development Process

The idea for Saffron grew from the realization that parts of the Sammamish Plateau were being rapidly transformed from rural areas to urban enclaves: commercial centers designated by the county thus represented important opportunities for leadership in design and development.

In the early 1990s, a consortium that included Joe Blattner and Michael Corliss purchased the site, along with two nearby parcels, as a passive investment. At the time the property was purchased, mixed-use zoning in unincorporated sections of King County was unheard of—and, in any case, a moratorium on water and sewer construction precluded development of the property.

When King County upzoned the parcel for mixed-use development, Blattner and Corliss decided to consolidate their interest and buy the other partners out. In 1995, they founded Tarragon, a limited liability company that develops, builds, leases, and manages real estate in the Puget Sound region. Tarragon is owned by Joe Blattner and Evergreen Capital Trust, which was founded by Mike Corliss. The firm has developed more than 10 million square feet (930,000 square meters) of commercial and multifamily real estate projects, including suburban shopping centers and industrial parks.

For the Saffron site, Blattner and Corliss were not interested in the usual response to the county's upzoning, which would have been to build a wall of retail along the street edge at the intersection and to place condominiums at the back of the site. Instead, they wanted to create

Pedestrians often walk from Saffron to the public library across the street. A wheelchair and stroller ramp add accessibility. Tarragon Development

a walkable place that could serve as the beginnings of a pedestrian-friendly, mixed-use downtown for the city of Sammamish. A conventional approach would have been better understood by potential residential and retail tenants, and would therefore have yielded higher short-term profit. But because of their ownership interest and long-term horizon for returns, Blattner and Corliss were willing to consider a promising, if less conventional, concept.

To help refine their ideas for the project, the Tarragon team took two important steps early on: they sought out an architect through a competitive process, and they brought in a retail marketing consultant. After soliciting statements of qualifications from a number of urban-design-oriented architects, Blattner and Corliss narrowed the field to three. They then paid each of the three firms $10,000 to cover some of their expenses for creating a concept for the site. The plan submitted by the Bumgardner Architects, a firm led by principals Mark Simpson and David Wright, offered an imaginative modernist vision for mixed-use development. The plan was a standout for its urban character: by creating a street grid, instead of simply surrounding development with parking lots, it would help to urbanize the existing suburban street pattern. The marketing consultant, the Retail Group, refined the concept, adding strategic elements to the plan and developing the overall approach to the promotional materials for Saffron.

Financing

Saffron was financed through a conventional construction loan with Wells Fargo Bank for 75 percent of the value of the property; Tarragon provided 25 percent of the project cost in the form of equity. Initial expectations were for a 25 percent internal rate of return and a 12 per-

Saffron's bold, contemporary architecture and bright colors are a departure from the traditional residential neighborhoods that surround it. Tarragon Development

cent cash-on-cash return. High returns were necessary because of the considerable risk: the project involved taking a mixed-use product from raw land through stabilized asset, in an environment where market acceptance was by no means assured.

Underwriting for the loan was based on residential rental rates of approximately $1.24 per square foot ($13.35 per square meter) and retail rental rates of approximately $26 per square foot ($280 per square meter), with operating costs, taxes, and insurance covered by tenants' rents. No preleasing was required for the construction loan.

The long-term, permanent financing was based on the same underwriting criteria as the construction financing and was provided by Aegon Life Insurance. To minimize the overall amount of capital needed to fund the project, Aegon also provided mezzanine financing for approximately 10 percent of the debt amount.

Approvals

The approval process involved an administrative rezoning from office mixed-use to commercial mixed-use, a request that was determined to be consistent with the height and density limits of the site and the market needs of the area. There were no design standards or public review requirements in place.

As the first mixed-use project to be permitted by King County, Saffron was subject to the discretionary review of an all-volunteer fire department based nearby. Once access to the multistory building was deemed acceptable, the permit was granted.

Planning and Design

Saffron is a small, pedestrian-friendly enclave within a region of single-family developments crossed by an irregular network of major arterials. It is designed to present an inviting, visually strong environment to passersby and to provide an interesting and comfortable place for residents to live and visitors to dine, shop, and pass the time.

Plantings and artwork add interest. Recalling the wildness that existed on the plateau, life-sized bronze animals populate Saffron's walls and walkways. Stefan Coe

Each of two buildings contains three stories of apartments above ground-floor storefronts, facing an inner pedestrian court.
Stefan Coe

For the designers and architects at Bumgardner, creating an urban environment in the midst of suburban sprawl meant deliberately calibrating new scales for massing and creating a street grid within the development. At the same time, the developer and the design team decided that the mixed-use project must engage the somewhat chaotic network of roads and view corridors that surrounded the parcel.

The designers chose to build "up and out" from the intersection at the development's southwest corner, placing eye-catching ground-level commercial storefronts near the corner and four-story residential buildings in the interior, facing an inner courtyard. One advantage of this transition from low to high is to provide parking and vehicular circulation that are visible from the surrounding arterials. At the same time, pedestrians can easily be seen from outside the development. The designers realized that the mixed-use development had to be approachable for cars as well as hospitable to pedestrians. The development offers many sheltered and landscaped opportunities for sitting outdoors, including 18-inch- (0.45-meter-) high walls and movable seating on the wide sidewalks.

Interior circulation for the site is defined by a midblock driveway entered from Northeast 8th Street, which divides the multistory, mixed-use buildings on the west side of the site from the one-story retail buildings on the east. A diagonal drive fronts the retail area, with its wide sidewalks and awnings, and leads to a broad set of steps that go down to the corner of Northeast 8th Street and 228th Avenue Northeast. In addition to the steps, a wheelchair- and stroller-accessible ramp leads from the development to the pedestrian crossing on 228th Avenue Northeast, between Saffron and the new county library. Shoppers sometimes park at Saffron, do some shopping, then walk over to the library and back. The steps and the diagonal drive that lead into the heart of Saffron extend the path of a third major arterial, Inglewood Hill Road, which meets 228th Avenue Northeast and Northeast 8th Street at the intersection.

Two apartment blocks, each with three stories of apartments above ground-floor storefronts, face an inner parking and pedestrian court. Buildings and surface parking both have underground parking beneath.

Early in the development process, Tarragon decided to go for an edgy, urban look that would depart from the traditional, conservative styles of the surrounding developments. Taking its inspiration from the drive-ins of the 1950s, Bumgardner designed the project with bright colors, quirky angles, sculptural elements, and metal details.

Standing high in the center of the development, where the one-story retail area meets the residential court, is a glass-fronted commercial space with a tilted-out roof. The angles, irregular volume, and height of the interior display space—visible from the corner pedestrian portal and from the parking lot of the strip mall across Northeast 8th Street—draw visitors' eyes into the heart of Saffron

Other signature elements include a triangular, free-standing, one-story retail building at the intersection. The building's awnings seem to be supported by thin, canted posts; at the edge of the awnings, the posts break free of the roof line and continue along the street as a free-standing design element.

The three scales of signage at Saffron are layered, as part of a strategy to create an urban environment that appeals to pedestrians while acknowledging the speeds at which cars pass. One layer, scaled to catch the eyes of motorists passing by at highway speed, consists of a series of seven thin standards with "Saffron" spelled out in tall letters. Another level of signage—logos affixed to bright-yellow storefronts—is modestly sized to catch the eyes of nearby pedestrians and slower—30 miles (48 kilometers) per hour—automobile traffic. At the purely pedestrian scale, lighted blade signs hang from canopies just above head level.

Rectilinear in plan, and relatively massive in size, the apartment buildings are characterized by metal siding, deep colors, and irregular angles at the ends overlooking the commercial areas. At the street-facing side of the apartment block, the concrete parking structure is exposed to provide an elevated platform for outdoor seating in the restaurant space that fills much of the first floor of the building.

With its bright colors and rich palette of metal siding and details, Saffron is a standout. The stylistic features contrast vividly with the traditional, false-front facades in the commercial strip across the street, and with the sprawling, garage-door-dominated landscape of the surrounding residential developments.

Abundant plantings and artworks soften the edginess of the architecture. In evocation of the wildness that existed until recently on the plateau, life-sized bronze animals—raccoons, turtles, and deer, fabricated by a local artist as specified by the project's landscape architects—populate Saffron's walls and walkways. A buck stands on the stairway at the sentinel corner, and a doe looks up from a stone well in the court beside the storefronts. Special paving mimics the path of a watercourse to the well.

The three top floors of the residential blocks are wood-frame construction with metal siding, built upon a poured-in-place concrete parking structure and first-floor retail. The one-story retail buildings on the west side of the development are steel and wood-frame construction, with slab on grade foundation. To satisfy the seismic requirements for an earthbound structural system, steel rods were used to tie the roof to the concrete foundation.

Judicious placement of four types of metal siding modulates and deepens the visual complexity of the development: corrugated metal, diagonal-shingle metal, and box-rib siding, which is used both seam-side-out and reversed, to expose the other side and achieve a more subtle texture.

Marketing and Management

The name Saffron comes from the rare spice; the name was chosen to evoke the upscale lifestyle that owners Joe Blattner and Mike Corliss envisioned in the development. Their research, which confirmed a strong market for high-quality dining and retail uses on the plateau, was based on the success of other recently completed pedestrian developments in the region, including University Village, in Seattle, and Redmond Town Center, to the north. "Living, shopping, dining" became part of the concept label for Saffron.

Completed in the spring of 2000, Saffron came online just as its most important marketing targets—young high-tech workers—were being laid off by the thousands in greater Seattle. Despite this accident of timing, residential and retail spaces both leased very quickly, at above-market rates for the area.

Rents for retail space ranged from $25 to $30 per square foot ($269 to $324 per square meter), depending on street exposure and location within the complex. Comparable rates for the area ranged from $18 to $22 per square foot ($194 to $237 per square meter) at the time. While the limited square footage precludes a retail anchor at Saffron, 76 percent of the retail space was leased before construction—a noteworthy phenomenon, given the economic climate at the time. Rents have increased at an average annual rate of 6 percent, whereas rents in the adjacent strip mall have remained flat.

Commercial tenants include health care services, fitness facilities, restaurants, and retailers. This mix follows established formulas for mixed-use lifestyle centers, where commercial tenants provide services that add convenience and market appeal for residential tenants. Major tenants include Evergreen Community Health Care, in the base of the south apartment block, and Columbia Fitness, in the north block. There are also a dentist, a skin care specialist, and a plastic surgeon. Pacific Bicycle, a sales and repair shop, now occupies the lofty "flagship" location, so called because of its striking shape and prominent position in the middle of the site. Consolidated Restaurants, owner of Seattle's landmark Metropolitan Grill, opened DC Steakhouse in the base of the south residential block, a prominent location with outdoor seating that faces Northeast 8th Street.

For the residential portion, an on-site rental office, managed by Investco, was furnished and open on May 1, 2000. Before Saffron had even obtained an occupancy permit, prospective tenants had picked out their favorite units on a Web site. By the time the development was open for occupancy, 17 units were already leased. Although there were flyers and local newspaper ads, most of the subsequent tenants had first seen the development while driving by.

Initial rental rates for studios and one-bedroom flats were the same as those being paid for nearby townhouses that included attached garages and separate entries. Moreover, Saffron commanded these rates without any of the typical free-rent incentives, and in the absence of standard amenities such as a clubhouse, media room, pool, or in-house fitness center.

Since that initial period, the combination of the local employment slump and low interest rates (which make homeownership affordable to more potential renters) has created a soft residential rental market. Investco's response has been to keep the property fully leased, even if that means reducing the rents. Despite the reductions, however, rents have remained above those for new rental units elsewhere on the plateau. To set rents, Investco put a considerable amount of time and effort into prorating the various property management and maintenance costs associated with the property. In some instances, prorating was done on a percentage-of-leasable-area basis, and in others on a percentage-of-value or percentage-of-footprint basis.

As projected, tenants are overwhelmingly single professionals, especially from the high-tech industry. Demand for studio apartments was the greatest, by a wide margin.

Saffron's residential component addresses an underserved rental-housing market. Underground parking makes the density possible and keeps the site from being overwhelmed by surface lots. Stefan Coe

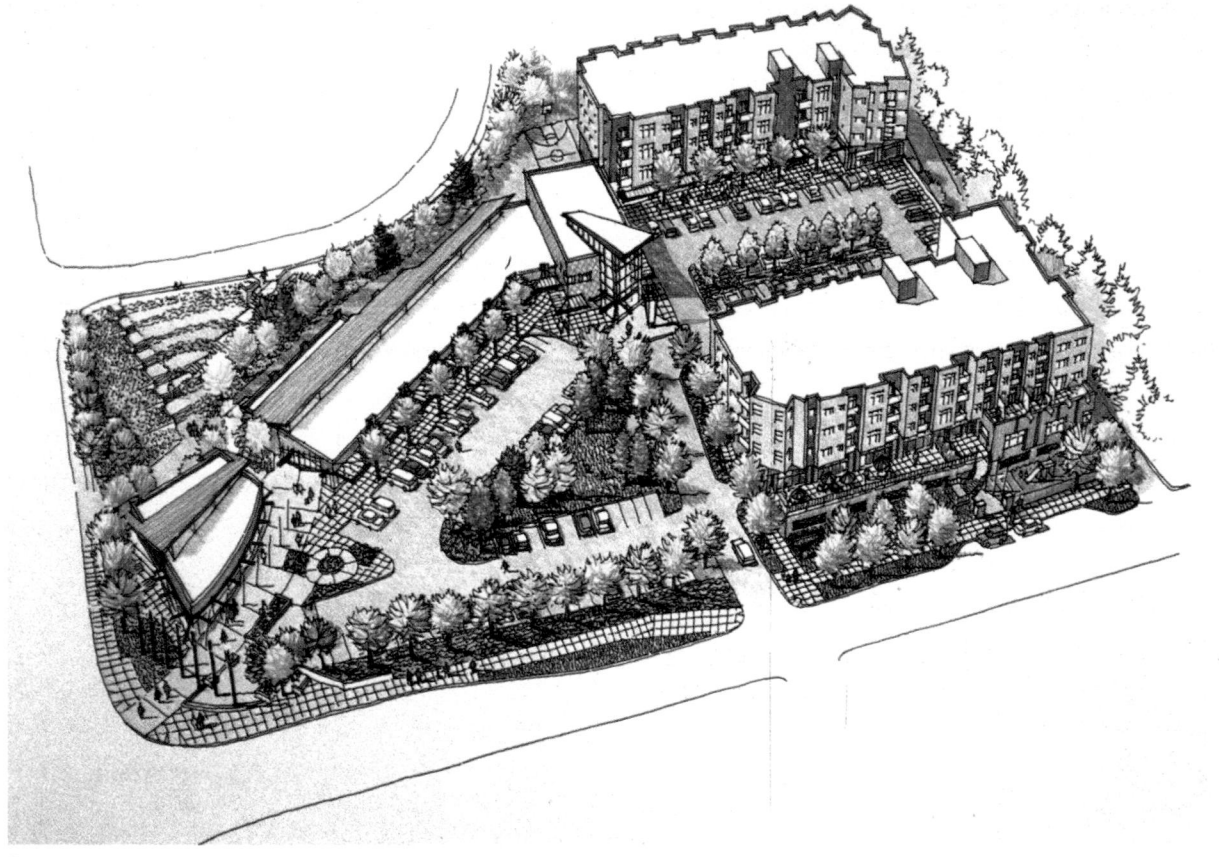

Site plan.

In explaining their reasons for choosing to live at Saffron, renters cite the convenience of being so close to shops and restaurants and the appeal of the streetscape. In good weather and especially on weekends, sidewalks are populated by pedestrians running errands, shopping, or just strolling. Bicyclists ride to and from Pacific Bicycle for repairs, even through the winter months, and bike racks are provided every 20 feet (six meters) on site. Shoppers cross 228th Avenue Northeast to the library and back. An ice cream shop draws business from teenagers at a nearby high school.

Experience Gained

From the standpoint of day-to-day management and operations, designing for retail and residential tenants in the same complex is challenging. Residents' privacy must be balanced with shoppers' access and convenience. And while residents clearly appreciate the proximity of restaurants and services, they are not necessarily prepared to accommodate the realities of shared parking and common garbage disposal.

The more unique and ambitious the design, the more likely that decisions involving significant capital must be made during construction. It is better, in such cases, if the developer acts as construction manager because the developer's close management of the construction process can preclude an overwhelming number of change orders.

Despite the operational challenges that go along with a unique design concept and a small, mixed-use community, Saffron has demonstrated the following:

■ It is possible to create an attractive example of contemporary urban living within a decidedly suburban environment. Both observation and market experience confirm that visitors and residents respond positively to the attractions and comforts of Saffron's street-oriented, pedestrian environment. Outdoor walkways and seating are well used in good weather. Bicyclists are a common sight in and around the development, and students walk to Saffron from a local high school. Visitors are willing to walk across the street to the library before returning to their cars.

■ Designing a mixed-use complex around a pedestrian environment creates a framework for good design decisions—decisions that will make the project attractive as both a destination and a living environment. Demand for residential units and for retail space at Saffron has exceeded expectations, despite a sharp regional and local economic downturn.

■ Investment in high-quality urban design for a project that also meets ambitious public goals for density and pedestrian amenities can pay off in the form of future opportunity for public/private partnerships. After Saffron was complete, Tarragon went on to compete for—and win—the right to develop a 550,000-square-foot (51,000-square-meter) retail, office, entertainment, and residential complex in Kent, Washington, on city-owned land. The project, formally known as Kent Station, is strategically located to become an identifiable town center for the Seattle suburb.

Saffron

Sammamish, Washington

Land Use Information

Site area (acres/hectares)   4.4/1.8

Gross Building Area

	Square Feet/Square Meters	
Use	**Existing**	**Planned**
Retail	47,300/4,390	49,700/4,620
Residential	82,800/7,690	95,200/8,840

Residential Information

Unit Type	Unit Size (Square Feet/ Square Meters)	Number Leased	Initial Rental Prices
Studio/efficiency	590/55	42	$850
1 bedroom/1 bath	864/80	27	$1,050
1 bedroom/1 bath + den	871/81	3	$1,075
2 bedroom/2 bath	1,060–1,239/98–115	12	$1,275–$1,485
2 bedroom/2 bath + den	1,239–1,314/115–122	15	$1,425–$1,575

Retail Information

Percentage of gross leasable area occupied	100
Annual rents (per square foot/square meter)	$24–$35/$258–$377
Typical length of lease	5–15 years

Tenant Classification	Number of Stores	Gross Leasable Area (Square Feet/Square Meters)
Food service	5	14,400/1,340
Clothing, accessories	1	1,500/140
Home furnishings	1	1,600/150
Hobby, special interest	1	4,100/380
Gifts, specialty	1	1,300/120
Personal services	7	16,400/1,520
Recreational and community facilities	1	8,100/750
Total	17	47,400/4,400

Development Costs

Land	$3,675,000

Soft Costs

Architectural fees	$793,000
Permits and fees	701,000
Contingency fees	311,000
Leasing and marketing fees	411,000
Loan fees and costs	1,490,000
Administrative costs	894,000
Subtotal, soft costs	$4,600,000

Hard Costs

On-site improvements	$1,355,000
Off-site improvements	170,000
Parking garage	2,080,000
Building 1	3,138,000
Building 2	3,767,000
Building 3	916,000
Building 4	276,000
Retail tenant improvements	499,000
General conditions	181,000
Sales tax (8.6%)	1,065,000
Subtotal, hard costs	$13,447,000
Total	$21,722,000

Development Schedule

Site purchased	June 1997
Planning started	June 1997
Construction started	July 1998
Leasing started	October 1999
Phase I completed	May 2000

Development Team

Developer

Tarragon

Seattle, Washington

www.tarragon.com

Architect

The Bumgardner Architects

Seattle, Washington

www.bumgardnerseattle.com

Landscape Architect

Berger Partnership, P.S.

Seattle, Washington

www.bergerpartnership.com

Consulting Engineers

Barghausen Consulting Engineers

Kent, Washington

www.barghausen.com

Baxter Village

Fort Mill, South Carolina

Baxter Village is a livable, walkable community that aims to meet all its residents' daily needs. It will set the standard for other projects in an area that is beginning to suburbanize. The mixed-use plan combines 1,325 residential units with 300,000 square feet (27,900 square meters) of commercial and civic space and over 500 acres (202 hectares) of parkland. Homes are a mix of for-sale townhouses and single-family houses. Recreational facilities include a community center with tennis courts and swimming pools and a new YMCA complex. A public library, an elementary school, and an urgent-care medical center round out the community.

Baxter's open-space plan consists of a series of community parks and playgrounds, all linked by a trail network. The 12-acre (five-hectare) Allison Park includes a playground, a bandstand, and a walk-through fountain. Neighborhood pocket parks provide identity for streets as well as additional open space.

Baxter Village was designed with walkability in mind. Streets connect, and are lined with tree-shaded sidewalks. Everything in the village is accessible by foot. Urban Design Associates

Baxter Village is an example of creating a lifestyle from scratch. The developer had to face the dilemma that always confronts new town centers: homes had to be built to support the town center, but early home sales were hindered by the absence of the very services that the town center would eventually provide.

Site

Baxter Village is located in Fort Mill, South Carolina, a suburbanizing area to the south of Charlotte, North Carolina. Fort Mill was chartered in 1783. The local textile industry began in 1887, with a mill that later became Springs Industries, makers of the Springmaid brand. A thriving busi-

ness and a major local employer for about 100 years, the mill closed in the mid-1980s and later burned down. The site of the mill is now a park, and the historic district surrounding the park is occupied mostly by antique shops and restaurants.

Baxter Village is located about two miles (3.2 kilometers) from Fort Mill's historic district, just off Interstate 77, at its interchange with Highway 160. The main entrance is off Highway 160, at Assembly Drive. Instead of being set off from the community by elaborate entrance features or gates, the development is integrated into its surroundings, with its town center clearly visible from the main road.

Baxter Village offers a variety of housing types that cover a wide range of price points. Shown here are the Summerville Cottages, which are among the smaller housing types. Clear Springs

The area immediately surrounding Baxter Village is dotted with small business parks, strip shopping centers, and residential subdivisions. Much of the land is still undeveloped. Directly to the south of Baxter Village is Sutton Place, a residential development being built by Ryan Homes. To the east is a shopping center anchored by a Winn Dixie supermarket. Across Highway 160 from Baxter Village is West Town Market, which opened in 2004 and is anchored by a Harris Teeter grocery store.

Baxter Village occupies 1,032 acres (418 hectares) of land that was once farmland, orchards, and woodlands. The terrain is quite varied, and the land slopes steeply along the gullies that run through much of the site. The property was difficult to develop, but its slopes and woodlands have made for an attractive setting.

Development and Approvals

The members of the Close family, heirs to Spring Industries and major landowners, were interested in preserving the local character while bringing economic growth to the town. In the early 1990s, the family created the Clear Springs Plan, which allocated 6,200 acres (2,509 hectares) of family-owned land for development and open-space preservation, including 2,300 acres (931 hectares) for a greenway. In 1997, the family formed Clear Springs Development Company to oversee the remaining acreage. However, before setting out to develop Baxter Village, the family worked with York County and the state of South Carolina to build an employment base in the region. With the state's help, the family developed business parks and recruited businesses to the area, bringing about 3,000 new jobs to the region. It also built a number of shopping centers. Once the employment base was established, the family was ready to begin a residential community.

The Close family had owned the land on which Baxter Village was developed for about 200 years when, beginning in the early 1980s, the family was approached by developers interested in the site. Instead of working with a developer, family members consulted with several design firms, exploring options to develop the land themselves. They eventually hired LandDesign, Inc., a local planning firm; they also hired Celebration Associates, a real estate development consulting firm formed by Don Killoren and Charles Adams, former executives at Disney's Celebration project, in Florida. In 1997, the Clear Springs Development Company began to develop Baxter Village with an in-house staff. In 2000, Don Killoren was hired as chief executive officer of Clear Springs Development Company. Clear Springs also hired Urban Design Associates (UDA) to create a pattern book and help with the land planning. (UDA had also worked on Celebration.)

The approvals process began when LandDesign began working with the county to create a traditional neighborhood development (TND) code that would allow Baxter Village to be developed as intended. It took about a year and a half to work through this process; even today, the development team makes recommendations to the county regarding revisions to the code.

Once the code was developed, it took another year to gain approvals for the concept plan. As part of this process, the developer agreed to allocate a site near the entrance to the community for the Fort Mill Public Library. In 1997, the developer received permits for the first infrastructure. The first homes were begun in late 1998, and home sales began in 1999. The Fort Mill Public Library broke ground the same year.

The project is zoned for a maximum of 1,500 residential units and up to 500,000 square feet (46,500 square meters) of nonresidential space, but only 1,325 homes and 300,000 square feet (27,900 square meters) of commercial space will actually be developed. Some local residents, accustomed to lots that were one acre (0.4 hectares) or larger (typical of the region at the time), objected to the project because they felt that the lots were too small. But the project was able to move forward, and now that it is well underway, most local residents are pleased with it.

Much of the land is too steep to build on, which made it easier to meet the county's requirements that at least 50 percent of the site remain open space. The county requires

Pocket parks are accessible to every neighborhood. They offer residents green views and space to play. Clear Springs

The creation of an improvement district would allow the developer to create mixed-use communities that would yield greater net fiscal benefit to the county than short-term, conventional financing would permit. An improvement district would also facilitate long-term thinking about commercial facilities in the early stages of development, when infrastructure costs are high and demand for residential space may be stronger than for commercial space.

Town centers need time to mature as the residential component is built out. Baxter Village's town center has grown to include a range of neighborhood-serving retailers, restaurants, and services. Urban Design Associates

a 100-foot- (30.5-meter-) deep buffer on the perimeter of all TNDs, which hinders meaningful connections to surrounding developments. The county also requires a minimum of 80 acres (32 hectares) for any site that is to be developed as a TND, which precludes smaller infill development. As the project progresses and the development team learns what works and what doesn't, the team has been working with the county to further refine the code. So far, no other development in the county has come along to use the TND ordinance.

The developer has also been working with the county for several years to create an improvement district, so that public bonds can be used to pay for future infrastructure.

Land Plan

The Baxter Village land plan could serve as a model for other communities in suburban—or even rural—districts. The town center is the hub of density and activity. High-density residential neighborhoods fan out from the town center, affording residents of those blocks walkable access

An on-site elementary school means that most children can walk to school. Clear Springs

it a step further. They particularly liked the idea of mixing a variety of housing types at varying price points and lot sizes throughout the development, a goal of TND that is rarely implemented. Market research did not support this kind of mixing, and production builders resisted, but the developer went ahead anyway. Large builders are not used to working at scattered sites throughout a development. They typically gain efficiencies and economies by building an entire section of homes at once.

Because of the difficult terrain and the major infrastructure costs, Baxter Village had high upfront costs. The lack of services and amenities in the newly developing area initially kept home sales at a slow pace. It was not possible, however, to develop Baxter's town center until enough homes were occupied to support the town center businesses.

The community is designed on a pedestrian scale. Except for Sutton Road, all streets are narrow and are cut into short blocks, so that traffic is naturally calmed. On-street parking further slows traffic. Sidewalks and curbside planting strips line both sides of every street. Nearly all homes are within easy walking distance of the town center, the elementary school, and recreational amenities.

The areas outside Baxter Village, however, are not conducive to pedestrian activity. While sidewalks and signaled crosswalks do exist, the larger environment would benefit from better connections between projects. For example, pedestrians could easily handle the distance between Baxter Village and the shopping centers across the road; but outside the development, wide arterials and mandatory buffers between projects create the sense of being in a no-man's-land.

to the town center. The outer edges of the development offer meandering streets where large and small homesites overlook the wooded ravines that slice through the terrain. Thus, the plan offers buyers a wide range of homes, lifestyles, and neighborhood character.

A major goal of the Close family was to minimize the environmental impact of the development. The family also wanted Baxter Village to blend into the natural and architectural surroundings. LandDesign had discussed the TND concept with the family, and family representatives had visited Disney's Celebration project in Florida. The members of the Close family liked the concept: they wanted to create a "front porch" environment with open-space preservation, lots of pocket parks, and a real sense of community—like Celebration. But they wanted to take

Baxter's town center is a focal point of commercial activity, with shops, restaurants, and offices housed in mixed-use, two- and three-story traditional "main street" buildings. Although the town center is not directly on Highway 160, the fact that the center is located on high ground provides it with visibility from the road. The 1,400-foot- (427-meter-) long Market Street is the core of the town center. Market Street is lined with on-street parking, and additional parking lots are located to the rear of the buildings. The result is that the main street is a pedestrian-focused district with tree-lined sidewalks and outdoor cafés. The town center parking lots also serve the public library and the YMCA, encouraging visitors to park once, then travel to multiple destinations on foot.

As the number of residents has become large enough to support the businesses, retail leasing has improved. Office leasing has been slower, partly because of a weak economy, but also because it takes time to become established as a desirable location for office space. In the first phase of the town center is the Springmaid Building, a three-story, 35,000-square-foot (3,250-square-meter) mixed-use building that combines restaurant, retail, and office space. Pittsburgh-based UDA and a local architectural firm, Studio A1, designed the building, which recalls the nearby historic downtown in character and style and sets the tone for the rest of the town center. While much development remains to be done, the town center is already a gathering place for residents and nearby workers.

Branching off to the northwest of Market Street, the town center continues to a traffic circle where the public library and the visitors' center are located. The visitors' center is zoned commercial so that it can be converted to

Allison Park is a meandering, 12-acre (4.8-hectare) nature preserve that runs through the community. The woodland trails are popular with walkers, bikers, and joggers. Clear Springs

commercial uses when home sales are completed. To the south of the retail district is the YMCA, which includes a fitness center, indoor and outdoor pools, and playing fields, and helps to round out the vision of Baxter Village as an active-living community.

The pattern book developed by UDA sets the requirements for the landscape plan. Street trees, installed by the developer and maintained by homeowners, follow the traditional patterns of the area, in both species and spacing. In addition to having sidewalks on all streets, Baxter Village offers a trail network that will eventually link all its open spaces and other destinations, including the town center, the library, the elementary school, and the community center. Where the trail meets Sutton Road, a tunnel allows bikers and hikers to avoid having to cross the road.

The community center, designed to resemble a historic South Carolina courthouse, includes an aerobics room, party rooms with a service kitchen, a conference room, an outdoor swimming pool, and a children's pool with adjoining snack bar. A full-time recreation director plans activities for residents. Baxter Village's Walkers' Club meets at 9:00 a.m. and 6:00 p.m. for daily walks.

Working with the U.S. Army Corps of Engineers, the developer created a low-impact solution for stormwater detention. The method, called online detention, allows stormwater to percolate through the soil, usually for no more than 24 hours after a storm. A major advantage of the approach is that the filtering process improves water quality. In addition, because no detention ponds are needed, the method eliminates the maintenance and extra land that such ponds entail.

Architecture and Homebuilders

The architecture of Baxter Village is the legacy of up-country towns and villages that developed in this part of South Carolina during the 19th century and early 20th century. These structures are admired today for their character and for the quality of their architecture.

After a design process that included holding charrettes with homebuilders, UDA created a pattern book. Designs and materials were selected to allow production homebuilding techniques, so that the homes would be affordable to a wide range of buyers. Although certain high-end building materials and designs were rejected, few compromises were needed.

The many exterior materials used in Baxter Village homes include brick, stucco, stone, and clapboard siding. Roofs are mostly asphalt shingle; some are standing-seam metal.

The homebuilders chosen to build at Baxter Village had to create all-new house designs. They started with their most successful floor plans, then "Baxterized" the elevations to fit the character of the community. Generally, this meant moving garages to the rear and reconfiguring the footprint to fit lots that are typically narrower and deeper than standard suburban lots.

Residential lots of varying sizes, from 45-foot- (13.7-meter-) wide cottage lots to 90-foot (27.4-meter-) wide estate lots, are mixed throughout the development rather than clustered in neighborhoods. The result is a real town, with a rich and varied streetscape, where every home is distinct. A full-time coordinator works with the builders to site houses on lots and to ensure the diversity of facades and palettes while maintaining the overall design themes.

About half the homes have rear alleyways with rear garages. Of the homes that are not on alleys, many still have detached rear garages accessed by single-lane driveways from the street. Front garages must be pushed back from the facade.

Homebuilders were selected for their experience in building high-quality homes and providing exceptional customer service. Six homebuilders are active in Baxter Village. Production homebuilders include the regional firm

Allison Park includes a bandstand and a splash fountain. Clear Springs

boards. Baxter Village has a visitors' center, which is rare in its market. The center explains the origins and goals of the community and educates potential homebuyers about the advantages of this kind of development.

Actual home sales are conducted by the individual builders, four of whom have fully furnished on-site model homes with staffed sales offices. Lots are sold only to builders—about 200 per year, resulting in about 130 home sales per year. In the local market, Baxter Village ranks among the top five communities in home sales. About 35 percent of the buyers are relocating from out of state or from other parts of the state; about 42 percent are from the Charlotte metro area; the rest are from the immediate Fort Mill area. Buyers are a diverse mix that includes single people, empty nesters, and families with children.

Saussy Burbank and national firms Beazer Homes, David Weekley Homes, and D.R. Horton. Local builders S.E. Miller Custom Homes and Evans Coghill Homes offer custom homes designed within the parameters of the Baxter Village pattern book.

Marketing and Management

Regionally, 65 percent of home sales occur through real estate agents, so Baxter's marketing effort has been largely targeted to agents in the area. The firm also initiated a multimedia campaign that included print, radio, and bill-

Unlike some developments, which have strong neighborhood identities—with separate names, housing types, homeowners' associations, and amenities—Baxter Village is a single cohesive community. Housing types are distributed throughout the development, as they would be in a traditional town. The Baxter Village Homeowners' Association is responsible for architectural review and for maintaining all parks, trails, and recreational amenities.

The community has an underground fiber-optic system and features a password-protected Web site that electronically links all homes, businesses, the public library, and the elementary school. Every home includes a state-of-the-art wiring package that allows for high-speed networking.

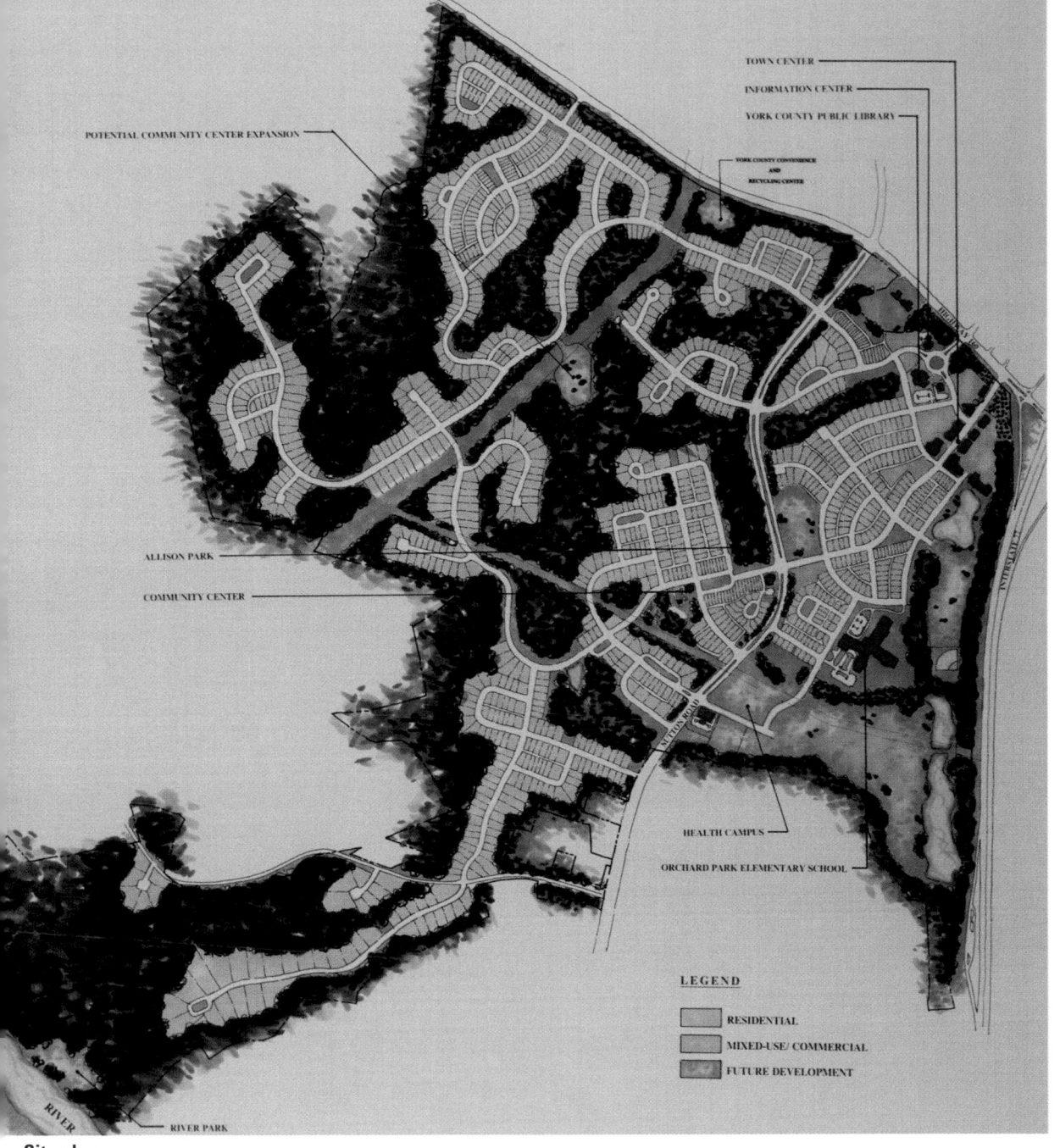

Site plan.

Experience Gained

The steep and varied terrain of the Baxter Village site made development difficult and expensive. In retrospect, instead of relying on a costly cut-and-fill process to force the land to accommodate the site plan, the developer would have tailored the plan more to the contours of the land.

In newly developing areas, the developer, local planning staff, and others involved in a project have to go through a learning curve. Working together helps everyone get up to speed. Baxter's development team worked with the county, for example, to help create the TND code, and has continued to make its expertise available as the project proceeds.

At lower price points, incorporating the design details that are critical to TND is a challenge, but it can be done. If homebuilders are included as part of the development team early in the design process, they have a chance to weigh proposed designs and materials against economic reality, and can help devise compromises that balance design excellence and affordability. To ensure that utilities are integrated into the plan in ways that will minimize their visual impact on the streetscape, representatives from all local utilities should be included early in the planning process as well.

Baxter Village

Fort Mill, South Carolina

Land Use Information

Site area (acres/hectares)	1,032/418
Total dwelling units planned	1,325
Gross nonresidential building area (acres/hectares)	73/29.5
Gross density (units per acre/per hectare)	1.4/3.5
Average net density (units per acre/per hectare)	3/7.4

Land Use Plan

Use	Acres/Hectares	Percentage of Site
Residential	443/179.2	42.9
Retail	4.2/1.6	0.4
Office	68.9/27.9	6.7
Common open space	516/208.8	50.0
Total	1,032.1/417.5	100.0

Residential Information

Unit Type	Lot Size (Square Feet/ Square Meters)	Unit Size (Square Feet/ Square Meters)	Number of Units Planned	Current Sales Prices
Single family	3,450–20,000/321–1,858	1,250–5,000/116–465	1,277	$139,900–$505,000
Townhouse	1,140–2,875/106–267	1,100–2,200/102–204	48	$115,000–$235,000

Retail Information

Gross leasable area occupied (square feet/square meters)	53,900/5,000
Annual rents (per square foot/square meter)	$16–$20/$172–$215
Average annual sales (per square foot/square meter)	$200–$300/$2,150–$3,230
Typical length of lease	5 years

Tenant Classification	Number of Stores	Gross Leasable Area (Square Feet/Square Meters)
Grocery, specialty foods, drugs	1	14,000/1,300
Restaurants, food service	6	20,000/1,860
Clothing, shoes, accessories	1	1,400/130
Hobby, special interest, gift	1	2,200/200
Personal services	5	8,000/740
Financial services	3	6,500/600
Bicycles	1	1,800/170
Total	18	53,900/5,000

Office Information

Gross building area (square feet/square meters):	200,000/18,600
Number of tenants:	20 to 30
Average rents (per square foot/square meter):	$16–18/$172–$194
Lease terms:	NNN
Typical length of lease:	5–10 years

Development Costs Expected at Buildout

	In Millions
Site acquisition	$3.1
Site improvement	60.3
Construction	6.7
Total	$70.1

Development Schedule

Site purchased	1995
Planning started	1996
Construction started	November 1997
Home sales started	April 1999
First closing	May 1999
Phase I completed	April 2001
Estimated project completion	2009

Development Team

Developer
Clear Springs Development Company
Fort Mill, South Carolina
www.clearspringsdevelopmentcompany.com

Site Planners
LandDesign, Inc.
Charlotte, North Carolina
www.landdesign.com

Urban Design Associates
Pittsburgh, Pennsylvania
www.urbandesignassociates.com

ColeJenest & Stone
Charlotte, North Carolina
www.colejeneststone.com.

Architects
Urban Design Associates
Pittsburgh, Pennsylvania
www.urbandesignassociates.com

Studio A1
Fort Mill, South Carolina
www.studioa1.com

Gray Houghland Architects
Charlotte, North Carolina
www.houghlandarchitecture.com

The Lawrence Group
Davidson, North Carolina
www.thelawrencegroup.com

Homebuilders
David Weekley Homes
Charlotte, North Carolina
www.davidweekleyhomes.com

Beazer Homes
Charlotte, North Carolina
www.beazer.com

Saussy Burbank
Charlotte, North Carolina
www.saussyburbank.com

S.E. Miller Custom Homes
Charlotte, North Carolina

D.R. Horton
Charlotte, North Carolina
www.drhorton.com

Evans Coghill Homes
Charlotte, North Carolina
www.evanscoghill.com

WaterColor and Seaside

Seagrove Beach, Florida

"It's relatively easy to be called 'a place.' It's a lot harder to be truly thought of as a place," says chairman and chief executive officer Peter Rummell, of the St. Joe Company. St. Joe is the developer of WaterColor, a 499-acre (202-hectare) coastal resort community on the Florida panhandle along the Gulf of Mexico. At buildout, the community will include 1,020 homes, 100,000 square feet (9,290 square meters) of commercial space, a 60-room boutique hotel, and a wealth of recreational amenities. Nearly half the site will be preserved as open space.

The community is adjacent to the Grayton Beach State Recreation Area and is bisected by Scenic Highway 30A, which runs parallel to the shore. The WaterColor site has a unique advantage: it wraps around the community of Seaside, the town that established the new urbanism as a force in community design. WaterColor's town plan was designed by Cooper, Robertson & Partners. The concept is in keeping with that of Seaside; together, the two communities create a large, pedestrian-friendly district in which residents can leave their cars parked and walk to everything they need.

WaterColor and Seaside are an example of the whole being greater than the sum of its parts. Together they create a large walkable district.
Cooper, Robertson & Partners

The Importance of Seaside

It is impossible to understand WaterColor without first learning about Seaside, the adjacent development that started the resort-development movement on Florida's panhandle.

Seaside is an 80-acre (32.4-hectare) beach-resort town developed by Robert Davis and his wife, Daryl. In 1946, J.S. Smolian bought the coastal property to build a summer camp for the employees of his Birmingham-based department store. But the site was so remote that no one wanted to go there. In the 1970s, Smolian's grandson, Robert Davis, a developer in southern Florida, inherited the land. Davis assembled a group of young architects—

most notably Andrés Duany and Elizabeth Plater-Zyberk— and began to formulate a vision of the kind of beach town he remembered from his childhood. The spatial basis for this kind of town was the five- to ten-minute walk: the distance a person would comfortably walk to take care of daily needs. Seaside opened in 1981, and became the prototype for what would become the new urbanism. Seaside also became the ultimate pedestrian-oriented development. Today, Seaside's residents and visitors leave their cars parked and walk or bike everywhere. The community is organized so that all homes are within a short

Seaside re-created the casual lifestyle of a beach town where everything is accessible by foot. Adrienne Schmitz

walk of the town center, the beach, and other carefully located facilities. In Seaside, the public domain takes precedence over the private. The sparkling white beach is public, and offers no parking lots for visitors: everyone walks or bikes. Nine boardwalks arch over the dunes, providing access to the beach while protecting the dune grasses from foot traffic. Each boardwalk is capped by its own individually designed pavilion overlooking the beach; in addition to offering shade and seating, the pavilions serve as neighborhood landmarks.

The houses, all of which have front porches, are set close to the street, so that the street is an extension of the homes' outdoor space. Traffic is minimal, and travels at a speed of only 15 miles per hour (24 kilometers per hour), so pedestrians can safely walk in the street, and children can play along its edge. The streets are very narrow—essentially one lane—and paved in brick, with shoulders of crushed shell. A network of unpaved footpaths provides interesting vistas and backyard views and allows pedestrians to take shortcuts through blocks.

The town center, the community's focal point, includes all the day-to-day basics (a grocery store, a bookstore, a post office, a bike-rental shop, and a range of restaurants) as well as luxuries like art galleries and jewelers. The fact that all the businesses, which are organized around a grassy amphitheater, are locally owned adds to the sense of community. On upper floors and tucked behind storefronts are medical offices, insurance agents, and other services. Civic institutions include the Seaside Charter School, the Seaside Institute (an educational facility for architecture, planning, and urban affairs), and the Seaside Interfaith Chapel. The town center is a place to greet neighbors, get a newspaper, and have ice cream with the kids. If all this sounds familiar, it's only because Seaside has been so influential that many of the best communities now strive to achieve the same kind of livability.

In economic terms, Seaside has been an enormous success: between 1982 and 1995, homesites appreciated an average of 25 percent annually. The first residential lots sold in 1982 for $15,000. In 2003, the final section of non-beachfront lots was released for sale at $500,000. In 2005, one unbuilt lot in that section was offered for $900,000. One of the few remaining beachfront lots was listed in 2005 for over $3.5 million. Cottage prices in 2005 ran from about $1 million to more than $4 million. Properties are snapped up quickly, often by current owners who either move up or increase their holdings. Vacation rentals are a thriving business in Seaside; out of 480 homes, 275 are rented to vacationers at least part of the time. Rentals are managed through an on-site office that provides hotel-level service to guests. The cottages, townhouses, and flats command high prices, and vacancies are rare.

The market for Seaside's shops and restaurants has expanded beyond the town's boundaries; Seaside's town center now attracts visitors from the entire coast, enabling

WaterColor's town center was conceived to fill in the elements that were missing at Seaside, rather than to compete with it. Cooper, Robertson & Partners

a broad range of businesses to emerge and succeed. Retail sales in 2002 totaled over $24 million, or about $640 per square foot ($6,889 per square meter). By comparison, in 2002, median sales per square foot at neighborhood shopping centers throughout the south were $237 ($2,551 per square meter). The unique environment created by Seaside's town center is its major draw. People come to walk around, to people watch, and to enjoy the outdoors.

Another measure of Seaside's success is the way it has set the stage for development along Florida's Gulf Coast, from Pensacola to Panama City. In terms of both quality and design, Seaside has been the model for much of the development that followed it. The coast is home to five new urbanist communities in various stages of completion: Seaside, WaterColor, WaterSound Beach, Rosemary

Beach, and Camp Creek. Seaside has also driven up real estate values along the coast, which are competitive with those of the very best resort properties in the country.

The WaterColor Site

WaterColor is located in northwest Florida, directly on the Gulf of Mexico. The property, which the St. Joe Company has owned since 1927, is irregularly shaped and relatively flat, and offers a variety of natural advantages, including coastal pine forests, freshwater marshes, saw-grass wetlands, a large lake, and 1,400 linear feet (427 meters) of beachfront on the renowned soft white beaches of Walton County. Much of the site is wooded, and the developer has taken care to preserve the existing vegetation. As noted earlier, one of the site's unique advantages is that parts of its southern and eastern edges border Seaside.

Planning and Design

At full buildout, the community will include 1,020 residences; 100,000 square feet (9,290 square meters) of commercial space; a full-service, 60-room hotel; beach, tennis, and swimming facilities; dune walkovers and

Cerulean Park, the heart of the community, defines a long water axis that connects the Gulf to Western Lake. A linear water canal creates the pedestrian corridor. Left: Cooper, Robertson & Partners. Right: Adrienne Schmitz

boardwalks; and a lake with a boathouse, surrounded by a lakefront park. Nearly half the site is being devoted to open space and to the preservation of natural habitats. The site plan is based on the principles of the new urbanism, a decision that was influenced by WaterColor's adjacency to use of the marshes, creeks, and wooded lake frontage as natural settings for the neighborhoods.

To ensure easy pedestrian access from every home in the community, the designers located destinations—the town center, the inn, and the recreational facilities—on

The WaterColor Beach Club is an amenity for residents, vacation renters, and hotel guests. It features a beachfront pool with hotel-style dining and services. Cooper, Robertson & Partners

Seaside. WaterColor is designed for connectivity with Seaside: view corridors between the two communities were taken into account in the design of WaterColor, and walking paths connect, although neighborhood streets do not. WaterColor homes that back up to Seaside were even designed to be compatible with Seaside's more exuberant palette and architectural styles.

The plan emphasizes walkable neighborhoods: houses are on small lots, and streets interconnect, to facilitate foot travel between destinations such as the town center, the beach, and Seaside's town center. The plan also respects the site's diverse natural environment, making

the central axis. Beach access is by way of footpaths that cross the dunes at two-block intervals. The beach is public and draws tourists, who also frequent the businesses at the town center. Seaside generates additional foot traffic. Unlike most Florida resort communities, WaterColor is not gated, and the interaction between residents and tourists adds to the sense of community.

The character of the residential neighborhoods is defined by tree-lined, pedestrian-scale streets and narrow alleys. The houses are designed in vernacular southern styles, with an emphasis on casual simplicity. Deep porches and overhanging roofs provide relief from the Florida sun. The palette combines pale neutrals and rich, deep shades. Materials—metal roofs, shingle and wood siding, and simple wood trim—are drawn from traditional southern beach houses.

In keeping with the casual atmosphere of a beach town, pedestrian walkways are made of crushed shell, as are the roadsides at Seaside. Boardwalks span the inland lake and lead to the beach. The landscape design relies on native plants, which are best suited to the environment and lend an appropriate character. A staff naturalist teaches residents about the importance of retaining the native plants on their own lots, instead of clearing the land and installing lawns.

A relaxed atmosphere is essential to a resort community, and the developers believe that a pedestrian focus enhances that atmosphere. Once people arrive, they can escape from their daily routines—which includes escaping from their cars and from traffic woes. Residents have clearly taken to this kind of lifestyle. Caravans of families biking to the beach are a common sight. Bicycles are included in cottage rentals, creating a wonderful incentive for guests to embrace the WaterColor lifestyle. The developers report that the parking spaces near the beach are rarely in use.

Residences at WaterColor include condominiums, townhouses, cottages, and large single-family houses. Above: Cooper, Robertson & Partners. Right: Adrienne Schmitz

WaterColor is made up of nine neighborhoods being built in three phases. Buyers select a lot and then choose a St. Joe home or hire an architect to design a home for their lot. The St. Joe homes were designed by five nationally recognized architects: Allison Ramsey Architects, Florida Haus, Historical Concepts, Kiara Designs, and Looney Ricks Kiss. For inspiration for the home designs, the architects drew on the indigenous, somewhat rustic architecture of nearby Grayton Beach and Defuniak Springs, and the Carpenter-style houses of lower Alabama and coastal Florida. They also drew on architectural influences from Key West and the Caribbean.

The architectural themes are carried out in every detail, right down to the door pulls and light fixtures (the footbridge over Western Lake, for example, is lit by a series of handmade copper-and-stained-glass cattails).

The Town Center

WaterColor's planners recognized Seaside's town center as the main commercial hub of the area. Their goal for WaterColor's town center was not to duplicate the existing center but to enhance it, filling in whatever elements were missing. So a major component of WaterColor's town center is the WaterColor Inn, the only full-service hotel in the area.

WaterColor's town center brings together residents and visitors in a mixed-use commercial and residential hub. In addition to the WaterColor Inn, the town center includes the Beach Club, a major recreational amenity; street-level shops and restaurants; and upper-level residential flats. The layout was influenced by the public squares of French and Spanish colonies. Adjacent to the town center is the central green, Cerulean Park. A landscaped canal and fountain run along the length of the park and lead to a wooden pedestrian bridge that crosses Western Lake, providing convenient access between the Phase III residential neighborhoods and the town center and beachfront.

The town center offers 70,600 square feet (6,570 square meters) of retail space, with 106 residential units on upper floors. As is typical of town centers in new communities, retail space was slow to lease until enough housing units were occupied to generate sufficient retail sales. Because the town center is an important amenity for homebuyers, the St. Joe Company worked hard to ensure that the town center was up and running as early as possible in the life of the development. Advantis Real Estate Services Company, the commercial real estate services arm of the St. Joe Company, worked with a list of desirable tenants and offered incentives to draw them to the town center. In addition to the town center, WaterColor also has a 140,000-square-foot (13,000-square-meter) shopping center, which is located at the edge of the community and anchored by a Publix grocery store.

The WaterColor Inn

The WaterColor Inn is a key component of WaterColor's marketing strategy. Homeowners usually start out as visitors, and the inn provides an opportunity for potential buyers to spend time enjoying the WaterColor experience. Opened in 2003, the 60-room inn is the first boutique hotel in northwest Florida. Now a part of the exclusive Small Luxury Hotels of the World association, the WaterColor Inn quickly gained favor among sophisticated travelers.

Architect David Rockwell designed the inn building with its natural setting in mind. All rooms have beach views and private balconies or patios. Six ground-floor rooms that face the dunes feature canvas-enclosed outdoor showers. The hotel includes meeting space, a restaurant, a fully equipped gym; a gift shop; a library; a beachfront pool deck with a heated swimming pool and a hot tub; and guest access to community amenities.

Community Amenities

WaterColor offers a wealth of recreational facilities that are available to residents, hotel guests, and those who are staying in vacation rentals. The Beach Club features a

All WaterColor vacation rentals include bicycles. Families typically bike to the beach and other destinations, leaving their cars behind. Adrienne Schmitz

beachfront pool with hotel-style services and a poolside dining facility. Various kinds of recreational equipment are available, including kayaks and snorkeling equipment.

WaterColor Workout, a gym, is also part of the community's amenity package. Instead of being part of a recreational complex, it is located at the town center, an arrangement that encourages residents to combine their workout with errands. The BoatHouse on Western Lake provides sailboats, canoes, kayaks, fishing gear, and boat storage, and features a restaurant, tennis courts, and an additional swimming pool. Other amenities include an extensive trail system for hiking and biking, an outdoor

amphitheater, and picnic and play areas. WaterColor's resident staff features a horticulturist, a naturalist, and an artist. An "art-of-living director" serves as a social director and ombudsman, helps to foster a sense of community among residents, and works with event planners and the homeowners' association.

Children who are full-time residents can attend the Seaside Charter School or the nearby Butler Elementary School, both of which are part of the public school system.

The St. Joe Company believes that opportunities for adult education are an important draw for people who are considering buying a second home but who eventually plan to make WaterColor their primary home, and the firm plans to expand adult educational amenities. Because residents can easily function at WaterColor without a car, aging in place is a likely possibility for many buyers.

Marketing and Sales

Although the potential market for second homes at WaterColor includes the entire southeastern United States, about 90 percent of the buyers who purchase second homes in WaterColor are from Alabama, Georgia, Louisiana, Tennessee, or Texas; the largest number are from the Atlanta area. The average age of buyers is 46 to 48, and most are families with young children.

Surveys show that buyers want outdoor places where they can walk and socialize. They also want the openness of a nongated community. WaterColor's marketing program focuses on this kind of lifestyle. The marketing effort began with a direct-mail campaign that relied on the St. Joe Company's extensive databases. Advertisements were placed in the regional editions of the *Wall Street Journal* and *USA Today*, as well as in the *Atlanta Journal-Constitution*. The WaterColor Inn is regarded as a marketing tool because it enables hotel guests to experience the WaterColor lifestyle before they consider purchasing a home.

Public events are part of the effort to familiarize potential buyers with the development. MountainFilm, a touring version of the internationally known Telluride Film Festival, is an annual event that brings cutting-edge films and filmmakers to Marina Park Amphitheater at WaterColor. The WaterColor Inn offers special weekend packages in conjunction with the festival.

As noted earlier, WaterColor buyers purchase lots from the developer, then select a St. Joe home or work with an approved architect. Even with the developer's high price assumptions, which were based on those at Seaside, sales have been very strong. Lot prices have far surpassed expectations. Typical lots are 55 by 110 feet (16.8 by 33.5 meters). When sales started in 2000, lots sold for about $250,000. In 2005, lot prices ranged from $625,000 to $2,800,000, with lakefront lots among the most expensive. All factors seemed to line up at the same time: the members of the baby boomer market were old enough and wealthy enough to be buying second homes, and many were rejecting the suburban lifestyle and seeking a more pedestrian-oriented environment in which children could be more independent. According to sales manager Tom Dodson, "WaterColor is incredibly successful by every measure."

Homeowners' Association

Except for the commercial components, WaterColor will eventually be owned and managed by the homeowners. The community has a single homeowners' association for the entire development. The developer has learned that most residents prefer minimal fees and restrictions. The average homeowners' fee is $660 per quarter, which covers all common-area maintenance and all amenities: the BoatHouse, the Beach Club, and so on. The residential units located above retail in the town center have an additional maintenance fee. These units are not condominiums

Site plan. Cooper, Robertson & Partners

but "freehold space," which means that the land is owned by the master association, and the homeowner owns the air space and the inside of the unit.

Developer

The St. Joe Company, a publicly held company based in Jacksonville, is one of Florida's largest real estate operating companies. It is engaged in town, resort, commercial, and industrial development; land sales; and commercial real estate services. The firm also has significant interests in timber.

The St. Joe Company has been fortunate in that demographic trends are working in its favor. As the number of people purchasing second homes and retirement homes expands, St. Joe is in a position to meet the demand: it has an abundant supply of high-quality, low-basis land in all regions of Florida and other southern states. St. Joe is disciplined about releasing new products, timing them to allow values to appreciate. In the words of Peter Rummell, chairman and chief executive officer of the St. Joe Company, "We are setting our pace and phasing our development to maximize value."

Experience Gained

The St. Joe Company is extremely pleased with Water-Color: it is a highly attractive, financially successful product. The town center concept—a profit center as well as an amenity and a hub for the community—will undoubtedly be replicated elsewhere. The lake and the boathouse complex have also become a template for other St. Joe communities, as has the idea of linking the beach to the neighborhoods by way of pedestrian trails. Finally, the openness that comes from being a nongated community has proven successful and is yet another feature that the company will implement in other projects.

The developer places great emphasis on enhancing the experience of residents and guests. The pedestrian-focused planning fits in with this emphasis by fostering a feeling of relaxation. The St. Joe Company believes that open space, pathways, and gathering areas add to the sense of community, and should be important components in any residential project.

A few aspects of the project might have been done differently. Now that most of the town center retail space is leased, it has become clear that more commercial space would have been feasible. The retail market, instead of being limited to WaterColor residents, has turned out to be countywide. It was initially assumed that the town center market would be a neighborhood-oriented corner store for basics like bread and milk. But with the broadened market and the upscale tone of the community, it has evolved into a highly successful gourmet market.

The Beach Club is owned and run by the homeowners' association. In future developments, such facilities will remain part of the St. Joe portfolio so that they can be used as profit centers. The town squares and other gathering places could use more seating, and more will probably be added. In some cases, the crushed shell paths are not functional, and might be changed.

The sense of place created at WaterColor is important for the community's profitability. As sales manager Tom Dodson says, "Special places create special values."

WaterColor

Seagrove Beach, Florida

Land Use Information

Site area (acres/hectares)	499/202
Number of dwelling units planned	1,020
Gross density (units per acre/per hectare)	2/5
Average net density (units per acre/per hectare)	5.5/13.6

Residential Information

Unit Type	Units Planned	Lot Size (Square Feet/ Square Meters)	Unit Size (Square Feet/ Square Meters)	Sales Prices (2005)
Single family	152	4,000–7,000/372–650	1,250–4,400/116–409	$1,600,000–$5,300,000
Multifamily	117	—	1,250–3,070/116–285	$1,125,000–$3,600,000
Lots only	751	4,000–7,000/372–650	—	$625,000–$2,800,000
Total	1,020			

Retail Information

Percentage of gross leasable area occupied	100
Annual rents (per square foot/square meter)	$20–$30/$215–$323
Average annual sales (per square foot/square meter)	$300/$3,229
Typical length of lease	4 years

Tenant Classification	Number of Stores	Gross Leasable Area (Square Feet/Square Meters)
Grocery, specialty foods	1	50,000/4,650
Restaurant, food service	2	8,500/790
Clothing, shoes, accessories	1	1,500/140
Home, kitchen, accessories	1	2,100/200
Hobby, special interest, gift	1	4,400/410
Other retail	1	4,100/380
Total	7	70,600/6,570

Land Use Plan

Use	Acres/Hectares	Percentage of Site
Residential	210/84.9	42.1
Retail and office	14/5.7	2.8
Resort, resort services	6/2.4	1.2
Governmental	3/1.2	0.6
Common open space	16/6.5	3.2
Recreation	9/3.6	1.8
Public parking	2/0.8	0.4
Open water[1]	32/12.9	6.4
Wetlands	103/41.6	20.6
Uplands setbacks	104/42	20.8
Total	499/201.6	100.0

1. Part of a 220-acre (89-hectare) coastal dune lake.

Hotel Information

Gross square feet/square meters	22,800/2,120
Number of guest rooms	60
Occupancy rate	60%
Average room rate per night	$231

Development Costs to Date

Site Improvement	In Millions
Excavation, grading, sewer, water, and drainage	$24
Landscaping and irrigation	5.5
Fees and general conditions	10.5
Subtotal, site improvement	$40

Construction	
Beach Club	$6
Tennis center	2
Marina and pool	5
CampWaterColor	2
Other	3
Subtotal, construction	$18

Soft costs	$10
Total	$68

Development Schedule

Site purchased	1927
Planning started	Quarter 1, 1998
Construction started	Quarter 2, 1999
Sales started	Quarter 2, 2000
First closing	Quarter 2, 2000
Phase I completed	Quarter 2, 2002
Phase II completed	Quarter 3, 2003
Phase III completed	Quarter 3, 2004
Phase IV completed	2005

Development Team

Developer
St. Joe
Jacksonville, Florida
www.arvida.com/watercolor

Site Planner and Architect
Cooper, Robertson & Partners
New York, New York
www.cooperrobertson.com

Master Code Consultant
Urban Design Associates
Pittsburgh, Pennsylvania
www.urbandesignassociates.com

Landscape Architects
Nelson Byrd Landscape Architects
Charlottesville, Virginia
www.nelson-byrd.com

Homebuilder
St. Joe
Santa Rosa Beach, Florida

Engineer
Post Buckley Schuh + Jernigan
Tallahassee, Florida
www.pbsj.com

Environmental Support
Environmental Services, Inc.
Destin, Florida
www.ecoserve.com

Inn Architect
Rockwell Architecture, Planning
 and Design, P.C.
New York, New York
www.rockwellgroup.com

Residential Architects
Historical Concepts
Peachtree City, Georgia
www.historicalconcepts.com

Looney Ricks Kiss
Memphis, Tennessee
www.lrk.com

Kiara Designs
Santa Rosa Beach, Florida

Graham Gund
Cambridge, Massachusetts
www.grahamgund.com

Glover Smith Bode, Inc.
Oklahoma City, Oklahoma
www.gsb-inc.com

Allison Ramsey Architects, Inc.
Beaufort, South Carolina
www.allisonramseyarchitect.com

Seaside

Seagrove Beach, Florida

Land Use Information

Site area (acres/hectares)	80/32.4
Number of dwelling units	480
Gross density (units per acre/per hectare)	9/22
Average net density (units per acre/per hectare)	15/37

Land Use Plan

Use	Acres/ Hectares	Percentage of Site
Residential	23.6/9.6	29.3
Commercial	2.5/1.0	3.1
Beach	14.0/5.7	17.4
Parks and squares	16.5/6.7	20.5
Streets	11.6/4.7	14.4
Other	12.4/5.0	15.4
Total	80.6/32.7	100.0

Development Schedule

Planning started	1970s
Construction started	1981
Sales started	1982
Status as of 2004	16 of 19 phases completed

Development Team

Developer
Seaside Community Development Corporation
Santa Rosa Beach, Florida

Master Planner
Duany Plater-Zyberk & Company
Miami, Florida
www.dpz.com

Master Plan Consultant
Leon Krier, Architect and Town Planner
Claviers, France